ZHUANGZI

THE ESSENTIAL WRITINGS

ZHUANGZI

THE ESSENTIAL WRITINGS

WITH SELECTIONS FROM
TRADITIONAL COMMENTARIES

Translated, with Introduction and Notes, by

BROOK ZIPORYN

Hackett Publishing Company, Inc.
Indianapolis/Cambridge

For further information, please address:

Hackett Publishing Company, Inc.
P.O. Box 44937
Indianapolis, IN 46244-0937

www.hackettpublishing.com

Cover design by Abigail Coyle
Text design by Carrie Wagner
Composition by Agnew's, Inc.

Library of Congress Cataloging-in-Publication Data

Zhuangzi.
  [Nanhua jing. English. Selections]
  Zhuangzi : the essential writings with selections from traditional commen-
taries / translated, with introduction and notes, by Brook Ziporyn.
    p. cm.
  ISBN 978-0-87220-911-4 (pbk.) — ISBN 978-0-87220-912-1 (cloth)
  I. Ziporyn, Brook, 1964– II. Title.
  BL1900.C5E5 2009
  299.5'1482—dc22

                                                    2008052827

The paper in this publication meets the minimum requirements of American
National Standard for Information Sciences—
Permanence of Paper for Printed Library
ANSI Z39.48-1984

CONTENTS

INTRODUCTION

About Zhuangzi

Not much is known about Zhuang Zhou (ca. 369–286 B.C.E.), who was also called Zhuangzi ("Master Zhuang"), the ostensible author of this work of the same name. What we do know about the man himself, as opposed to his work, is limited to the brief biography written by Sima Qian (145–86 B.C.E.), telling us simply that Zhuangzi was a native of Meng in the state of Song (present-day Henan Province), and served as a minor official in an otherwise unknown locale described as "the lacquer-tree park of Meng." One brief anecdote about the man is appended: King Wei of the state of Chu, hearing of Zhuangzi's talents, sent a messenger to offer him financial support and perhaps to invite him to serve as prime minister in his government. Zhuangzi is said to have laughed and replied to the messenger:

> A thousand measures of gold is a substantial profit, and a prime ministership is an exalted position indeed. But haven't you ever heard about the ox offered in the official sacrifice? He is generously fed for years and dressed in the finest embroidered fabrics, so that he may one day be led into the Great Temple for slaughter. When that day comes, though he may wish that he were just a little orphaned piglet instead, it is too late! So scram, you! Do not defile me! I'd rather enjoy myself wallowing in the filth than let myself be controlled by some head of state. I'd rather remain without official position to the end of my days, enjoying myself whichever way I wish.[1]

It is probably safe to assume that this story is less factual than rhetorical. That is also true of the tales about the character named "Zhuangzi" that we find in the book that bears his name. Even in this brief sketch, however, we begin to see that convergence of apparently contradictory identities that make Zhuangzi so fascinating: acerbic mystic, subtle rustic, bottom dweller and high flyer, unassuming rebel, abstruse jester, frivolous sage. Profound comedians have always been hard to come by; funny philosophers perhaps even more so.

---

[1] Sima Qian, *Shiji*, juan 63, "Laozi Hanfei liezhuan."

To enter into this work attributed to Zhuangzi is to find oneself roused and en-raptured not only by its intellectual and spiritual depth, but also by its provoca-tive humor and its sonorous beauty. But what is perhaps even more precious and unusual here is that these three heady torques seem to erupt in this work all at once: it is precisely Zhuangzi's humor that is beautiful, his beauty that is profound, his profundity that is comic. This work defies the dreary but preva-lent notion that the serious is the important, that the playful is the inconse-quential, and above all that we are under some obligation to draw conclusions about ourselves and our world and then stick to them. Zhuangzi refuses to let himself be completely known; indeed, he seems to deny the possibility and even desirability of total understanding, of himself or of anything else. But at the same time he shows himself to us, an unignorable and unforgettable pres-ence that is all the more vivid and evocative for its staunch evasion of ultimate knowability or definitive identity. Encountering Zhuangzi opens a window into a world of enlivening confusions, taunting misdirections, surreal grotes-queries, merciless satire, virtuoso reasonings, insouciant despair, mischievous fallacies, morbid exuberances, impudent jokes, and jolting nonsequiturs, which nonetheless has the most profoundly consequential things to say about the gravest human problems of living, dying, and knowing. Who is this man? What is this book?

About This Book

This volume is organized around a certain way of reading the highly complex text attributed to Zhuangzi. The present version of the original Chinese work consists of thirty-three chapters, edited down from a no longer extant fifty-two chapter version. Most traditional readers took this work to be a single integrated text written by one person. The varying viewpoints expressed in these chapters were thus regarded as in some sense compatible, being expressions of different aspects of a single coherent point of view. Some classical literati, as well as modern scholars such as A. C. Graham and Liu Xiaogan,[2] however, have seen the text as the work of various different authors with related ideas which may or may not be ultimately compatible with one another. A still more extreme view, embraced by Graham, is that even the first seven chapters (known as the "Inner Chapters," generally regarded as the most reliably attributable to the historical Zhuang Zhou himself) are "mutilated" and cannot be read coherently as they stand without forced interpretations that distort their original intent, which can only be speculatively reconstructed.

---

[2] See www.hackettpublishing.com/zhuangzisup, "About the *Zhuangzi*," for an overview of recent scholarly classifications of the chapters of the text.

Given what we know about the *Zhuangzi*'s textual history, then, there are several ways to read this material. Some have suggested that we can interpret the *Zhuangzi* as a coherent thirty-three chapter text expressing a unified viewpoint, recognizing the unifying hand as that of its compiler and editor, the brilliant commentator Guo Xiang, rather than that of a certain shadowy figure named Zhuang Zhou. Guo at least saw this entire text as expressing a single consistent vision, and we can interpret the text so as to understand *this* viewpoint, Guo's, rather than that of the historical Zhuang Zhou, of which we have no certain knowledge. The opposite extreme is to read each of the sections independently, trying to discern the various authors' individual ideas, as Graham and Liu (and some traditional commentators such as Wang Fuzhi) have done.

The arrangement of this translation is based on an interpretive stance somewhere between these two extremes. The first seven chapters of the traditional text, known as the Inner Chapters, are here regarded as forming a single, coherent work, expressing an integrated and intelligible philosophical point of view, attributable to the historical figure of Zhuang Zhou. In accord with scholarly consensus, the remaining sections of the text are taken to be the work of multiple authors, written within a hundred and fifty years or so of Zhuangzi's death.[3] These remaining sections—known as the "Outer Chapters" (8 through 22) and "Miscellaneous Chapters" (23 through 33)—might be read as various *receptions and responses* to the main text: commentaries, extensions, ruminations, domestications, and developments building upon the themes of the Inner Chapters. Each of these "responses" would have developed within the differing contexts of the philosophical concerns and historical circumstances of their authors, and these are worth discussion in their own right, as Graham and Liu have attempted. We might also read this series of responses to Zhuangzi's original writings (the Inner Chapters) as instances of the ways in which their implications have ramified over time.

It is in accordance with such considerations that this book is arranged. The first section presents a translation of the entire original work of Zhuang Zhou, the seven Inner Chapters (pages 1–54). This is followed by selections from the remaining chapters (8 through 33) of the traditional *Zhuangzi* text (pages 55–125), to be regarded as the earliest stratum of ancient "responses" to and interpretations of the Inner Chapters. About two-thirds of the entire thirty-three-chapter traditional *Zhuangzi* is included in this volume (complete translations of chapters 1 through 7, 8 through 10, 17, 19, 22, 23, 27, and 33, and selections from chapters 14, 20, 24 through 27, and 32). My choices concerning which parts of the Outer and Miscellaneous Chapters to include are neces-

---

[3] I accept this view for textual and philological reasons, as developed in Liu Xiaogan's work, not for literary or philosophical reasons. There is really no reason to believe that a single person cannot express wildly different moods and positions at different times, particularly a person such as Zhuangzi, who offers such good reasons for doing so.

sarily influenced by personal preference, and it is inevitable that some readers will find their own favorite passages left out, as we all have our own tastes in these matters. But beyond the question of personal inclinations, I have favored those parts of the texts that seem to me most *distinctive* to the *Zhuangzi*, rather than those that are most *representative* of Chinese thought or "Daoism" in general. The intent behind this choice is to make what is unique to this text available to English readers, stressing those philosophical and literary motifs that are difficult or impossible to come across elsewhere. For this reason, one will find a relative dearth of the passages described as "syncretist"—combining Daoist, Confucian, and Legalist motifs, or beginning to patch together the types of cosmological speculations that would become common in later Daoist-leaning works such as the *Huainanzi*. Instead, the more peculiar—and more difficult—passages, especially those which take up the unique style and attitude of the Inner Chapters, have been privileged.

The last part of this volume consists of still *later* "receptions and responses," in the form of selections from the traditional interlineal commentaries on the Inner Chapters—commentaries that accumulated over the course of the subsequent two-plus millennia of traditional Chinese cultural history and were written by scholars of diverse orientations representing various stripes of Buddhism, Confucianism, and Daoism (pages 129–212). These are indexed to the Inner Chapters translation by means of chapter and comment numbers (e.g., "3:6" appears in the margin beside the end of the sixth passage in Chapter 3 for which comments are appended; those comments are found following the same set of numbers, 3:6, in Selections from Traditional Commentaries). The reader, coming across a passage in the Inner Chapters that intrigues or confounds, can check for a number in the margin, then turn to the commentary section to see what traditional commentators had to say about it.

The Inner Chapters are thus the core text here, the stimulus that has elicited the various responses (the selections from the Outer and Miscellaneous Chapters of the traditional *Zhuangzi*, and also from the works of various later commentators) that constitute the remainder of this volume. I have chosen those commentaries which I think bring the most to the text, which contribute ideas about how to interpret, connect, and interlink apparent disjunctions in it or offer surprising or interesting insights about its structure, imagery, or philosophy. All commentators necessarily come to any text with their own ideas and commitments, which are inevitably reflected to some extent even in purely philological and literary comments. But I have tried to avoid presenting to the English reader those comments wherein the interpreters present starkly original ideas of their own, however fascinating, which are only peripherally connected to the problem of reading and understanding the original *Zhuangzi* text. The central criterion of choice here is what English readers, trying to wend their way through Zhuangzi's strange and sometimes jarring writings, might find useful as an example or precedent of how others, over the course of Chinese intellectual history, have tried to find their bearings in this work, ways in which they connected apparently unrelated passages, their understandings of the implications of various metaphors and rhetorical flourishes, and their general dialogue with the sequence of ideas and stories that make up this piece of writing. I have focused on these commentators as interpreters, rather than as philosophers. Hence, when a thinker like Guo Xiang uses a passage from the *Zhuangzi* as a springboard from which to develop ideas distinctive to himself, with no obvious relation to the text at hand, that comment has been passed over. The same is true for those cases when, for example, a Buddhist commentator such as Shi Deqing matches Zhuangzi's terms to particular items in Buddhist technical vocabulary or specific Buddhist practices, or when a Confucian thinker such as Wang Fuzhi takes the opportunity to explain Zhuangzi's words in terms of his own metaphysics of "vital force" (*qi*). But when any of these commentators proposes an insightful or intriguing way to interpret the imagery of the text and its relation to what precedes and follows, attempts a daring method of spelling out the unstated steps to be interposed between Zhuangzi's apparent premises and his apparent conclusions, suggests what Zhuangzi means to imply with a certain story or rhetorical question, or has an argument for why one part of the text is meant provisionally or jestingly while another part expresses Zhuangzi's real intention, I have tried to include those comments. These comments are selected because they provide an attempt to understand what would otherwise likely be a puzzling aspect of the text to English as well as Chinese readers, connecting it thematically to the rest of the passage or to the work as a whole. I have privileged comments that suggest connections that likely would not occur to a contemporary English reader otherwise and give a good example of how a traditional Chinese exegete handles difficult turns in the text, as a contribution to the project of reading and making sense of the *Zhuangzi* and understanding how this was done in the context of traditional Chinese literary culture. For our topic here is the *Zhuangzi* text, how to understand it, and how others have tried to understand it, as a written document. Most of these commentators are brilliant thinkers in their own right and well worth our attention and study. It is hoped that the reader will be able to get some sense of their style and approach from the selected remarks, in conjunction with the appended biographies and summaries of their work. Readers who come to conceive an interest in any of these thinkers based on the ways they find the commentators interacting with the *Zhuangzi* text would, it is hoped, be motivated to learn more about them from other sources specifically devoted to their more general ideas and commitments.

Sometimes the commentators read the original text differently than I do in my translation, even parsing sentences differently. I have indicated such occurrences in the translations of the commentaries with an asterisk (*) placed prior to the line in question, and in cases of extreme divergence I have appended a footnote. The assumption is that it will be self-evident which phrase in the translation is being given the alternate interpretation and also that this will help the non-Chinese-reader appreciate the diversity of understandings the text has traditionally engendered.[4] Brief biographies of the commentators have been provided at the end of this volume, together with some remarks on the general point of view and approach characterizing their respective commentaries to this text ("About the Commentators," pages 221–227).

In this way I have striven to include the maximum variety in viewpoints about this work, to give the English reader some sense of what it is like to read the text in Chinese. The *Zhuangzi* has been read for the past two millennia alongside its commentaries, as part of an ongoing dialogue, a consortium of diverse voices providing alternate perspectives. The extent of the text's ambiguity is perhaps difficult to imagine for an English reader without the use of this expedient. The reading of the widely discrepant views of the various commentaries on sections of this text will also convey some sense of just how many possible ways the text can be read and how freely these alternate readings have been adopted and given full play by traditional Chinese literati.

Historical and Philosophical Background

Zhuangzi was born into a time of great political and philosophical upheaval and ferment known as the Warring States Period (ca. 475–221 B.C.E.). To get a sense of that period, one must look back to the political situation emerging from the collapse of the Western Zhou empire (ca. 1050–771 B.C.E.) and its aftermath.

The Western Zhou had unified the central area of what is now China under a single regime. When it fell apart, a number of de facto independent principalities cropped up, vying for supremacy, each attempting to unify the other states under its own aegis. This provided a kind of open marketplace of potential sponsors for a new class of intellectuals, as all of the rulers of these states were looking for an ideology and set of policies that would both establish their legitimacy as heirs to the Zhou dynasty and allow them to accomplish political unification under their own hegemony.

In this climate, advocates of many contending philosophical schools eventually emerged. The earliest of these private reformers and educators, putting forth a doctrine independent of any particular political power but marketed to various contenders, was Confucius (Kong Qiu 孔丘; ca. 551–479 B.C.E.). Confucius, as represented in the *Analects* (*Lunyu*), advocated the cultivation of certain personal qualities — "virtues" — that would allow those who mastered them to form an educated class capable of presiding wisely, benevolently, and

---

[4]   Where substitute characters from alternate editions or speculative reconstructions are used for the translation, however, I have avoided annotation or attribution in all but extreme cases, on the grounds that to those who are familiar with the textual materials in Chinese the provenance will be obvious, while to those who are not it will be irrelevant.

effectively over its subjects, inspiring the people to emulate these virtues without having to be commanded to do so, ideally bringing about both social order and personal harmony without recourse to coercion. The virtues in question involved a return to an idealized version of the earlier Zhou ritual forms of social organization, rooted in the relations of the family that were hierarchical but also cemented by bonds of spontaneous affection. The trademark virtues of the Confucians were Humanity (*ren* 仁), Responsibility (*yi* 義), Ritual Propriety (*li* 禮), and Filial Piety (*xiao* 孝).[5]

The development of Confucian thought was continued by Mencius (Meng Ke 孟軻, ca. 372–289 B.C.E.), a contemporary of Zhuangzi's (although neither explicitly mentions the other). Mencius defends the Confucian virtues by asserting that their seeds are in some sense built into the human person at birth, such that their cultivation and development are at the same time the maximal satisfaction of the natural "Heaven-conferred" dispositions of human beings, which motivates Mencius's famous slogan, "Human nature is good." The exact sense in which this was meant continues to be the subject of much scholarly disagreement.

The work of Confucius was opposed by Mozi (Mo Di 墨翟; ca. 450–390 B.C.E.). Mozi rejected the primacy of the family, and the spontaneous but biased affections that come with it, as a model for social organization. Instead, he proposed a more abstract notion of moral obligation rooted in a utilitarian calculation of maximized material benefits for all, justified not by human fellow-feeling but by an anthropomorphic deity, Heaven, whose will was to benefit all equally, and the punishments and rewards enforced by this deity and many lesser ghosts and spirits. In place of filial piety, which prescribed special duties toward one's family, Mozi put "all-inclusive love" (*jian ai* 兼愛), meaning the concern for the benefit (construed almost exclusively as enjoyment of material resources) of all equally, kin and nonkin. Rituals such as lavish funeral services and musical ceremonies, which Confucians saw as important expressions of family sentiment and methods for harmonious social consolidation, were seen by Mozi as a useless waste of resources.

The Mohists and the Confucians each have their own "course" (*dao* 道). The term *dao* is cognate with the term for "to lead or guide" (*dao* 導) and can also mean "to speak." Hence, its prescriptive force is particularly pronounced. When used in Confucian and Mohist texts of this period, it could perhaps be translated as "guiding (dis)course." The term originally meant a set of practices designed to guide one's behavior in some specific way so as to promote the attainment of a predetermined value or objective: social harmony, personal contentment, material benefit. The term *dao* ("course," "way," "method," "path") is thus initially used by both the Confucians and Mohists to denote

---

[5] See Glossary for a further discussion of the notion of "virtue" (or "Virtuosity") in general and of the Confucian virtues of Humanity and Responsibility.

their "way" of doing things, their particular tradition of valuations and behaviors, including the exemplary deeds of a teacher and the guiding discourse prescribing a course of study and emulation, and the resulting set of practices (e.g., the system of traditional ritual) which lead to the attainment of the preconceived value. When these practices are mastered and internalized, one has "attained (i.e., mastered) the Course" or "the Way" in question, and this "attainment" (*de* 得) is what is known as "Virtuosity" or "Virtue" (*de* 德).

Thus, there are many *daos*, many courses: the course of the ancient kings, the course of Heaven, the course of charioteering, the course of swordsmanship, the course of all-inclusive love, the course of filial piety, the course of Confucius, the course of Mozi. One studies and practices one of these courses, thereby mastering a predetermined skill, a virtuosity that involves both dividing up the world in the way prescribed by the system of terms employed in the guidance provided by that course and in turn valuing and disvaluing things and acting accordingly. The courses advocated by the Confucians and Mohists in some ways contradicted each other: some of what one affirmed as right (e.g., filial piety, lavish funerals, or conversely all-inclusive love and frugality in funerals) the other negated as wrong.

Sometime after Mozi, another position, later known as "Daoist," came to be articulated in a probably gradually compiled, multiauthored text known as the *Daodejing*, later associated with the mythical figure Laozi (or Lao Dan, as he is usually called in the *Zhuangzi*). This text marks a major break, indeed a deliberate 180-degree turnaround, from the understanding of *dao* found in the Confucian and Mohist schools, developing a new and profoundly different, *ironic* meaning of the term *dao*.[6] In this context, *dao* is precisely what is *free of* purpose and specific guidelines, the exact opposite of the traditional meaning of *dao*. Yet it is still called a *dao*. Why? Because it does in fact do what the traditional *daos* promised to do: generate the things we see, know, and want. Most *daos* were seen as generating these things through deliberate human action, and initially even the Course of Heaven was seen as involving Heaven's intention. But as the concept of Heaven came to be increasingly naturalized in this period, among Confucians if not among Mohists, Heaven's Course came to be seen as producing what we see, know, and want *without* any deliberate intentions, explicit commands, or purposive actions.[7] The Course of Heaven is thus closely associated with the shift in the meaning of *dao* effected by the early Daoists, and the term "Heaven" occurs frequently in Daoist works, though now Heaven, formerly a commanding and controlling deity, is also explicitly divested of conscious knowing and moral desiderata. Indeed, central to the Daoist idea is a critique of conscious knowledge and moral ideals as such.

---

[6]   See "The Dao of the *Daodejing*" at www.hackettpublishing.com/zhuangzisup for a fuller exposition of the meaning of *dao* in the *Daodejing*.

[7]   See Glossary for a fuller discussion of term "Heaven."

Our attention is directed away from the foreground purposes of human activity and toward the background, that is, what normally escapes our purpose-driven awareness. This move reorients our focus toward the spontaneous and purposeless processes in nature and man that undergird and produce things, begin things, end things, compose the stuff of things, and guide things along their courses by not deliberately guiding them at all. This can be viewed as a new stress on Nature as opposed to Man, but only if "nature" is understood precisely as "spontaneity," that is, what is so without conscious planning or purpose, not nature understood as a product of a purposive creator that abides by the laws He imposes upon it and reveals thereby the glory of His intelligence and goodness.

The *Daodejing* is never quoted or directly alluded to in the Inner Chapters (though it is often quoted verbatim in the rest of the *Zhuangzi*), but some similar ideas concerning *daos* and the ironic *Dao* are found there. For example, we find Zhuangzi saying, "when the Course becomes explicit, it ceases to be the Course" (2:35), which could stand almost as an exact paraphrase of the first line of the received version of the *Daodejing*. It is impossible to know whether these considerations are arrived at independently, or if the tradition that produced the *Daodejing* also had some influence on Zhuangzi. But in any case, it is to these philosophical controversies over alternate *daos* that we find Zhuangzi responding in the Inner Chapters.

There is another development in Chinese thought that had a deep impact on Zhuangzi, setting the stage quite directly for his work and marking it off sharply from other Daoist texts. This is the emergence of a form of logical disputation represented here by Zhuangzi's best friend, sparring partner, straight man, and arch-foil, Huizi (Hui Shi 惠施; ca. 370–310 B.C.E.). Huizi figures prominently throughout the Inner Chapters, even when he is not explicitly named.[8] The standard thirty-three-chapter version of the *Zhuangzi*, furthermore, con-

---

[8]   He appears explicitly at 1:14, 1:15, 2:28, and 5:23, but implicit references and critiques of his thought are found much more frequently. Indeed, the rhetorical framing of Zhuangzi's first chapter (its opening trope and its final two dialogues) might suggest the hypothesis that the Inner Chapters were written by Zhuangzi precisely as a response to Huizi, perhaps intended for the latter's eyes in particular, almost as a private joke. We are told, after all, that Zhuangzi considered Huizi the only one who really understood his words, the only one for whom he spoke or wrote (see Chapter 24). Chapter 1 begins with a vast fish that transforms into a vast bird and is then ridiculed for his high flying by smaller birds gazing up at him from the ground. It ends with two dialogues between Zhuangzi and Huizi that closely parallel the structure of the relationship between Peng and the little birds. Another story of a confrontation between Zhuangzi and Huizi (Chapter 17) supports the view that the large-and-small-bird trope symbolizes Zhuangzi's view of their relationship. There, Zhuangzi, after hearing that Huizi believes him to be after his official position, tells the story of a tiny creature who screeches at a vast one uncomprehendingly. The rhetorical trope there ("In the southern region there is a bird, and its name is . . ." and so on) closely parallels the opening tale of Peng and the little birds, with Huizi likened to the latter and Zhuangzi to the former.

cludes with a long description of Huizi's work and a heartfelt but biting lament over his shortcomings (see Chapter 33). On the basis of these descriptions, it seems that Huizi developed a method of overturning commonsense assertions by showing that the distinctions on which they are based depend on the particular perspectives from which they are drawn, making them inherently negotiable. Thus, all our usual distinctions about units of time and space, and even of "sameness" and "difference" in general, are relative and malleable. It would seem that part of Huizi's object in pressing this point was to show the contradiction entailed in making any distinctions at all, for the sole positive ethical pronouncement attributed to him in Chapter 33, at the end of a long string of paradoxes, is the following: "Love all things without exception, for Heaven and earth are one body." As Graham has suggested, just as Zeno's paradoxes are generally interpreted as intended to support the Parmenidean thesis of absolute oneness of Being, Huizi would seem to be using a similar sort of *reductio ad absurdum* as a support for a crypto-Mohist injunction to love all things equally. Zhuangzi has much in common with Huizi: the method of revealing the presuppositions underlying seemingly unproblematic claims, the mastery of dialectic, the thesis of relativity to perspective, the penchant for paradox, the suspicion of distinctions, and the interest in the oneness of all things. Indeed, it seems possible if not likely that Zhuangzi directly adopted all these *from* Huizi, taking them over from him wholesale. And yet, Zhuangzi objects most strenuously to his friend's position, the ridicule of which is one of the most vital motifs running through this entire work. For it appears to Zhuangzi that Huizi wants to win arguments by *proving* that all things *are really* one, and therefore that one really *should* choose the path of loving all equally. Huizi provides an answer to the questions: what is the case (all things are one body), how can I know it (through reasoning and dialectic, which relativize all distinctions), and therefore how should I live my life (love all things equally). In doing so, he implicitly asserts the unique ascendancy of his own position and practices, as the one who can victoriously demonstrate and proclaim this. It is to this, it would seem, that Zhuangzi lovingly and laughingly objects, undermining it by means of a further extension of Huizi's own premises. Zhuangzi seems to adopt everything from Huizi except his answers—and his concomitant status as "the one with the answers."

The question Zhuangzi faces is indeed among the most fundamental human problems: How should I live my life? Which of the alternate courses should I take as my guide? How is it that I come to choose one course over another? Given that there are alternate ways to see things, why do I, and why *should* I, see things the way I do rather than another way and thus follow one path rather than another? Zhuangzi's response to this problem, simply stated, is this: This question can never be answered in the terms in which it has been put, because our understanding consciousness can *never* know why it sees things one way rather than another, can *never* ultimately ground its own judgments, and is actually in no position to serve as a guide for living. To consciously weigh alternatives, apply your understanding to making a decision about what is best, and then deliberately follow the course you have decided on—this is the fundamental structure of all purposive activity and conscious knowledge, the basis of all ethics, all philosophy, all politics, all human endeavors at improvement, and this is precisely what Zhuangzi seems to consider ridiculous and impossible. Knowledge is unreliable; Will is unreliable; Tradition is unreliable; Intuition is unreliable; Logic is unreliable; Faith is unreliable. But what else is there?

Multiple Perspectives of the Inner Chapters

There has been considerable diversity of opinion in understanding Zhuangzi as a philosopher, somewhat exacerbated by recent attempts by Western readers to fit him into a familiar Occidental philosophical category. Is Zhuangzi, as represented in the Inner Chapters, a mystic? A skeptic? A metaphysical monist? A spirit-body dualist? An intuitionist? A theist? A deist? An agnostic? A relativist? A fatalist? A nihilist? A linguistic philosopher? An existentialist? Or perhaps a poet uncommitted to any particular philosophical position? All of these have been suggested and aggressively argued for, and indeed none of these interpretations is without support in the text. There are places where Zhuangzi speaks as if he were a mystic in the traditional sense, or a skeptic, or a monist, a dualist, an intuitionist, a theist, a deist, an agnostic, a relativist, and so on. Readers would do well to note as they proceed through the text the passages that, taken on their own, might lead to these conclusions. Like a mystic, Zhuangzi often seems to speak of a state that transports one beyond ordinary reason and sensation and puts one in touch with an alternate, life-changing realm of experience (e.g., at 2:36, 2:41, 4:10, 6:54). Like a skeptic, he has many cutting observations to make about the limits of all possible forms of knowledge and ridicules the dogmatism of anyone who claims to know anything conclusively (2:14–33). Like a monist, we find in his work the repeated assertion that "all things are one" (2:32, 5:5). Like a spirit-matter dualist, he tells stories of the negligibility of the physical body, however deformed it may be, in favor of "what moves the physical form" (5:4–20). Like an intuitionist, his dismissal of rational knowledge sometimes seems to point to some alternate type of knowing that can escape the skeptical objections he presents (2:15–24, 3:3–5). Like a theist, he presents characters who speak piously of submitting to the will of an anthropomorphized "Creator of Things" (6:40). Like a deist, he presents a softer version of this trope that severely limits what can be known of this creator, even its personal character and relationship to human beings (6:41–42, 6:52). Like an agnostic, he finally questions even his ability to know what the Heavenly is, whether the Heavenly is not really the Human or vice versa (6:5). Like a relativist, he asserts that all words are acceptable, all courses right, in relation to the perspective from which they are pronounced (2:16–21). Like a fatalist, he speaks of Fate as something about which nothing can be done, something that is simply to be accepted as unavoidable (5:15, 6:57). Like a nihilist, he denies the distinction between right and wrong, and even whether we can know whether knowing is knowing or not-knowing (2:38–39). Like a philosopher of language, he presents devastating insights into the character of discourse and its effect on our beliefs about the world and about values (2:14–17, 2:30–33). Like an existentialist, he seems to conceive the range of human transformation as unbounded, suggesting that the values that guide it lie in the hands of each individual, to be renewed moment by moment (2:18, 2:24, 2:40, 5:5, 5:17, 6:28–29, 7:9–10).

This list could be extended. But it is obvious that many of these positions seem to be starkly opposed or at least incompatible. Does Zhuangzi somehow really combine them all? Can the contradiction be alleviated by judging some of these impressions to be plain misreadings, not really intended in the text? Or are some of them additions by later editors who did not understand the *Zhuangzi's* philosophy? Is there some hierarchy of provisional and more ultimate formulations that would allow us to order them, so that some are to be taken as rhetorical, therapeutic, or jocular formulations while others express Zhuangzi's real position? Are all these positions just thrown together incoherently? Or is there some coherent way to integrate all these different strands into one vision?

As does any translator, I have my own opinions about what I think Zhuangzi is getting at here and about how his text has been devised to express that vision. Readers interested in understanding the philosophical interpretation that informs this translation are invited to consult "Zhuangzi as Philosopher" on this volume's title support page at www.hackettpublishing.com/zhuangzisup, where an extended analysis of the philosophical arguments and implications of the Inner Chapters, and their manner of solving the apparent contradictions between relativism and absolutism, between skepticism and mysticism, is offered. (In addition, the reader will find there an account of recent scholarly analysis of the grouping and dating of chapters of the text, a more detailed discussion of the notion of *dao* as developed in the *Daodejing*, and notes on the method of translation and conventions used in this volume.) But conclusions are perhaps the least important thing to be gained from reading the *Zhuangzi*, and I hope that the delicious experience of grappling with and being jostled about by this text will allow readers to come to their own conclusions about it—and then perhaps to question those conclusions and try out some others.

I am deeply grateful to Shuen-fu Lin, Scott Cook, Alan Cole, Douglas Skonicki, Loy Hui Chieh, Shuman Chen, Paul Dambrasio, Alan Dagovitz, Brian Loh, Diana Lobel, Elena Park, Edward Russell, and Deborah Wilkes for reading and commenting on early versions of parts of this translation and introduction. Their responses and suggestions have been invaluable. Thanks are due also to Northwestern University, the Fulbright-Hays Foundation, the American Council of Learned Societies, and the National Endowment for the Humanities for making available the time and support necessary to complete this work.

THE INNER CHAPTERS

CHAPTER ONE
Wandering Far and Unfettered

There is a fish in the Northern Oblivion named Kun,[1] and this Kun is quite huge, spanning who knows how many thousands of miles. He transforms into a bird named Peng,[2] and this Peng has quite a back on him, stretching who knows how many thousands of miles. When he rouses himself and soars into the air, his wings are like clouds draped across the heavens. The oceans start to churn, and this bird begins his journey toward the Southern Oblivion. The Southern Oblivion—that is the Pool of Heaven.

The Equalizing Jokebook,[3] a record of many wonders, reports: "When Peng journeys to the Southern Oblivion, the waters ripple for three thousand miles. Spiraling aloft, he ascends ninety thousand miles and continues his journey without rest for half a year."

—It's a galloping heat haze![4]—It's a swirl of dust!—It's some living creature blown aloft on a breath of the air! And the blue on blue of the sky—is that the

---

[1]   The name Kun 鯤 literally means "fish egg." The character consists of a "fish" radical beside a phonetic element that literally means "elder brother." If we were to take this as a kind of visual pun, the name might be rendered "Big Brother Roe." The paradoxes implicit in this name are not irrelevant. The largest fish is thus also the smallest speck of pre-fish, the tiny fish egg. The youngest newborn here, the not-yet-fish, is also the elder brother.

[2]   The name Peng 鵬 is cognate with *feng* 鳳, meaning "phoenix," a mythical bird of enormous proportions. The phonetic of the form used by Zhuangzi here is the character *peng* 朋, meaning a "friend" or a "classmate," "comrade" or "peer." If we wished to render the visual pun, we might translate the name as "Peer Phoenix." Again, the paradox is of some importance. Peng is vast, and his superiority to other birds seems to be stressed in what follows, but his name also includes a reference to parity and companionship.

[3]   "Qi Xie" could be the name of either a person or a book, and could also be interpreted to mean, "The Equalizing Harmony."

[4]   Literally, "wild horse(s)." Some commentators suggest this is a term for a miragelike heat haze, which moves through the air like a pack of wild horses seen at a distance, but it is an unusual usage. Some take it literally, construing these three lines as describing the results of Peng's stirring ascent, like the rippling of waters, or else what he sees when looking downward. Here, it is interpreted as what Peng might look like from below, the guesses made by those on the ground. He is unknown, has no "definite identity," only because he is so lofty, and he has to be so lofty only because he is so big.

sky's true[5] color? Or is it just the vast distance, going on and on without end, that looks that way? When Peng looks down, he too sees only this and nothing

1:4   more.

Now, if water is not piled up thickly enough, it has no power to support a large vessel. Overturn a cupful of water in a hole in the road and you can float a mustard seed in it like a boat, but if you put the cup itself in there it will just get stuck. The water is too shallow for so large a vessel. And if the wind is not piled up thickly enough, it has no power to support Peng's enormous wings. That is why he needs to put ninety thousand miles of air beneath him. Only then can he ride the wind, bearing the blue of heaven on his back and unob-

1:5   structed on all sides, and make his way south.

The cicada and the fledgling dove laugh at him, saying, "We scurry up into the air, leaping from the elm to the sandalwood tree, and when we don't quite make it we just plummet to the ground. What's all this about ascending ninety thousand miles and heading south?"

If you go out on a day trip, you can return with your belly still full. If you're traveling a hundred miles, you'll need to bring a day's meal. And if you're traveling a thousand miles, you'll need to save up provisions for three months before you go. What do these two little creatures know? A small consciousness cannot keep up with a vast consciousness; short duration cannot keep up with long duration. How do we know? The morning mushroom knows nothing of the noontide; the winter cicada knows nothing of the spring and autumn. This is what is meant by short duration. In southern Chu there is a tree called Mingling, for which five hundred years is as a single spring, and another five hundred years is as a single autumn. In ancient times, there was even one massive tree whose spring and autumn were each eight thousand years long. And yet nowadays, Pengzu[6] alone has a special reputation for longevity, and every-

1:6   one tries to match him. Pathetic, isn't it?

Tang's questions to Ji also have something about this:

> In the barren northland there is a dark ocean, called the Pool of Heaven. There is a fish there several thousand miles across with a length that is as yet unknown named Kun. There's a bird there named Peng with a back like Mt. Tai and wings like clouds draped across the heavens. Whorling upward, he ascends ninety thousand miles, breaking through the clouds and bearing the blue of the sky on his back, and then heads south, finally arriving at the Southern Oblivion. The quail laughs at him, saying, "Where does he think *he's* going? I leap into the air with all my might, but before I get farther than a few yards I drop to the ground. My twittering and fluttering between the bushes and branches is the utmost form of flying! So where does he think *he's* going?" Such is the difference between the large and the small.

And he whose understanding[7] is sufficient to fill some one post, whose deeds meet the needs of some one village, or whose Virtuosity[8] pleases some one ruler, thus winning him a country to preside over, sees himself in just the same way. Even Song Rongzi[9] would burst out laughing at such a man. If the whole world happened to praise Song Rongzi, he would not be goaded onward; if the whole world condemned him, he would not be deterred. He simply made a sharp and fixed division between the inner and the outer and clearly discerned where true honor and disgrace are to be found. He did not involve himself in anxious calculations in his dealings with the world. But nonetheless, there was still a sense in which he was not yet really firmly planted.

1:7

Now, Liezi rode forth upon the wind, weightlessly graceful, not heading back until fifteen days had passed. He did not involve himself in anxious calculations about bringing good fortune to himself. Although this allowed him to avoid the exertions of walking, there was still something he needed to depend on.

But suppose you were to chariot upon what is true[10] both to Heaven and to earth, riding atop the back-and-forth of the six atmospheric breaths,[11] so that

---

7 "Understanding" is *zhi* 知, elsewhere translated as the "understanding consciousness," "knowing consciousness," "conscious knowing," "knowledge," "cleverness," or "wisdom." See Glossary.

8 Virtuosity is *de* 德. See Glossary.

9 Song Rongzi is another name for the philosopher Song Xing, to be discussed at greater length in Chapter 33. His doctrine that "to be insulted is not a disgrace" is acknowledged by Zhuangzi here as a salutary first step toward independence from the opinions and value judgments of convention. But as the commentators point out, this is still just a first step, which rests on making a clear and fixed distinction between self and other, safeguarding one's identity against external influence.

10 "True" is *zheng* 正. See Glossary. This echoes the question at the beginning of the chapter about the "true" color of Heaven as seen from the earth (1:4, note 5). Now Zhuangzi speaks of riding upon what is true both to Heaven *and* to earth, what he later calls "Walking Two Roads" (2:24). Cf. also 2:39, 2:44.

11 *Liu qi* 六氣, literally, the six *qi*. For *qi*, see Glossary. According to Sima Biao, the six are yin, yang, wind, rain, darkness, and light. Cheng Xuanying, citing Li Yi 李頤, interprets them as the atmospheric conditions of dawn, high noon, sunset, and midnight, together with the energies of Heaven and earth generally. Zhi Daolin 支道林, more simply, takes them to be the four seasons together with the general energies of Heaven and earth. The character *bian* 辯, translated as "back-and-forth," means disputation, the central topic of much of the following chapter. See Glossary. The usage is odd, and several substitutions have been suggested, including "transformation" and "differentiation," other important Zhuangzian themes. But replacing the character seems to efface the resonance with the trope of the wind-storm sounds as disputations that opens the next chapter. Each atmospheric state is, as it were, making an "argument," presenting what is right to it. We are urged to ride what is true both to Heaven and to earth and similarly to hitch our chariots to the disputational deposition of each contrasting atmospheric state in turn.

your wandering could nowhere be brought to a halt. You would then be depending on[12]—what? Thus I say, the Consummate Person has no fixed iden-
1:8   tity, the Spirit Man has no particular merit, the Sage has no one name.

When Yao[13] went to cede the empire to Xu You, he said, "To keep the torches
burning in broad daylight would be making needless trouble for oneself. To
continue watering one's garden during heavy rainfall would be pointless labor.
Now, you, sir, so much as appear in the world and at once it is well-ordered.
And yet here I am, playing the master and acting like I control it all. I feel I am
1:9   greatly deficient. Please accept the rulership of this world from me."

Xu You replied, "You rule the world, and the world is thus already ruled
however you rule it. If I were nonetheless to take your place, would I be doing
it for the name? But name is merely a guest of what is really substantial. Shall
I then play the role of the guest? The tailorbird lives in the depths of a vast forest but uses no more than a single branch to make its nest. When the beaver
1:10   drinks from the river, it takes only enough to fill its belly. Go home, my lord!
I have no use for an empire. Although the cook may not keep the kitchen in
order, that doesn't mean the spirit-medium or the priest needs to leap over the
1:11   sacrificial vessels to replace him!"[14]

Jian Wu said to Lian Shu, "I was listening to the words of the madman Jieyu.[15]
He talked big without getting at anything, going on and on without getting
anywhere. I was shocked and terrified by what he said, which seemed as limitless as the Milky Way—vast and excessive, with no regard for the way people
really are."

Lian Shu asked, "What in the world did he say?"

---

12   "Depending on" is *dai* 待. See 2:44, 2:45, 2:48, 4:9, 6:5, 6:29, 7:15, and Glossary.

13   Mythical ancient sage-emperor who ceded his empire not to his son but to the most
worthy man in the realm, Shun, also subsequently revered as a sage. The current incident,
in which Yao tries and fails to cede it to the hermit Xu You, suggests that Shun was a second
choice at best.

14   The reference is to a ritual sacrifice to the ancestors, where the spirit-medium is a
stand-in for the dead ancestors, occupying their place and thus receiving the offerings. The
priest is the one who arranges the ritual vessels. The cook prepares the food to be used as sacrificial offerings. Xu You compares himself to the medium, in whose person presence and
absence, life and death, coincide. He is silent, inactive, majestic, awe-inspiring, sacred. He
is the one who receives the offerings of the "cook," that is, the ruler, and yet he does not really receive them; they pass through him. If he were to leap over the vessels to take the place
of the cook, because the food was ill-prepared, he would be relinquishing precisely the qualities that make him worthy of the offering and thus undermine the ritual even more disas-
trously than the poor-quality food does. The ruler may be offering unpalatable fare, but to
try to fix it would be to give up an even more sacred position, one that alone makes the whole
arrangement meaningful.

15   Jieyu ridicules Confucius in the *Analects* (18.5) and thus serves as a classic symbol of
anti-Confucian sentiment. He appears again at the end of Chapter 4 and passim.

"'There is a Spirit-Man living on distant Mt. Guye with skin like ice and snow, gentle and yielding like a virgin girl. He does not eat the five grains but rather feeds on the wind and dew. He rides upon the air and clouds, as if hitching his chariot to soaring dragons, wandering beyond the four seas. He concentrates his spirit, and straightaway all things are free from sickness and the harvest matures.' I regard this as crazy talk, which I refuse to believe."

"That's just as it should be. The blind have no access to the beauty of visual patterns, and the deaf have no part in the sounds of bells and drums. It is not only the physical body that can be blind and deaf; the faculty of understanding[16] can also be so. If you were then to 'agree' with his words, you would be acting like a virgin girl who has just reached her time.[17] A man like the one described in these words blankets all things with his Virtuosity, allowing the present age to seek out its own chaotic order.[18] How could he be bothered to try to manage the world? This man is harmed by no thing. A flood may reach the sky without drowning him; a drought may melt the stones and scorch the mountains without scalding him. From his dust and chaff you could mold yourself a Yao or a Shun. Why would he bother himself over mere *beings*? A ceremonial cap salesman of Song once traveled to Yue, where the people shave their heads and tattoo their bodies—they had no use for such things. After Yao brought all the people of the world under his rule and put all within the four seas into good order, he went off to see four of these masters of distant Mt. Guye at the bright side of the Fen River. Astonished at what he saw there, he forgot all about his kingdom."

1:12

1:13

Huizi said to Zhuangzi, "The King of Wei gave me the seed of a great gourd. I planted it, and when it matured it weighed over a hundred pounds. I filled it with liquid, but it was not firm enough to lift. I cut it in half to make a dipper, but it was too large to scoop into anything. It was big and all, but because it was so useless, I finally just smashed it to pieces."

Zhuangzi said, "You are certainly stupid when it comes to using big things. There was once a man of Song who was skilled at making a balm to keep the hands from chapping. For generations his family had used it to make a living washing silk through the winter. A customer heard about it and asked to buy

---

16 *Zhi.* See Glossary.

17 Many commentators suggest that this sentence should be read to mean, "This describes you perfectly," taking *shi* 時 as a loan for *shi* 是, and *nü* 女 as a loan for *ru* 汝. This is feasible, but the more literal translation given here suggests that it is only right for Jian Wu to consider these words untrue, for if someone who is "blind and deaf" in this way were to blindly "agree" with them (literally, "consider these words right," *shi qi yan* 是其言 (cf. 2:43); for *shi*, see Glossary), that person would be like a flirtatious virgin girl who has not experienced, and does not really understand, to what she is agreeing.

18 The term *luan* 亂 normally meant "disorder" in Zhuangzi's time, but it has an archaic meaning of just the opposite, "to govern" or "to put in order." Zhuangzi seems to be playing on this double meaning here.

the recipe for a hundred pieces of gold. The family got together and consulted, saying, 'We've been washing silk for generations and have never earned more than a few pieces of gold; now in one morning we can sell the technique for a hundred. Let's do it.' The customer took the balm and presented it to the king of Wu. When Yue started a war with him, the king made the man a general who led his soldiers through a winter water battle with the men of Yue and beat them big. The man was then enfeoffed as a feudal lord. The power to keep the hands from chapping was one and the same, but one man used it to get an enfeoffment and another couldn't even use it to avoid washing silk all winter. The difference is all in the way the thing is used. You, on the other hand, had a gourd of over a hundred pounds. How is it that you never thought of making it into an enormous vessel for yourself and floating through the lakes and rivers in it? Instead, you worried that it was too big to scoop into anything, which I guess means our greatly esteemed master here still has a lot of tangled weeds

1:14   clogging up his mind!"

Huizi said to Zhuangzi, "I have a huge tree which people call the Stink Tree. The trunk is swollen and gnarled, impossible to align with any level or ruler. The branches are twisted and bent, impossible to align to any T-square or carpenter's arc. Even if it were growing right in the road, a carpenter would not give it so much as a second glance. And your words are similarly big but useless, which is why they are rejected by everyone who hears them."

Zhuangzi said, "Haven't you ever seen a wildcat or weasel? It crouches low to await its prey, pounces now to the east and now to the west, leaping high and low. But this is exactly what lands it in a trap, and it ends up dying in the net. But take a yak: it is big like the clouds draped across the heavens. Now, that is something that is good at being big—but of course it cannot catch so much as a single mouse. You, on the other hand, have this big tree, and you worry that it's useless. Why not plant it in our homeland of not-even-anything, the vast wilds of open nowhere? Then you could loaf and wander there, doing lots of nothing there at its side, and take yourself a nap, far-flung and unfettered, there beneath it. It will never be cut down by ax or saw. Nothing will harm it. Since it has nothing for which it can be used, what could entrap or

1:15   afflict it?"

CHAPTER TWO
Equalizing Assessments of Things[1]   2:1

Ziqi of the Southern Wall was reclining against a low table on the ground, releasing his breath into Heaven above, all in a scatter, as if loosed from a partner.

Yancheng Ziyou stood in attendance before him. "What has happened here?" he said. "Can the body really be made like dried wood, the mind like dead ashes? What reclines against this table now is not what reclined against it before."

Ziqi said, "A good question, Yan! What has happened here is simply that *I* have lost *me*. Do you understand? You hear the piping of man but not yet the   2:2 piping of the earth. You hear the piping of the earth but not yet the piping of Heaven."   2:3

Ziyou said, "Please tell me more."

Ziqi replied, "When the Great Clump belches forth its vital breath,[2] we call it the wind. As soon as it arises, raging cries emerge from all the ten thousand hollows. Don't tell me you've never heard how long the rustling continues, on and on! The towering trees of the forest, a hundred spans around, are riddled with indentations and holes—like noses, mouths, ears; like sockets, enclosures, mortars; like ponds, like puddles. Roarers and whizzers, scolders and sighers, shouters, wailers, boomers, growlers! One leads with a ycee! Another answers with a yuuu! A light breeze brings a small harmony, while a powerful gale makes for a harmony vast and grand. And once the sharp wind has passed, all these holes return to their silent emptiness. Have you never seen all the tempered attunements, all the cunning contentions?"   2:4

Ziyou said, "So the piping of the earth means just the sound of these hollows. And the piping of man would be the sound of bamboo panpipes. What, then, is the piping of Heaven?"

Ziqi said, "It gusts through all the ten thousand differences, allowing each

---

1   "Assessment" here renders *lun* 論, meaning a verbally expressed viewpoint or discussion on some matter, a discourse that weighs relevant factors with much or little argument and explanation, but generally with the intent of rendering a judgment and expressing a position on what is so and what is right. An attempt is made here to preserve the ambiguity of this title, *Qiwulun* 齊物論 which can be parsed either as 2-1 or as 1-2, thus meaning either "Assessments that Equalize Things" or "Equalizing the Assessments Made by All Things and, by Extension, All Things So Assessed." The word *wu* 物, rendered as "thing(s)" here, is in other contexts translated as "being(s)" and denotes not only inanimate objects but also living creatures and even sometimes abstract entities. In the "commentaries" section, the word *lun* is rendered "theories," as the sense of the term had taken on this more formal implication by the times in which they were written.

2   The "Vital breath" is *qi* 氣. See Glossary.

to go its own way. But since each one selects out its own, what identity can
2:5 there be for their rouser?"³

A large consciousness is idle and spacey; a small consciousness is cramped and
circumspect. Big talk is bland and flavorless; petty talk is detailed and frag-
2:6 mented. We sleep and our spirits converge; we awake and our bodies open outward. We give, we receive, we act, we construct: all day long we apply our
minds to struggles against one thing or another—struggles unadorned or struggles concealed, but in either case tightly packed one after another without gap.
The small fears leave us nervous and depleted; the large fears leave us stunned
and blank. Shooting forth like an arrow from a bowstring: such is our pre-
sumption when we arbitrate right and wrong. Holding fast as if to sworn oaths:
such is our defense of our victories. Worn away as if by autumn and winter:
such is our daily dwindling, drowning us in our own activities, unable to turn
back. Held fast as if bound by cords, we continue along the same ruts.⁴ The
mind is left on the verge of death, and nothing can restore its vitality.

Joy and anger, sorrow and happiness, plans and regrets, transformations and
stagnations, unguarded abandonment and deliberate posturing—music flowing out of hollows, mushrooms of billowing steam! Day and night they alternate before us, but no one knows whence they sprout. That is enough! That is
2:7 enough! Is it from all of this, presented ceaselessly day and night, that we come
to exist? Without *that* there would be no me, to be sure, but then again with-
2:8 out *me* there would be nothing selected out from it all.⁵ This is certainly something close to hand, and yet we do not know what makes it so. If there is some
controller behind it all, it is peculiarly devoid of any manifest sign. Its ability
to flow and to stop makes its presence plausible, but even then it shows no definite form. That would make it a reality with no definite form.

The hundred bones, the nine openings, the six internal organs are all present here as my body. Which one is most dear to me? Do you delight in all
2:9 equally, or do you have some favorite among them? Or are they all mere servants and concubines? Are these servants and concubines unable to govern
each other? Or do they take turns as master and servant? If there exists a gen-

---

³   An alternate rendering of this important line is: "It blows forth in ten thousand different ways, allowing each to go as it will. Each takes what it chooses for itself—but then who
could it be that activates them all?" And another: "Gusting through this multitude, every one
of them different, it yet allows each to go its own way. The taking up of something is done
by themselves, so what rouser could there be?" Many commentators accept the textual vari-
ant *yi* 已 ("to cease") for *ji* 己 ("oneself"), so that the line would perhaps mean: "It blows
forth the ten thousand differences but also allows them to cease on their own. They take up
both [their beginning and their ending] on their own accord—who, then, is the rouser?"

⁴   The translation is based on Wang Fuzhi's reading.

⁵   Analogously, without the wind there would be no sound, but without the holes there
would be no particular tone selected out from it and actualized.

uine ruler among them, then whether we could find out the facts about him or not would neither add to nor subtract from that genuineness.   *2:10*

If you regard what you have received as fully formed[6] once and for all, unable to forget it, all the time it survives is just a vigil spent waiting for its end. In the process, you grind and lacerate yourself against all the things around you. Its activities will be over as quickly as a horse galloping by, unstoppable— is it not sad? All your life you labor, and nothing is achieved. Worn and exhausted to the point of collapse, never knowing what it all amounts to—how can you not lament this? What good does it do if others say, "To us he is not dead"? The body has decayed and the mind went with it. Can this be called anything but an enormous sorrow? Is human life always this bewildering, or am I the only bewildered one? Is there actually any man, or anything in a man, that is not bewildered?   *2:11*

If we follow whatever has so far taken shape, fully formed,[7] in our minds, making that our teacher, who could ever be without a teacher? The mind comes to be what it is by taking possession of whatever it selects out of the process of alternation—but does that mean it has to truly understand that process? The fool takes something up from it too. But to claim that there are any such things as "right" and "wrong" *before* they come to be fully formed in someone's mind in this way—that is like saying you left for Yue today and arrived there yesterday.[8] This is to regard the nonexistent as existent. The existence of the nonexistent is beyond the understanding of even the divine sage-king Yu—so what possible sense could it make to someone like me?   *2:12*   *2:13*

"But human speech is not just a blowing of air. Speech has something *of which* it speaks, something it refers to." Yes, but what it refers to is peculiarly unfixed. So is there really anything it refers to? Or has nothing ever been referred to? You take it to be different from the chirping of baby birds. But is there really any difference between them? Or is there no difference? Is there any dispute, or is there no dispute? Anything demonstrated, or nothing demonstrated?   *2:14*

How could courses be so obscured that there could be any question of genuine or fake among them? How could words be so obscured that there could be any question of right or wrong among them? Where can you go without it being a course? What can you say without it being affirmable? Courses are obscured by the small accomplishments already formed and completed by them.[9] Words are obscured by the ostentatious blossoms of reputation that come with them. Hence we have the rights and wrongs of the Confucians and Mohists, each affirming what the other negates and negating what the other

---

6   "Fully formed" is *cheng* 成. See Glossary.

7   *Cheng*. See Glossary.

8   A phrase attributed to Hui Shi; see Chapter 33.

9   "Fully formed and completed" is the rendering for *cheng* here. See Glossary.

affirms. But if you want to affirm what they negate and negate what they affirm, nothing compares to the Illumination of the Obvious:[10]

There is no being that is not "that." There is no being that is not "this." But one cannot be seeing these from the perspective of "that": one knows them only from "this" [i.e., from one's own perspective].[11] Thus, we can say: "That" emerges from "this," and "this" follows from "that." This is the theory of the simultaneous generation of "this" and "that." But by the same token, their simultaneous generation is their simultaneous destruction, and vice versa. Simultaneous affirmability is simultaneous negatability, and vice versa. What is circumstantially right is also circumstantially wrong, and vice versa. Thus, the Sage does not proceed from any one of them alone but instead lets them all bask in the broad daylight of Heaven. And that too is only a case of going by the rightness of the present "this."

"This" is also a "that." "That" is also a "this." "THAT" posits a "this" and a "that"—a right and a wrong—of its own. But "THIS" also posits a "this" and a "that"—a right and a wrong—of its own. So is there really any "that" versus "this," any right versus wrong? Or is there really no "that" versus "this"? When "this" and "that"—right and wrong—are no longer coupled as opposites—that is called the Course as Axis, the axis of all courses.[12] When this axis finds its place in the center, it responds to all the endless things it confronts, thwarted by none. For it has an endless supply of "rights," and an endless supply of "wrongs." Thus, I say, nothing compares to the Illumination of the Obvious.

To use this finger to show how a finger is not a finger is no match for using not-this-finger to show how a finger is not a finger. To use this horse to show that a horse is not a horse is no match for using not-this-horse to show that a horse is not a horse. Heaven and earth are one finger. All things are one horse.[13]

2:15
2:16
2:17
2:18
2:19

---

10   The phrase *yiming* 以明 (literally, "use of the light/obvious") is here rendered as "Illumination of the Obvious." See *yiming* in the Glossary.

11   This line constitutes an essential turning point in the discussion, but it is very hard to construe. Here, it is interpreted to mean that since we are each restricted to our own perspective—our "this"—but at the same time we manifestly have an awareness of other possible perspectives—since we can say both "this" and "that"—both the "this" and the "that" are present here in the "this." The rest of this paragraph follows from this consideration.

12   Neither a singular nor a plural reading of *dao* 道 will suffice in this context. The text says literally "is called the Course-Axis." This could imply either the axis *of* the Course or that the Course *is* an axis.

13   An alternate reading of this passage would be something like the following: "To stand in the perspective of what is indicated [i.e., 'this'] to show how what is not indicated ['that'] is entailed in every indication ['this'] is no match for standing in the perspective that is not indicated ['that'] to show how what is not indicated ['that'] is entailed in every indication ['this']." The rejected alternative in this version is a caricature of a proposition attributed to the "logician" Gongsun Long (who is also mentioned in Chapters 17 and 33): "all things are capable of being pointed out [lit., 'fingered'], but pointing out can never be pointed out"

Something is affirmative because someone affirms it. Something is negative because someone negates it. Courses are formed[14] by someone walking them. Things are so by being called so. Whence thus and so? From thus and so being affirmed of them. Whence not thus and so? From thus and so being negated of them. Each thing necessarily has some place from which it can be affirmed as thus and so, and some place from which it can be affirmed as acceptable.   2:20

So no thing is not right, no thing is not acceptable. For whatever we may define as a beam as opposed to a pillar, as a leper as opposed to the great beauty Xishi, or whatever might be [from some perspective] strange, grotesque, uncanny, or deceptive, there is some course that opens them into one another, connecting them to form a oneness. Whenever fragmentation is going on, formation, completion,[15] is also going on. Whenever formation is going on, destruction is also going on.   2:21

Hence, all things are neither formed nor destroyed, for these two also open into each other, connecting to form a oneness. It is only someone who really gets all the way through them that can see how the two sides open into each other to form a oneness. Such a person would not define rightness in any one particular way but would instead entrust it to the everyday function [of each being]. Their everyday function is what works for them, and "working" just means this opening up into each other, their way of connecting. Opening to   2:22

(*wu wu fei zhi, er zhi fei zhi* 物無非指，而指非指). This is seemingly meant to show that the act of indicating "this" always fails to indicate itself, and thus every act of "the pointing out of this" is never pointed out as "this," so the act of indicating some "this" is never it self "this." All other things are "this," but the pointing out of "this" can never be "this." A "pointer out" or "indicator" can also be interpreted to mean what is pointed out, i.e., "a meaning." The implication is then that the meaning of a statement is also not the meaning, and whatever something may mean, it also means something else besides, which arrives the long way around at Zhuangzi's own point. Zhuangzi too wants to show that "this" is never merely "this," but he suggests an alternate method: to show that *this* is also *that*, simply use the Illumination of the Obvious to look at *this* from the perspective of *that*. *This* is then immediately seen as a *that*. A similar point is then made with respect to another paradox attributed to Gongsun: "A white horse is not a horse." The point here is that "white horse" and "horse" are, strictly speaking, two distinguishable meanings: one indicates a shape and a color, and the other indicates only a shape; indicating a shape and color is not the same as indicating only a shape. So he is using a (white) horse to show that a horse is not a (white) horse. Instead, Zhuangzi wants to arrive at the same conclusion—a horse is not a horse, "this" is not merely "this" but also "that"—but does so merely by pointing out that if "horse" is defined as "this," it must posit "nonhorseness" as its corresponding "that," which will also be a "this" with its own perspective, for which "horse" is no longer "this." Whatever I point out as horse must follow the "this/that" structure, and the defining of it as "horse" is internal to the perspective of the "this," which is thus undermined when the "this" shifts to the other, nonhorse side. Hence, a horse is not a horse.

14   "Formed" is *cheng*. See Glossary.

15   "Completion" is *cheng*. See Glossary.

form a connection just means getting what you get: go as far as whatever you happen to get to, and leave it at that. It is all just a matter of going by the rightness of the present "this." To be doing this without knowing it, and not because you have defined it as right, is called "the Course."

2:23   But to labor your spirit trying to make all things one, without realizing that it is all the same [whether you do so or not], is called "Three in the Morning."

What is this Three in the Morning? A monkey trainer was distributing chestnuts. He said, "I'll give you three in the morning and four in the evening." The monkeys were furious. "Well then," he said, "I'll give you four in the morning and three in the evening." The monkeys were delighted. This change of description and arrangement caused no loss, but in one case it brought anger and in another delight. He just went by the rightness of their present "this." Thus, the Sage uses various rights and wrongs to harmonize with others and yet remains at rest in the middle of Heaven the Potter's Wheel.[16] This is called

2:24   "Walking Two Roads."

The understanding of the ancients really got all the way there. Where had it arrived? To the point where, for some, there had never existed so-called things. This is really getting there, as far as you can go. When no things are

2:25   there, nothing more can be—added!

Next there were those for whom things existed but never any definite boundaries between them. Next there were those for whom there were boundaries but never any rights and wrongs. When rights and wrongs waxed bright,

---

16   Or "the Heavenly Potter's wheel," "the Potter's Wheel of the Heavenly," "the Potter's Wheel of Heaven." In all of Zhuangzi's coinages involving the word "Heaven," it is useful to experimentally substitute the words "Natural," "Undesigned," "Spontaneous," or "Skylike." Hence, one might retranslate this phrase as either "Potter's Wheel of Nature" or, perhaps more strikingly, "the Skylike Potter's Wheel." (See *tian* in Glossary.) The character used here for "Potter's Wheel" also means "equality." The two meanings converge in the consideration of the even distribution of clay made possible by the constant spinning of the wheel: the potter's wheel's very instability, its constant motion, is what makes things equal. Note also that Chinese cosmology considers Heaven, the sky, to be "rotating": the stars and constellations turn in the sky, and the seasons—the sky's varying conditions—are brought in a cyclical sequence. This turning of the seasons is what makes things exist and grow. The turning of the Potter's Wheel sky brings life, as the potter's wheel creates pots. The "Qifa" chapter of the *Guanzi*, a text of "Legalist" orientation, states, "To give commands without understanding fixed principles is like trying to establish [the directions] of sunrise and sunset while standing on a turning potter's wheel." It is significant that Zhuangzi uses an image of instability that others employ to critique the relativism of shifting perspectives as a solution to the same. This shows the deliberate irony of the use of the verb "rest" in this context, which is connected to the idea of the unmoving center of the spinning wheel, the stability that exists in the midst of this instability without eliminating it: Walking Two Roads. Cf. "the Tranquility of Turmoil" of Chapter 6, specifically 6:38.

the Course began to wane. What set the Course to waning was exactly what brought the cherishing of one thing over another to its fullness.[17]   2:26

But is there really any waning versus fullness? Or is there really no such thing as waning versus fullness? In a certain sense, there exists waning versus fullness. In that sense, we can say that the Zhaos are zither players. But in a certain sense, there is no such thing as waning versus fullness. In that sense we can say, on the contrary, that the Zhaos are no zither players.   2:27

Zhao Wen's zither playing, Master Kuang's baton waving, Huizi's desk slumping—the understanding these three had of their arts flourished richly. This was what they flourished in, and thus they pursued these arts to the end of their days. They delighted in them, and observing that this delight of theirs was not shared, they wanted to make it obvious to others. So they tried to make others understand as obvious what was not obvious to them, and thus some ended their days debating about the obscurities of "hardness" and "whiteness," and Zhao Wen's son ended his days still grappling with his father's zither strings. Can this be called success, being fully accomplished at something? In that case, even I am fully accomplished. Can this be called failure, lacking the full accomplishment of something? If so, neither I nor anything else can be considered fully accomplished.   2:28

Thus, the Radiance of Drift and Doubt is the sage's only map. He makes no definition of what is right but instead entrusts it to the everyday function of each thing. This is what I call the Illumination of the Obvious.   2:29

Now I will try some words here about "this." But I don't know if it belongs in the same category as "this" or not. For belonging in a category and not belonging in that category themselves form a single category! Being similar is so similar to being dissimilar! So there is finally no way to keep it different from "that."   2:30

Nevertheless, let me try to say it. There is a beginning. There is a not-yet-beginning-to-be-a-beginning. There is a not-yet-beginning-to-not-yet-begin-to-be-a-beginning. There is existence. There is nonexistence. There is a not-yet-beginning-to-be-nonexistence. There is a not-yet-beginning-to-not-yet-begin-to-be-nonexistence. Suddenly there is nonexistence. But I do not-yet know whether "the existence of nonexistence" is ultimately existence or nonexistence.

Now I have said something. But I do not-yet know: has what I have said really said anything? Or has it not really said anything?   2:31

Nothing in the world is larger than the tip of a hair in autumn, and Mt. Tai is small. No one lives longer than a dead child, and old Pengzu died an early death. Heaven and earth are born together with me, and the ten thousand things and I are one.   2:32

---

[17] The single word *cheng*, depending on its antonym in each case, is translated variously as fullness, completion, formation, fully formed, success, or accomplishment in this and the preceding passages. See Glossary.

But if we are all one, can there be any words? But since I have already declared that we are "one," can there be no words? The one and the word are already two, the two and the original unnamed one are three.[18] Going on like this, even a skilled chronicler could not keep up with it, not to mention a lesser man. So even moving from nonexistence to existence we already arrive at three—how much more when we move from existence to existence! Rather than moving from anywhere to anywhere, then, let us just go by the rightness of whatever is before us as the present "this."

2:33

Now, courses have never had any sealed borders between them, and words have never had any constant sustainability.[19] It is by establishing definitions of what is "this," what is "right," that boundaries are made. Let me explain what I mean by boundaries: There are right and left, then there are classes of things and ideas of the proper responses to them,[20] then there are roles and disputes, then there are competitions and struggles. Let's call these the Eight Virtues! As for the sage, he may admit that something exists beyond the six limits of the known world, but he does not further discuss it. As for what is within the known world, he will discuss it but not express an opinion on it. As for historical events, he will give an opinion but not debate it. For wherever a division is made, something is left undivided. Wherever debate shows one of two alternatives to be right, something remains undistinguished and unshown. What is it? The sage hides it in his embrace, while the masses of people debate it, trying to demonstrate it to one another. Thus I say that demonstration by debate always leaves something unseen.

The Great Course is unproclaimed. Great demonstration uses no words.

2:34

Great Humanity is not humane. Great rectitude is not fastidious. Great courage is not invasive. For when the Course becomes explicit, it ceases to be the Course. When words demonstrate by debate, they fail to communicate. When Humanity is constantly sustained, it cannot reach its maturity.[21] When rectitude is pure, it cannot extend itself to others. When courage is invasive, it

---

[18]   A. C. Graham's comment on this passage is unimprovable:

Hui Shih [Huizi] had said that 'Heaven and earth are one unit' [see Chapter 33]. At first sight one might expect [Zhuangzi] to agree with that at least. But to refuse to distinguish alternatives is to refuse to affirm even "Everything is one" against "Things are many." He observes that in saying it the statement itself is additional to the One which it is about, so that already there are two (Plato makes a similar point about the One and its name in *The Sophist*). It may be noticed that [Zhuangzi] never does say that everything is one (except as one side of a paradox [Chapter 5, specifically 5:5]), [but rather] always speaks subjectively of the sage treating [all things] as one (Graham, *Chuang Tzu*, p. 56).

[19]   "Constant sustainability" is *chang*. See Glossary.

[20]   "Proper responses" is *yi*. See *ren yi* in Glossary.

[21]   "Maturity" is *cheng*.

cannot succeed.[22] These five are originally round, but they are forced toward squareness.

     Hence, when the understanding consciousness comes to rest in what it does not know, it has reached its utmost. The demonstration that uses no words, the Course that is not a course—who "understands" these things? If there is something able to "understand" them [in this sense], it can be called the Heavenly Reservoir—poured into without ever getting full, ladled out of without ever running out, ever not-knowing its own source.[23]

     This is called the Shadowy Splendor.

In ancient times, Yao asked Shun, "I want to attack Zong, Kuai, and Xu'ao, for though I sit facing south on the throne, still I am not at ease. Why is this?"

     Shun said, "Though these three may continue to dwell out among the grasses and brambles, why should this make you ill at ease? Once upon a time, ten suns rose in the sky at once, and the ten thousand things were all simultaneously illuminated. And how much better are many Virtuosities than many suns?[24]

Nie Que[25] asked Wang Ni, "Do you know what all things agree in considering right?"

     Wang Ni said, "How could I know that?"

     Nie Que said, "Do you know that you don't know?"

     Wang Ni said, "How could I know that?"

     Nie Que said, "Then are all beings devoid of knowledge?"

     Wang Ni said, "How could I know that? Still, let me try to say something about this. How could I know that what I call 'knowing' is not really 'not-knowing'? How could I know that what I call 'not-knowing' is not really 'knowing'?

2:35

2:36

2:37

2:38

---

[22]   "Succeed" is *cheng*.

[23]   Or "Skylike Reservoir" instead of "Heavenly Reservoir." Here, the Heavenly Reservoir (*tianfu* 天府) is construed as a name not for "the Course that is not a course," but for what would be able to "understand it"—i.e., to know it by not knowing it, by coming to rest in what it does not know. In other words, the Heavenly Reservoir is the Daoist's wild-card mind, rather than its object, the Course. Note the similar Zhuangzian phrases for Daoist subjectivity, e.g., the "Numinous Reservoir" (*lingfu* 靈府 ; see 5:16). Both "know" and "understand" in this passage are renderings of *zhi* 知 (see Glossary).

[24]   For Yao and Shun, see 1:9, note 13. According to the *Huainanzi*, "In the time of Yao, ten suns rose in the sky at once, scorching the grains and crops, killing the plants and grasses." The story is meant to show that there can be only a single ruler, just as there can be only a single sun. Many suns will be "too much of a good thing," killing off the crops. Hence, Yao had nine of the suns shot out of the sky, thereby establishing unified rule. Zhuangzi's parody turns this point on its head. Yao thinks ten different standards of "rightness" will lead to chaos—there must be a single unified truth, a single ruler. Zhuangzi here allows all things their own rightness—and thereby there will be all the more illumination, with each thing its own sun.

[25]   Cf. p. 50 and p. 87.

But now let me take a stab at asking you about it. When people sleep in a damp place, they wake up deathly ill and sore about the waist—but what about eels? If people live in trees, they tremble with fear and worry—but how about monkeys? Of these three, which 'knows' what is the right[26] place to live? People eat the flesh of their livestock, deer eat grass, snakes eat centipedes, hawks and eagles eat mice. Of these four, which 'knows' the right thing to eat? Monkeys take she-monkeys for mates, bucks mount does, male fish frolic with female fish, while humans regard Mao Qiang and Lady Li as great beauties—but when fish see them they dart into the depths, when birds see them they soar into the skies, when deer see them they bolt away without looking back. Which of these four 'knows' what is rightly alluring? From where I see it, the transitions of Humanity and Responsibility and the trails of right and wrong are hopelessly tangled and confused. How could I know how to distinguish which is right among them?"

Nie Que said, "If that's the case, then you can't even tell benefit from harm. Does the Consummate Person really fail to distinguish between benefit and harm?"

2:39   Wang Ni said, "The Consummate Person is miraculous, beyond understanding! The lakes may burst into flames around him, but this can't make him feel it is too hot. The rivers may freeze over, but this can't make him feel it is too cold. Ferocious thunder may crumble the mountains, the winds may shake the seas, but this cannot make him feel startled. Such a person chariots on the clouds and winds, piggybacks on the sun and moon, and wanders beyond the four seas. Even death and life can do nothing to change him—much less the

2:40   transitions between benefit and harm!"

Ju Quezi asked Chang Wuzi, "I have heard the Master relating the claim that the sage does not engage in projects, does not seek benefit, does not avoid harm, does not pursue happiness, does not follow any specific course. He says something by saying nothing, and says nothing by saying something, and thus does he wander, beyond the dust and grime. The Master considered these rude and careless words, but I believe they are the practice of the Mysterious Course. What do you think?"

Chang Wuzi said, "These words would send even the Yellow Emperor into fevers of confusion. How could Confucius understand them? And you, on the contrary, are judging far too prematurely. You see an egg and try to get it to crow at dawn; you see a crossbow pellet and try to roast it for your dinner. I'm going to try speaking some reckless words. How about listening just as recklessly? While the mass of men are beleaguered and harried, the sage is dim and dense, standing shoulder to shoulder with the sun and moon, scooping up time

---

26   "Right" is *zheng* 正 , the same word translated in Chapter 1 as "true," as in the "true color [of the sky]" (1:4) and "chariot upon what is true both to Heaven and to earth" (1:8). See Glossary.

and space and smooching them all together, leaving them all to their own slippery mush so that every enslavement is also an ennobling. He is there taking part in the diversity of ten thousand harvests, but in each he tastes one and the same purity of fully formed maturation.[27] For to him each thing is just so, each thing is right, and so he enfolds them all within himself by affirming the rightness of each.

2:41

"How, then, do I know that delighting in life is not a delusion? How do I know that in hating death I am not like an orphan who left home in youth and no longer knows the way back? Lady Li was a daughter of the border guard of Ai. When she was first captured and brought to Qin, she wept until tears drenched her collar. But when she got to the palace, sharing the king's luxurious bed and feasting on the finest meats, she regretted her tears. How do I know that the dead don't regret the way they used to cling to life? 'If you dream of drinking wine, in the morning you will weep. If you dream of weeping, in the morning you will go out hunting.'[28] While dreaming you don't know it's a dream. You might even interpret a dream in your dream—and then you wake up and realize it was *all* a dream.

2:42

"Perhaps a great awakening would reveal all of this to be a vast dream. And yet, fools imagine they are already awake—how clearly and certainly they understand it all! This one is a lord, they decide, that one is a shepherd—what prejudice! Confucius and you are both dreaming! And when I say you're dreaming, I'm dreaming too. So if you were to 'agree' with these words as right, I would name that nothing more than a way of offering condolences for the demise of their strangeness.[29] For actually, even if some great sage shows up after ten thousand generations who knows how to unravel them, it would still be as if he arrived after only a single day.

2:43

"Suppose you and I get into a debate. If you win and I lose, does that really mean you are right and I am wrong? If I win and you lose, does that really mean I'm right and you're wrong? Must one of us be right and the other wrong? Or could both of us be right, or both of us wrong? If neither you nor I can know, a third person would be even more benighted. Whom should we have straighten

---

27   "Fully formed maturation" is *cheng*. See Glossary.

28   This sentence is phrased in the gnomic diction of a dream prognostication text, possibly quoting a well-known folk belief.

29   This phrase has given commentators many headaches. Zhuangzi's coinage, used in modern Chinese to translate "paradox," is usually glossed as something like the "Supreme Swindle," or the "Ultimate Monstrosity." Taking the phrase more literally, the present translation ("offering condolences for the demise of the strangeness") is a bit more adventurous. The implication is that to merely judge these paradoxical words as "true" or "right" (*shi qi yan*; 是其言 cf. Chapter 1, note 16) is a way of killing off their salutary strangeness and then eulogizing the corpse with these laudatory titles. Better to leave them unjudged and fully strange, evoking the Radiance of Drift and Doubt.

out[30] the matter? Someone who agrees with you? But since he already agrees with you, how can he straighten it out? Someone who agrees with me? But since he already agrees with me, how can he straighten it out? Someone who disagrees with both of us? But if he already disagrees with both of us, how can he straighten it out? Someone who agrees with both of us? But since he already agrees with both of us, how can he straighten it out? So neither you nor I nor any third party can ever know how it is—shall we wait for yet some "other"[31]?

2:44

"What is meant by harmonizing with them by means of their Heavenly Transitions[32]? It means 'right' is also 'not right,' and 'so' is also 'not so.' If right were ultimately right, its differentiation from not-right would require no debate. If so were ultimately so, its differentiation from not so would require no debate. Thus, even though the transforming voices may depend on one another, this is tantamount to not depending on[33] anything at all.[34]

2:45

"Harmonize with them all by means of their Heavenly Transitions, follow along with them in their limitless overflowings, and you will be able to fully live out your years. Forget what year it is, forget what should or should not be.[35] Let yourself be jostled and shaken by the boundlessness—for that is how to be lodged securely in the boundlessness!"

2:46

The penumbra[36] said to the shadow, "First you were walking, then you were standing still. First you were sitting, then you were upright. Why can't you decide on a single course of action?"

2:47

---

30   "Straighten out" is *zheng*, as in note 26 of this chapter. See Glossary.

31   "Wait for some 'other'" is *dai bi* 待彼. For *dai*, see 1:8, 2:44, 2:45, 2:48, 4:9, 6:5, 6:29, 7:15, and Glossary. *Bi*, here translated "other," is the word used for "that" as opposed to "this" earlier in this chapter.

32   "Heavenly Transitions" is *tian ni* 天倪. This might also be called their Natural Transitions or, more concretely, their nondeliberate, rotating "Skylike" Transitions. *Ni* means literally "beginnings" or "child" on the one hand and "borders" on the other, put together here to form the meaning "transitions"—a beginning that crosses a division. The term also figures importantly in Chapter 27.

33   "Depending on" is *dai* 待. See 1:8, 2:44, 2:45, 2:48, 4:9, 6:5, 6:29, 7:15, and Glossary.

34   The sounds of the wind, the voices of the debaters, may depend on and wait for each other to render a judgment on which is right and which is wrong, but in fact they can never straighten each other out, each being right from its own perspective, so in the end they are not mutually dependent at all for their rightness. In fact, it is just their full dependence on each other, the mutual entailment of "this" and "that," that renders them independent. Cf. 1:8.

35   "What should or should not be" is *yi*. See *ren yi* in Glossary.

36   The "penumbra" is a mythical creature, described as the shadow of the shadow, or the faint dimness around the edge of a shadow. But the name means literally "the neither of the two," presenting a conceptual rhyme with "Walking Two Roads."

The shadow said, "Do I depend on[37] something to make me as I am? Does what I depend on depend on something else? Do I depend on it as a snake does on its skin, or a cicada on its shell? How would I know why I am so or not so?"   2:48

Once Zhuang Zhou dreamt he was a butterfly, fluttering about joyfully just as a butterfly would. He followed his whims exactly as he liked and knew nothing about Zhuang Zhou. Suddenly he awoke, and there he was, the startled Zhuang Zhou in the flesh. He did not know if Zhou had been dreaming he was a butterfly, or if a butterfly was now dreaming it was Zhou. Surely, Zhou and a butterfly count as two distinct identities! Such is what we call the transformation of one thing into another.   2:49

CHAPTER THREE

The Primacy of Nourishing Life[1]   3:1

The flow of my life is always channeled by its own boundaries, but the mind bcn on knowledge never is.[2] A flow channeled by its own boundaries is endangered when forced to follow something that is not, and trying then to rescue it with the doings of the knowing mind only makes the danger worse. What-   3:2
ever "good" it[3] may do, it remains far from the reach of reputation. Whatever "evil" it may do, it remains far from the reach of punishment.[4] It tends to-

---

37   *Dai* again. See 1:8, 2:44, 2:45, 4:9, 6:5, 6:29, 7:15, and Glossary.

1   The title of this chapter could also be interpreted to mean, "Nourishing the Host [or Master] of Life," which is how many of our commentators take it. Alternately, it could mean, "What Is Primary in Nourishing Life."

2   This sentence is often interpreted to mean, "My life is limited, but knowledge is unlimited." On this reading, "life" refers to the duration of a human life span, while "knowledge" is interpreted as "the body of knowable things to be learned." The point would then be that my life span is too short to learn all there is to learn, and hence the pursuit of learning is a futile, even dangerous endeavor. But this reading of both *sheng* 生 (life) and *zhi* 知 (here translated as "the mind bent on knowledge") is not consistent with the usage of those words in the rest of the Inner Chapters, nor the usual usage in texts of this period generally, where the former refers to the process of coming to be, and the latter primarily to the faculty of knowing rather than the field of things to be known. See Glossary. Nonetheless, something of this sense of the inexhaustibility of knowables is not irrelevant to the points being made in this chapter.

3   I.e., the undirected flow of life.

4   These two lines are often read as conditional imperatives: "When you do good, stay away from reputation. When you do evil, stay away from punishment."

ward the current of the central meridian[5] as its normal course. And this is what enables us to maintain our bodies, to keep the life in them intact, to nourish those near and dear to us, and to fully live out our years.

The cook was carving up an ox for King Hui of Liang. Wherever his hand smacked it, wherever his shoulder leaned into it, wherever his foot braced it, wherever his knee pressed it, the thwacking tones of flesh falling from bone would echo, the knife would whiz through with its resonant thwing, each stroke ringing out the perfect note, attuned to the "Dance of the Mulberry Grove" or the "Jingshou Chorus" of the ancient sage-kings.

The king said, "Ah! It is wonderful that skill can reach such heights!"

The cook put down his knife and said, "What I love is the Course, something that advances beyond mere skill. When I first started cutting up oxen, all I looked at for three years was oxen, and yet still I was unable to see all there was to see in an ox. But now I encounter it with the spirit rather than scrutinizing it with the eyes. My understanding consciousness, beholden to its specific purposes, comes to a halt, and thus the promptings of the spirit begin to flow. I depend on Heaven's unwrought perforations[6] and strike the larger gaps, following along with the broader hollows. I go by how they already are, playing them as they lay. So my knife has never had to cut through the knotted nodes where the warp hits the weave, much less the gnarled joints of bone. A good cook changes his blade once a year: he slices. An ordinary cook changes his blade once a month: he hacks. I have been using this same blade for nineteen years, cutting up thousands of oxen, and yet it is still as sharp as the day it came off the whetstone. For the joints have spaces within them, and the very edge of the blade has no thickness at all. When what has no thickness enters into an empty space, it is vast and open, with more than enough room for the play of the blade. That is why my knife is still as sharp as if it had just come off the whetstone, even after nineteen years.

---

5   The "central meridian" is *du* 督. In Chinese medicine, this term, which in other contexts means "controller," is used for the current of energy that runs vertically through the middle of the human back. The image of a flowing current connects to the opening trope of the chapter. This flow tends toward the central (hence, if left to itself, never going too far toward either good or evil), is unseen (hence, it is opposed to "the knowing mind"), and is the real controller (as opposed to the knowing mind's pretensions to control and direct life). See Wang Fuzhi's comment.

6   "Heaven's unwrought perforations" are *tianli* 天理, which also could be translated as "Natural Perforations," "Spontaneous Perforations," or "Skylike Perforations." This is the only occurrence of the character *li* (see Glossary) in the Inner Chapters, and the first time in Chinese literary history that the binome *tianli* 天理 is used. This term would later come to stand for a crucial category in Neo-Confucian metaphysics, in which context it is sometimes translated as the "Principle of Heaven" or "Heavenly Pattern." The meaning here is much more literal. The term *li* can refer to the optimal way of dividing up and organizing a raw material to suit human purposes or to the nodes in the material along which such division can most easily be done. In this context, it remains closely connected to a still more literal meaning, the pattern of lines on skin.

"Nonetheless, whenever I come to a clustered tangle, realizing that it is difficult to *do* anything about it, I instead restrain myself as if terrified, until my seeing comes to a complete halt. My activity slows, and the blade moves ever   3:5
so slightly. Then all at once, I find the ox already dismembered at my feet like clumps of soil scattered on the ground. I retract the blade and stand there gazing at my work arrayed all around me, dawdling over it with satisfaction. Then I wipe off the blade and put it away."

The king said, "Wonderful! From hearing the cook's words I have learned how to nourish life!"   3:6

When Gongwen Xuan saw the Commander of the Right he was astonished. "What manner of man are you, that you are so singularly one-legged? Is this the doing of Heaven or of man?"

He answered, "It is of Heaven, not man. When Heaven generates any 'this,' it always makes it singular, but man groups every appearance with something else.[7] Thus, I know that whatever it is, it is Heaven, not man. The marsh pheasant finds one mouthful of food every ten steps, and one drink of water every hundred steps, but he does not seek to be fed and pampered in a cage. For though his spirit might there reign supreme, it does not do him any good."   3:7

When Lao Dan[8] died, Qin Yi went to mourn for him, but after wailing thrice he immediately departed. His disciple asked, "Weren't you a friend of the Master's?"

"Yes," he said.

"Then is this the proper way for you to mourn him?"

"Indeed, it is. At first I thought it would be his kind of people there, but then I saw that this was not the case. When I went in there to mourn, I saw the elders among them weeping as if for their sons, and the young among them weeping as if for their mothers. With such as these gathered there, I too would no doubt have proceeded to utter some unsought-for words and weep some unsought-for tears. But this would be to flee from the Heavenly and turn away from how things are, forgetting what one has received, which is why the ancients called such things 'the punishment for fleeing from Heaven.' When it came time to arrive, the master did just what the time required. When it came time to go, he followed

---

7   Following the suggestion of Hu Yuanjun.

8   Also known as Laozi, traditionally considered the author of the *Daodejing*, although there is no reference either to this text or to any such authorship in the Inner Chapters. This glaring absence has led many scholars—notably Qian Mu and A. C. Graham—to conclude that the Inner Chapters of the *Zhuangzi* actually predate the *Daodejing* and possibly even that Lao Dan was a character created right here in this passage of the *Zhuangzi* who later came to be connected to the *Daodejing*. The discovery of fragments of the present *Daodejing* in the Guodian bamboo slips, dated to around the middle of the fourth century B.C.E., have made the temporal priority of the Inner Chapters to *all* of the passages in the *Daodejing* less plausible, but the completion of that text, its assumption of its present form, and its linkage to the name "Lao Dan" are still unattested until well after Zhuangzi's death.

along with the flow. Resting content in the time and finding his place in the flow, joy and sorrow had no way to seep in. The ancients called that 'Liberation from the Lord's Dangle.' The finger can indicate only the doings of the firewood, but 3:8   meanwhile the fire has moved on. Its ending is unknown."

CHAPTER FOUR

4:1   *In the Human World*

Yan Hui went to see Confucius, asking leave to depart. Confucius said, "Where will you go?"

Yan Hui said, "I shall go to Wei."

"What will you do there?"

"I have heard that the ruler of Wei has reached the prime of his life and become quite autocratic in his ways. He makes frivolous use of his state without seeing his error. He thinks nothing of the death of his people—nationfuls of corpses fill the marshes, clumped in piles like bunches of plantains.[1] The people there are utterly without recourse. I have heard you say, Master, 'Leave a well-ordered state and go to one in chaos. At a physician's door there are always many invalids.' I wish to take what I have learned from you and to derive some standards and principles from it to apply to this situation. Perhaps then the state can be saved."

Confucius said, "Ah! You will most likely go and get yourself executed! If you're following a course, it's better not to mix anything extraneous into it. Mixing in the extraneous, you wind up with multiple courses, which leads to mutual interference, which means constant anxiety. And yet all your anxiety will 4:2   not save you.

"The Consummate Persons of old made sure they had it in themselves before they tried to put it into others. If what is in yourself is still unstable, what leisure do you have to worry about some tyrant?

"Do you know what it is that undermines real Virtuosity, and for what purpose, on the contrary, 'cleverness'[2] comes forth? Virtuosity is undermined by 4:3   *getting a name for it.* Cleverness comes forth from *conflict.* For a good name is

---

[1]   A nearly unintelligible sentence, for which many character substitutions and alternate readings have been suggested. The rendering here is an attempt to take the extant text literally. But the dead might be, for example, "as though ravaged by fire and slaughter" (Graham), "reckoned in swampfuls like so much grass" (Watson), or "as thick as heaps of fuel" (Legge).

[2]   "Cleverness" is *zhi* 知, elsewhere translated as "the understanding," "knowledge," or "wisdom." See Glossary. Here, the contrast is between genuine Virtuosity, which provides the real skill for dealing with such problems, and conscious and purposive manipulation of schemes and skills, based on preexisting knowledge of principles and standards applied to fixed purposes, such as Yan Hui is aspiring to here.

most essentially a way for people to one-up each other, and cleverness is most essentially a weapon for winning a fight. Both are inauspicious implements, not the kind of thing that can be used to perfect your own behavior.

"But even if your Virtuosity were ample, reliable, and firm, and you engaged in no contention for the sake of a good name, unless you somehow attained perfect comprehension of his mind and disposition, your high-handed display of regulating words about Humanity and Responsibility in the face of such a tyrant would just be a way of showing off your beauty at the expense of his ugliness. This is called plaguing others—and he who plagues others will surely be plagued in return. You are in danger of being plagued! Conversely, if he happens to be the type who takes delight in worthy men such as yourself while despising men of lesser quality, why would you want to change him in the first place? 4:4

"On the other hand, if you just agree with everything anyone says, the princes of the state will surely take advantage of you in their jostlings with one another. Your eyes will be dazzled by the struggle, your countenance flattened by it, your mouth busied with it, your face expressive of it—and finally your heart and mind will be completely made of it! Then it will be like using fire to put out a fire, or pouring water on a drowning man—I'd call that augmenting the excessive. Beginning in this way, you'll just keep following the flow until even your sincerest words are untrustworthy—and then you're certain to end up dead at the feet of the tyrant. 4:5

"In ancient times, Jie killed Guanlong Feng and Zhou killed Wangzi Biqian. These were men who cultivated their own persons, devoting themselves to their love of the masses below and thus resolutely remonstrating with their rulers above. The rulers did away with them because of their impeccable characters. This is what comes from love of a good name. Yao attacked Cong Zhi and Xun Ao and Yu invaded You Hu. These nations were laid to waste and their citizens slaughtered. They had been incessant in their use of force and insatiable in their quest for property, the things referred to by names. This is what comes from the quest for property and a good name. Hasn't anyone taught you even this? The allure of property and a good name cannot be contained even by sages—much less you! 4:6

"But I'm sure you've thought of some way around all this. Let's hear what you've got."

Yan Hui said, "Punctilious in bearing, I shall become empty and humble. Diligent in my work, I will make myself unified and focused. Would that work?"

Confucius said, "No, no! How could that ever work? Filled to overflowing with aggressive resolve but presenting an ever-changing appearance to the world so as to accommodate common opinion, manipulating the impressions of others to win a place in their hearts, I'd say even a gradually advancing Virtuosity will be unable to take shape, much less the Great Virtuosity. If you cling without transforming, externally accommodating but internally without any self-criticism—how could that ever work?" 4:7

Yan Hui said, "Then I shall be internally upright but externally adaptable, using preexisting doctrines linked to antiquity. To be internally upright is to be a follower of the ways of Heaven. Such a one knows that Heaven looks upon both himself and the 'Son of Heaven' equally as sons. Would he then care whether his words were pleasing or displeasing to others? Such a one is seen by others as an innocent child. This is what I mean by being a follower of Heaven.

"To be externally adaptable, on the other hand, means to be a follower of the ways of man. To bow and salute is the ceremony that goes with being someone's underling. Others do it, so would I dare not to? He who just does whatever others do will not be criticized by those others.

"To use preexisting doctrines linked to antiquity means to be a follower of the ways of the ancients. Although one seems to speak only accepted dogmas, in reality a criticism is hidden in it—but it was the ancients who said so, not me! In this way, although upright, one cannot be attacked. This is what I mean by being a follower of the ancients. Would this work?"

Confucius said, "No, no! How could that ever work? You're like a ruler with a great multitude of policies and methods but without any foreign intelligence. Although this might well allow you to get by without being faulted, that's about all you'll accomplish. How could it have any effect on the tyrant? You are still taking your mind as your instructor."

4:8

Yan Hui said, "I have nothing more. What then should I do?"

Confucius said, "You must fast! Let me tell you. To have something in mind and then go out and do that thing—do you think this is a simple matter? Majestic Heaven does not accommodate those who look on this as easy."

Yan Hui said, "My family is poor, and I have had no wine or meat for many months. Can this be considered fasting?"

Confucius said, "That's the fasting you do for a religious sacrifice. It is not the fasting of the mind."

Yan Hui said, "What is the fasting of the mind?"

Confucius said, "If you merge all your intentions into a singularity, you will come to hear with the mind rather than with the ears. Further, you will come to hear with the vital energy[3] rather than with the mind. For the ears are halted at what they hear. The mind is halted at whatever verifies its preconceptions.[4]

---

3   "Vital energy" is *qi* 氣. See Glossary.

4   Literally, "The mind stops at tallies." The reference is to a bamboo tally broken into two irregular parts that can subsequently be fitted together to ensure a match. The mind goes no further than what it can tally, which is what matches it, or what pieces it can match together into a preconceived notion of a coherent whole. Cheng Xuanying reads these two lines as imperatives: "Let your listening stop at the ears [i.e., not clinging to the objects heard]. Let your mind cease its merging into its objects."

But the vital energy is an emptiness, a waiting for the presence of beings.[5] The Course alone is what gathers in this emptiness. And it is this emptiness that is the fasting of the mind."

4:9

Yan Hui said, "Before I find what moves me into activity, it is myself that is full and real. But as soon as I find what moves me, it turns out that 'myself' has never begun to exist. Is that what you mean by being 'empty'?"

Confucius said, "Exactly. Let me tell you about it. With this you can play in his cage without impinging on his concern for a good name. When he's receptive, do your crowing, but when he's not, let it rest. Do not let him get to you, but do not harm him either. Seeing all possible dwelling places as one, let yourself be lodged in whichever cannot be avoided.[6] This will get you close to success. It is easy to wipe away your footprints, but difficult to walk without touching the ground. It is easy to use deception when you are sent into your activities at the behest of other humans, but difficult to use deception when sent into activity by Heaven. You have learned how to fly with wings, but not yet how to fly without wings. You have learned the wisdom of being wise, but not yet the wisdom of being free of wisdom.[7] Concentrate on the hollows of what is before you, and the empty chamber within you will generate its own brightness.

4:10

4:11

"Good fortune comes to roost in stillness. To lack this stillness is called scurrying around even when sitting down. Allow your ears and eyes to open inward and thereby place yourself beyond your mind's understanding consciousness.[8] Even the ghosts and spirits will then seek refuge in you, human beings all the more so! This is the transformation of all things, the hinge on which Shun and Yu moved, the lifelong practice of Fu Xi and Ji Qu.[9] How much more should it be so for others!"

4:12

Zigao of Shegong had been designated envoy to Qi. He asked Confucius for instruction, saying, "The king has given me a heavy mission. The people of Qi treat envoys with great respect but are slow to make any concessions. Even the ordinary folk there are unbudgeable—how much more so the feudal lords! I am quite terrified. You once said to me, 'In all affairs, large or small, a happy conclusion is rarely reached unless one follows the Course. Otherwise, if you fail, you will have troubles with other people, but to succeed you will have to trouble the balance of your own internal yin and yang. Only a person of Vir-

---

5 The word translated as "waiting" here is *dai* 待, which also means "to depend on." See 1:8, 2:44, 2:45, 2:48, 6:5, 6:29, 7:15, and Glossary.

6 Or, reversing the order of the first two characters, as most interpreters do, the line can be translated as follows: "Making your real home in the oneness, let yourself be temporarily lodged in whatever cannot be avoided."

7 *Zhi* appears four times in this sentence. See Glossary.

8 "Understanding consciousness" is *zhi*. See Glossary.

9 All four are ancient sage-emperors.

tuosity can remain untroubled whether he succeeds or fails.' I am a man who has no special dietary needs, and even when drinking a steaming broth I normally have no need for a cooler, but look at me now: I got my orders this morning and already I am sucking on ice chunks this evening, as if my insides were on fire! I have not yet begun the actual task and already my yin and yang are out of whack. And if the mission turns out to be a failure, I'll surely be menaced by the people around me. Given these two problems, it is just not worth it to be employed as someone's underling! Please give me some advice!"

4:13

Confucius said, "There are two great constraints in this world. One is fate, one's mandated limitations, and the other is responsibility, doing what fits one's position. A child's love for his parents is fate—it cannot be removed from his heart. An underling's service to a boss is responsibility, the response called for by his position; wherever he goes, he is in service to his boss. It cannot be avoided anywhere in this world. Thus I call these the great constraints. To be reconciled to wherever you may have to go to serve your parents is perfect filial piety, and to be reconciled to whatever may be involved in serving your boss is complete loyalty. And in the service one must render one's own heart, seeing that you likewise cannot change the joy and sorrow it sets before you, thus reconciling yourself to these too as a part of your fate, knowing them to be something else you can do nothing about—that is the utmost Virtuosity. Being a son or a subordinate, there will inevitably be things you cannot avoid having to do. Absorb yourself in the realities of the task at hand to the point of forgetting your own existence. Then you will have no leisure to delight in life or abhor death. That would make this mission of yours quite doable!

4:14

"Let me tell you a little more of what I've learned. Human interactions, when handled face-to-face, are founded on mutual trust. But when handled at a distance, they must depend on *words* to establish reciprocal loyalty. These words have to be transmitted by someone, and there is nothing in the world more difficult than communicating mutual esteem or mutual anger between two people. The esteem gets exaggerated into flattery and the anger into insult. These exaggerations then become outright lies, and once the lying starts trustworthiness is lost, and then the ability to communicate is destroyed—and perhaps the messenger as well. As the maxim says, 'Transmit their usual characteristic inclinations, not their occasional exaggerations, and your task will be close to success.'

"Another thing: when two people test their skills against each other, it starts out brightly enough but usually ends darkly; when it really gets extreme, they end up engaging in all sorts of outrageous tactics to defeat each other. A drinking ritual is orderly at first but usually ends up in turmoil, and when it gets really extreme, the amusements start to get perverse. All things are like this. They begin nicely enough but in the end it gets ugly. They start out simple but end up oversized and unwieldy. Words are like winds and waves, and actions are rooted in gain and loss. Winds and waves can easily shake a man, and gain and loss can easily endanger him. So the rage comes forth for no apparent reason, the cunning words fly off on a tangent, like the panicked cries of a dying ani-

4:15

mal with no time to choose. The breath and vital energy come to a boil, and with that everyone becomes bloody-minded. As the feeling of being threatened reaches its zenith the more unlovely states of mind come with it and nobody even notices it—and if they don't realize what is happening to them, there is no saying where it will all end! Thus, the maxim says, 'Do not compromise your mission, do not hurry it to completion, for these would take it beyond the beneficial measure. Compromised missions and hurried completions are dangerous things.' Beauty is something that comes from taking your time, and once the ugliness takes shape it is too late to change it. Can you afford to be careless? Let yourself be carried along by things so that the mind wanders freely. Hand it all over to the unavoidable so as to nourish what is central within you. That is the most you can do. What need is there to deliberately seek any reward? The best thing is just to fulfill what's mandated to you, your fate—how could there be any difficulty to that?"

4:16

When Yan He was appointed tutor to the crown prince of Wei, son of Duke Ling, he went to consult with Qu Boyu. "Here is a man who is just naturally no good. If I find no way to contain him, he will endanger my state, but if I try to contain him, he will endanger my life. His cleverness allows him to understand the crimes people commit, but not why they were driven to commit these crimes.[10] What should I do?"

Qu Boyu said, "Good question! Be careful and cautious and rectify yourself! Be compromising in appearance and harmonious in mind. But even these measures can present problems. Don't let the external compromise get inside you, and don't let your inner harmony show itself externally. If you let the external compromise get inside you, it will topple you, destroy you, collapse you, cripple you. If the harmony in your heart shows itself externally, it will lead to reputation and renown, until you are haunted and plagued by them. If he's playing the baby, play baby with him. If he's being lawless and unrestrained, be lawless and unrestrained with him. If his behavior is unbounded and shapeless, be unbounded and shapeless with him. You must master this skill to the point of flawlessness. Don't you know the story of the praying mantis? It flailed its pincers around to stop an oncoming chariot wheel, not realizing the task was beyond its powers. This is how it is for those with 'great talents.' Be careful, be cautious! If you irritate him by flaunting your talents, you will be in more or less the same position. Don't you know how the tiger trainer handles it? He doesn't feed the beast live animals for fear of arousing its lust for killing. He doesn't feed it uncut sides of meat for fear of arousing its lust for dismemberment. He carefully times out the feedings and comprehends the creature's propensity for rage. The tiger is a different species from man but can be tamed through affection for its feeder. The ones it kills are the ones who cross it. How-

---

[10] Guo Xiang and others take this to mean that the crown prince's own poor governance is the cause of the crimes committed by his subjects.

ever, a man who loves horses even to the point of gathering their shit and piss in jeweled boxes may still get his skull or chest kicked in if he smacks away a mosquito on the unbridled animal at the wrong time. Despite the best inten-
4:17   tions, his solicitousness backfires on him. Can you afford to be careless?"

Carpenter Shi was traveling in Qi when he came upon the tree of the shrine at the Qu Yuan bend. It was over a hundred arm spans around, so large that thousands of oxen could shade themselves beneath it. It overstretched the surrounding hills, its lowest branches hundreds of feet from the ground, at least a dozen of which could have been hollowed out to make into ships. It was surrounded by marveling sightseers, but the carpenter walked past it without a second look.

When his apprentice finally got tired of admiring it, he caught up with Carpenter Shi and said, "Since taking up my axe to follow you, Master, I have never seen a tree of such fine material[11] as this! And yet, you don't even deign to look twice at it or pause beneath it. Why?"

Carpenter Shi said, "Stop! Say no more! This is worthless lumber! As a ship it would soon sink, as a coffin it would soon rot, as a tool it would soon break, as a door it would leak sap, as a pillar it would bring infestation. This is a talentless, worthless tree. It is precisely because it is so useless that it has lived so long."

Back home, Carpenter Shi saw the tree in a dream. It said to him, "What do you want to compare me to, one of those *cultivated* trees? The hawthorn, the pear, the orange, the rest of those fructiferous trees and shrubs—when their fruit is ripe they get plucked, and that is an insult. Their large branches are bent; their small branches are pruned. Thus do their abilities embitter their lives. That is why they die young, failing to fully live out their natural[12] life spans. They batter themselves with the vulgar conventions of the world— and all other creatures do the same. As for me, I've been working on being useless for a long time. It almost killed me, but I've finally managed it—and it is of great use to me! If I were useful, do you think I could have grown to be so great?

"Moreover, you and I are both [members of the same class, namely], *beings* —is either of us in a position to classify and evaluate the other? How could a worthless man with one foot in the grave know what is or isn't a worthless tree?"

Carpenter Shi awoke and told his dream to his apprentice. The apprentice said, "If it's trying to be useless, what's it doing with a shrine around it?"

Carpenter Shi said, "Hush! Don't talk like that! Those people came to it for refuge of their own accord. In fact, the tree considers it a great disgrace to be surrounded by this uncomprehending crowd. If they hadn't made it a shrine, they could easily have gone the other way and started carving away at it. What

---

11   "Fine material" (*cai* 材) is translated as "talent" or "being worth something" below.

12   "Natural" (*tian* 天) is elsewhere translated "Heaven" or "Heavenly." See Glossary.

it values is not what they value. Is it not absurd to judge it by whether it does what is or is not called for by its position, by what role it happens to play[13]?"

Ziqi of Nanbo was traveling in the hills of Shang when he came across a huge tree. He marveled at it, for the horses from a thousand chariots could have cooled themselves in its shade. "What sort of tree is this?" said Ziqi. "It must be of unusually fine material." Looking up at its branches, he saw that they were too twisted and gnarled to be used for beams or pillars. Looking down at its trunk, he saw that it was too splotched and split to be used for a coffin. It stung and stabbed the tongue when licked and crazed and inebriated the mind for three days when sniffed. Ziqi said, "It turns out to be a worthless tree, and thus it has been able to grow so huge. Ah! This is the worthlessness that the Spirit Man relies on!

    "In the Jingshi region of Song grow the catalpas, cypresses, and mulberries. The tall ones are chopped down for monkey perches. Those that are three or four spans around are chopped down to make pillars for stately homes. Those that are seven or eight spans around are felled to make coffin shells for the wealthy. Thus, they fail to fully live out their natural life spans and die before their time under axes and saws. This is the trouble that comes from being worth something.[14] In the expiation ceremony, cows with white spots, pigs with upturned snouts, and humans with hemorrhoids are considered unfit to be offered as sacrifices to the river god. All shamans know this, and thus they regard these as creatures of bad fortune. But this is exactly why the Spirit Man regards them as creatures of very good fortune indeed!

"Now Shu the Discombobulated was like this: his chin was tucked into his navel, his shoulders towered over the crown of his head, his ponytail pointed toward the sky, his five internal organs were at the top of him, his thigh bones took the place of his ribs. With his sewing and washing, he could make enough to fill his mouth, and by pounding the divining sticks and exuding an aura of mystic power,[15] he could in fact make enough to feed ten men. When the authorities called for troops, he would just present himself among all the others, flailing his arms in his discombobulated way [without any danger of being drafted for military duty]; and when it came time to take on any great labors, his chronic condition exempted him from service. When the authorities handed out rations to the disabled, he got three large measures of grain and ten bundles of firewood. A discombobulated physical form was sufficient to allow him to nourish his body, so that he was able to live out his natural life span. And how much more can be accomplished with discombobulated Virtuosity!"

4:18

4:19

---

[13] "What is called for by its position" and "role . . ." render *yi* 義, which is translated as "Responsibility" when paired with the Confucian virtue of Humanity. See Glossary.

[14] "Worth something" is *cai*; see note 11 in this chapter.

[15] I am indebted to Donald Harper, through his student Alan Dagovitz, for suggesting this reading.

When Confucius went to Chu, the madman Jieyu wandered past his gate. He was singing this song:

> "Oh Phoenix! Oh Phoenix! How your Virtuosity declines!
> You cannot wait for a future era, nor can you recapture the past.
> When the Course is present in the world, the sage perfects himself with it.
> When the Course is lacking in the world, he lives his own life with it.
> But in the present age, avoiding execution is the best he can do with it.
> Good fortune is lighter than a feather, yet no one can carry it for long.
> Trouble is heavier than the earth, yet no one can get it to drop away.
> Confronting the world with your Virtuosity—let it rest, give it up!
> Drawing a straight line upon this earth and then trying to walk along it—
>   danger, peril!
> The brambles and thorns, which so bewilder the sunlight, they don't
>   impede my steps.
> My zigzag stride amid them keeps my feet unharmed.[16]

The mountain tree plunders itself. The candle fat scorches itself. The cinnamon tree is edible, and thus it gets chopped down. The lacquer tree is useful, and thus it is cut down. Everyone knows how useful usefulness is, but no one 4:20 seems to know how useful uselessness is."

CHAPTER FIVE

5:1   *Markers¹ of Full Virtuosity*

In the state of Lu there was a man called Wang Tai whose foot had been chopped off as a punishment. Yet somehow he had as many followers as Confucius himself. Chang Ji² questioned Confucius about it.

"Wang Tai is a one-footed ex-con, and yet his followers divide the state of Lu with you, Master. When he stands he offers no instruction, and when he

---

16   Jieyu's crazy words have already been referenced in Chapter 1 (1:12). The present song is a parody of his words in the *Analects* 18.15: "Phoenix! Phoenix! How your Virtuosity has declined! The past cannot be corrected, but the future can be still be pursued! Let it rest, give it up! To involve yourself in governing now can only lead to danger!"

1   "Markers" here is *fu* 符, a kind of tally that was broken in half as a security to guarantee the authenticity of an official order. Their jagged edges fit together like jigsaw pieces, ensuring a perfect match of two parts from the same original whole. Zhuangzi views the broken bodies of the cripples in this chapter through this trope. The same word is translated as "whatever verifies its preconceptions," i.e., what matches, at 4:9, note 4.

2   The name might be translated "Sustainable [or Constant] Season," a trope of some relevance to part of what follows in this chapter, e.g., 5:8 and 5:16–17. "Sustainable" is *chang.* See Glossary.

sits he gives no opinions. And yet, they go to him empty and return filled. Is there really such a thing as a wordless instruction, a formless way of bringing the mind to completion[3]? What kind of man is he?"

5:2

Confucius said, "That man, my master, is a sage. Only my procrastination has kept me from going to follow him myself. If he is master even to me, how much more should he be so to you. I shall bring not only the state of Lu but all the world to follow him!"

Chang Ji said, "Here he is, a one-legged ex-con, and yet you honor him as your teacher. He must be quite extraordinary! How exactly does he make use of his mind?"

Confucius said, "Life and death are a great matter, but they are unable to alter him. Even if Heaven and earth were to topple over, he would not be lost with them. He discerns what alone is unborrowed, so he is not transferred away with the things around him. He looks on the alterations of all things as his own fate, and thus holds fast to their source."

5:3

5:4

"Please tell me more."

"Looked at from the point of view of their differences, even your own liver and gallbladder are as distant as Chu in the south and Yue in the north. But looked at from the point of view of their sameness, all things are one. If you take the latter view, you become free of all preconceptions about which particular objects might suit the eyes and ears. You just release the mind to play in the harmony of all Virtuosities. Seeing what is one and the same to all things, nothing is ever felt to be lost. This man viewed the chopping off of his foot as nothing more than the casting away of a clump of soil."

5:5

5:6

5:7

"For his own sake then," Chang Ji said, "he uses his understanding[4] to discover [the capacities of] his mind[5] and then makes use of that mind of his to develop a mind for the constant.[6] But why then should other beings esteem him so?"

5:8

Confucius said, "People cannot see their reflections in running water, but only in still water. Only stillness can still the multitude to the point of genuine stillness. Though all life-forms receive their vitality from the earth, it remains constantly replete only in the pine and the cypress, so they remain lush and green both summer and winter. Although all life-forms receive their vitality

5:9

---

[3] "Completion" is *cheng* 成. See Glossary.

[4] "Understanding" is *zhi* 知. See Glossary.

[5] I.e., to realize that the mind has the power to view things in various different ways, as indicated by Confucius above.

[6] I.e., thereupon choosing to view things in the way that makes for a constant state of mind that sees the constancy and oneness of things. The term could mean either "a sustainable state of mind" or "a mind focused on what is sustainable," or, more likely, since in this passage these two seem to imply each other, both. Note that this term *chang* 常, meaning "sustainable" or "constant," is often rendered more grandiloquently as "eternal," which would have this passage speaking of the "Eternal Mind." See Glossary.

from Heaven, it is only Shun who got it straight and full,[7] so he had the ability to straighten out others as well. That alone is how he set them straight.

"The proof that one is holding fast to the origin can be seen in true fearlessness. A brave warrior will heroically throw himself into the thick of battle. His lust for glory enables him to restrain his fear. How much more fearless is a man who takes heaven and earth as his own bodily organs and the ten thousand things as his own guts, a man who is merely lodging for the moment in his particular limbs and trunk and head, a man who regards even his own eyes and ears as mere semblances. He takes all that his consciousness knows and

5:10   unifies it into a singularity, so his mind always gets through unslaughtered.[8] His death will be just like choosing a day to climb off into the distance.[9] It is others who have decided for themselves to follow him—how could such a man

5:11   have ever bothered his mind over mere *beings*?"

Shen Tujia, a one-footed ex-convict, was a fellow student of Zichan[10] under Uncle Dim Nobody. Zichan said to him, "When I leave, you wait behind for awhile, or if you leave first, I'll wait behind." The next day they were again seated side by side in the same small hall, and Zichan said, "I said you should wait behind when I leave, and I'd wait behind when you leave. Now I'm about to go—will you wait behind or not? You see a holder of political power and you don't give way—do you think you're equal to a holder of power?"

Shen Tujia said, "Here at our master's place is there really such a thing as a holder of power? You delight in your office and push others behind you. I have heard that a bright mirror gathers no dust; if dust gathers there, it wasn't really bright to begin with. Long interaction with a truly worthy man should free you from error. Now it is our master whom you claim to esteem, and yet you still talk like this. Is that not a mistake?"

Zichan said, "A man in your condition, and yet you still think you can wrangle over goodness with Yao the sage-king! In light of the state of your own Virtuosity, don't you think you should critique yourself instead?"

Shen Tujia said, "There are many who dress up their mistakes and thus think

---

7   "Straight and full" is *zheng* 正. See Glossary.

8   The strange locution here means literally "his mind has never once died." This presumably is a continuation of the "fearless in battle" comparison: his mind survives every engagement on the battlefield of constantly changing beings.

9   The term *dengxia* 登假 here means literally "to climb upon the borrowed," but it is usually interpreted through character substitution to mean, "to climb into the distance," or, using another substitution, "to ascend upon the rosy glow of the clouds." This is an official euphemism sometimes used to describe the death of an emperor—he has ascended into the distance, over the clouds. The implication of both death and ascension is to be retained in reading Zhuangzi's odd usage of this term. Cf. 6:6, note 8.

10   Zichan (d. 522 B.C.E.) was prime minister of Zheng during the Spring and Autumn Period; he died when Confucius was still young. Confucius praised him for both his policies and his personal qualities.

they should not lose a foot, but very few who do not dress up their mistakes, knowing they have no particular entitlement to retain that foot. Only a true Virtuoso can understand what is unavoidable and find peace in it as his own fate. If you play around near Archer Yi's target, lurking near the bull's-eye, it is only normal to get hit. If you manage to escape being hit, that's just fate, good luck.   5:12

"Many two-footed people laugh at me for having one foot, which always used to infuriate me. But as soon as I arrived here at our master's place, my rage fell away and I returned to normal. It's as if the master cleansed me with his goodness without my even realizing it. I have studied under him for nineteen years and never once have I been aware that I was one-footed. Here you and I wander together beyond shapes and bodies—is it not wrong of you to seek me within a particular body and shape?"

Zichan's face changed suddenly, jolted as if by a kick. "Don't tell anyone about this!" he said.

There was an ex-con in Lu, named Toeless Shushan, whose feet had been mutilated as a punishment. He heeled his way over to see Confucius, who said to him, "You were careless in your past behavior and thus have ended up in this condition. Isn't it a little late to come to me now?"

Toeless said, "I just didn't understand my duties and undervalued my own body, and so I now lack a foot, but I come to you with something worth more than a foot still intact. Heaven covers all things. Earth supports all things. I used to think that you, Sir, were just like Heaven and earth—I never imagined you would instead say something like this!"

Confucius said, "It was rude of me. Won't you please come in and teach me what you've learned?"

But Toeless departed. Confucius then said, "Learn from this, my disciples! For Toeless is a one-footed ex-convict, but he still endeavors to learn, so as to make up for the ugliness of his past behavior. How much more should you do so, you whose Virtuosity is still intact!"

Toeless told Lao Dan[11] about it, saying, "Confucius is certainly no match for the Consummate Person, is he? Why does he go around imitating you so subserviently? He must be seeking some bizarre, deceptive, illusory, freakish thing like a good name, not realizing that the Consummate Person views such things as handcuffs and leg chains."

Lao Dan said, "Why don't you simply let him see life and death as a single string, acceptable and unacceptable as a single thread, thus releasing him from his fetters? How would that be, do you think?"

Toeless said, "Heaven itself has inflicted this punishment on him—how can he be released?"   5:13

Duke Ai of Lu consulted with Confucius, saying, "There's this ugly man in Wei named Horsehead Humpback. When men are with him, they can think of

---

11   Laozi, legendary author of the *Daodejing*. See Chapter 3, note 8.

nothing else and find themselves unable to depart. When women see him, they plead with their parents, saying they would rather be this man's concubine than any other man's wife—this has happened at least a dozen times already! And yet he's never been heard to initiate anything of his own with them, instead just chiming in with whatever they're already doing. He has no position of power with which to protect their lives and no stash of wealth with which to fill their stomachs, and on top of that he's ugly enough to startle all the world. He chimes in with them instead of presenting anything new of his own, his understanding is limited to his immediate surroundings, and yet the men and women converge around him. I figured he must have something special, so I called him to my court to take a look at him. He was indeed ugly enough to astonish all the world. It took a few weeks before I could see him as actually human. But after a few months, I started to trust him. My state had no prime minister, so I offered the post to him. Looking trapped and put upon, he was vague and evasive when he finally responded, seeming to reject the idea. I was embarrassed, but in the end I prevailed upon him to accept control of the state. But before long he left me and vanished. I was terribly depressed, as if a loved one had died, unable to take any pleasure in my power. What kind of man is this?"

Confucius said, "I was once sent on a mission to Chu, where I saw some piglets still nursing at the teats of their dead mother. After a short while, they suddenly looked very startled and bolted away from her. They could no longer see themselves in her, could find no similarity to themselves there. What they loved in their mother was not her physical form but what moved that form. When a war casualty is buried, he does not care whether he is adorned with camouflage feathers, and a footless man has no love for shoes—in both cases the fundamental thing has already been lost. The women in the emperor's harem are not allowed to pare their nails or pierce their ears. When soldiers stationed abroad get married, they are for a time exempted from all missions. If such value is placed on an undamaged body, how much more accrues to a

5:14   person of undamaged Virtuosity?

"Now this Horsehead Humpback says nothing and yet is trusted, achieves nothing and yet is loved, to the point of inspiring you to hand over your state to him, fearing only that he wouldn't accept it. His innate powers must be whole and intact even though his Virtuosity takes no definite external form."

Duke Ai asked, "What does it mean, the innate powers being whole?"

Confucius said, "Death and life, surviving and perishing, failure and success, poverty and wealth, superiority and inferiority, disgrace and honor, hunger and thirst, cold and heat—these are the transformations of events, the

5:15   proceedings of fate. Day and night they come to us, one replacing another, and yet our understanding[12] can never compass what it is that begins them. So there is no need to let them disrupt our harmony, and we must deny them

---

12   "Understanding is *zhi.* See Glossary.

entrance into our Numinous Reservoir.[13] That is what allows the joy of its harmony to open into all things without thereby losing its fullness,[14] what keeps it flowing on day and night without cease, taking part everywhere as the springtime of each being. Connecting up with This, your own mind becomes the site of the life-giving time.[15] This is what is called keeping the innate powers whole."

5:16

5:17

"Then what do you mean by Virtuosity that takes no definite external form?"

"When water is perfectly still, it can serve as a standard of levelness. When the internal is preserved, the external will remain unshaken as well. Virtuosity is really just an ornamental form giving a definite shape to the fullness of the harmony within. So a Virtuosity that remains unexpressed in any definite physical form is something all beings find themselves unable to live without."[16]

5:18

5:19

On another day, Duke Ai told this story to Minzi, commenting, "I used to think that in sitting on my throne and ruling the empire by maintaining standards for the people and protecting them from death I was already doing a perfect job. Now that I have heard the words of the Consummate Person, I fear I have not lived up to my post. By neglecting my personal welfare, I've ruined my state. And Confucius and I, we are not ruler and subject. We are simply comrades in this Virtuosity."

Hunchback Limpleg the lipless cripple presented himself to Duke Ling of Wei, who was so delighted with him that when he saw the unimpaired their necks looked freakishly long to him. Jarsized Goiter presented himself to Duke Huan of Qi, and in that case too the ruler was so delighted that when he saw the unimpaired their necks looked freakishly long to him. Thus, where Virtuosity excels, the physical form is forgotten. But people are unable to forget the forgettable, and instead forget the unforgettable—true forgetfulness!

5:20

---

[13] Cf. "Heavenly Reservoir" at 2:36, which is similarly described. Both denote the ideal state of mind of the Zhuangzian person.

[14] Reading *chong* 充 (fullness) for *dui* 兌, as in the parallel passage in *Huainanzi*, "Jingshen xun."

[15] "This" is *shi* 是. See Chapter 2 and Glossary. Alternate interpretations of this very obscure sentence are as follows: "Taking up whatever comes, one's own mind gives rise to just the moment for it"; "Whatever you encounter, the timely [response] arises in your mind"; "Continuing every rightness, it is always the life-giving season in your mind"; "In contact with whatever is there, the moment springs to life in your own mind"; "Receiving the rightness of every 'this,' all its seasons come forth within your own mind!" "Taking up the rightness of every 'this,' it is in one's own mind that the life-giving season is ever emerging."

[16] As a consequence of the indeterminability of the source of the transforming perspectives, the Zhuangzian person is free of a fixed identity, empty of fixed forms. This is compared to still water, empty of any particular motion. This state "gives life" to each "this," like the springtime, affirming and enhancing each one. Hence, all creatures find themselves drawn to it, needing it for their existence as still water is needed as a standard of levelness.

The sage has his ways of wandering. For him, understanding[17] is merely a bastard son, obligations and agreements merely glue, Virtuosity a mere continuation of something received, skill merely salesmanship. The sage makes no plans, so what use would he have for understanding? He is unsplit, so what use would he have for glue? He loses nothing, so what use would he have for the attainments of Virtuosity? He is not for sale as a commodity, so what use would he have for salesmanship? These four are his nourishment from Heaven, the Heavenly Sustenance. Since he receives his sustenance from Heaven, what use

5:21   would he have for the human? He has the physical form of a human being, but not the characteristic inclinations of a human being. Since he shares the human form, he lives among men. Since he is free of their characteristic inclinations, right and wrong cannot get at him. Minute and insignificant, he is just another man among the others. Vast and unmatched, he is alone in per-

5:22   fecting the Heavenly in himself.

Huizi said to Zhuangzi, "Can a human being really be without the characteristic human inclinations?"

Zhuangzi said, "Yes."

"But without the characteristic human inclinations, how can he be called a human being?"

"The Course gives him this appearance, Heaven gives him this form, so why shouldn't he be called a human being?"

"Since you call him a human being, how can he be without the characteristic human inclinations?"

Zhuangzi said, "Affirming some things as right and negating others as wrong are what I call the characteristic inclinations. What I call being free of them means not allowing likes and dislikes to damage you internally, instead making it your constant practice to follow along with the way each thing is of itself, going by

5:23   whatever it affirms as right, without trying to add anything to the process of life."

Huizi said, "If he doesn't add to the process of life, how can his body be sustained?"

Zhuangzi said, "The Course gives him this appearance, Heaven gives him this physical form, and he doesn't allow likes and dislikes to damage him internally. Now you, on the other hand, treat your spirit like a stranger and labor your vitality, leaning against a door screen reciting your disputations or nodding off across your desk. Heaven chose your physical form, and here you are

5:24   using it to crow on about 'hardness' and 'whiteness'!"[18]

---

17   "Understanding" is *zhi*. See Glossary.

18   The status of abstract qualities like "hardness" and "whiteness," their relation to specific white and hard beings, and to what degree they can exist in separation from one another, were among the topics hotly debated by the ancient Chinese logicians, including Huizi. See Chapter 33, as well as the Introduction and the essay "Zhuangzi as Philosopher" at www.hackettpublishing.com.

CHAPTER SIX

The Great Source as Teacher

6:1

"To understand what is done by Heaven, and also what is to be done by Man, that is the utmost."[1]

6:2

To understand what is done by the Heavenly: just in being the Heavenly, as the way all beings are born, what it does is give birth to them all.[2]

6:3

To understand what is to be done by the Human: that would be to use what your understanding understands to nurture what your understanding does not understand. You could then live out all your natural years without being cut down halfway. And that would indeed be the richest sort of knowledge.[3]

6:4

However, there is a problem here. For our understanding can be in the right only by virtue of a relation of dependence[4] on something, and what it depends on is always peculiarly unfixed.[5] So how could I know whether what I call the Heavenly is not really the Human? How could I know whether what I call

---

[1]   As in 2:14, here we seem to have the putting forth of a tentative position, perhaps a conventional stance, which is then considered, analyzed, and deconstructed.

[2]   "Just in being the Heavenly . . . birth to them all" is *tian er sheng ye* 天而生也 This simple four-character phrase is extremely rich with ambiguities. Most literally, it might be rendered, "It is Heaven and birthing." The character *sheng* means "life, birth, generation, producing, emergence, and bringing about in general"; since no specific object is given, we can assume this applies to all beings. [It should be noted too that all "beings" here includes also all possible states and conditions, as when Zhuangzi uses this term to ask where various moods and states of mind and perspectives arise from (2:11)]. But it is not clear if this implies that "Heaven means simply the very generating of things" or that "Heaven is what generates things." Further, it could mean that "the Heavenly is, for any being, the condition in which it is born," or perhaps "Heaven is what simply produces," where this answers the question about "what Heaven does." The use of the noun "Heaven" here as a condition perhaps implies further, "Just by being Heaven, it is what simply produces," or "Just by being Heaven, it is the very emergence of things." Loosely translated, the whole phrase would then mean, "Since 'Nature' or 'Natural' means how things are when born, what Nature does is just to give birth to things." Since Zhuangzi notes several times that where all these states of being emerge from is something the understanding cannot know (2:7, 5:16), this "emergence per se" is presumably what the following phrase refers to as "what the understanding doesn't understand," to be nurtured by "what the understanding understands."

[3]   "Knowledge" *zhi* 知 has appeared in this passage nine times already. See Glossary. All the various senses of the term should be kept in mind throughout this passage: Understanding, intelligence, cleverness, knowing, consciousness, wisdom, and knowledge.

[4]   "Dependence" is *dai* 待. See Glossary.

[5]   According to the discussion in Chapter 2, the meaning of the terms by which the understanding identifies things depends on what we identify as "this" and "that" (*shi* and *fei*), which, as a function of our shifting perspectives, is peculiarly unfixed.

6:5
the Human is not really the Heavenly? Let us say instead, then, that there can be "Genuine Knowledge" only when there is such a thing as a "Genuine Human Being."[6]

And what do we mean by a "Genuine Human Being"? The Genuine Human Beings of old did not revolt against their inadequacies, did not aspire to completeness,[7] did not plan their affairs in advance. In this way, they could be wrong or they could be right, but without regret and without self-satisfaction. And thus they could ascend the heights without fear, submerge into the depths without getting drenched, enter the flames without feeling hot. Such was the way their understanding was able, in its very demise, to ascend through the re-

6:6
motest vistas of the Course.[8]

The Genuine Human Beings of old slept without dreaming and awoke without worries. Their food was plain but their breathing was deep. The Genuine Human Beings breathed from their heels, while the mass of men breathe from

6:7
their throats. Submissive and defeated, they gulp down their words and just as

6:8
soon vomit them back up. Their preferences and desires run deep, but the

6:9
Heavenly Impulse is shallow in them. The Genuine Human Beings of old understood nothing about delighting in being alive or hating death. They emerged without delight, submerged again without resistance. Swooping in they came and swooping out they went, that and no more. They neither forgot where they came from nor asked where they would go. Receiving it, they de-

6:10
lighted in it. Forgetting about it, they gave it back. This is what it means not to use the mind to push away the Course, not to use the Human to try to help the

6:11
Heavenly. Such is what I'd call being a Genuine Human Being.

Being thus, their minds were intent,[9] their faces tranquil, their foreheads broad and plain. They were cool like the autumn, warm like the spring; their

6:12
joy and their anger intermingled with the four seasons. They found something fitting in their encounter with each thing, and none could tell exactly what

6:13
their ultimate end might be. Hence, if the sage uses force, he may destroy nations without losing the hearts of the people. His kindness and bounty may ex-

---

6   This suggests that, in the literal sense, there is not really any such thing as Genuine Knowledge, in the sense of either true and justified objective knowledge or a reliable faculty for making cognitive judgments. Zhuangzi will henceforth use the term only to indicate the state of mind of the Genuine Human, as Zhuangzi sees him according to his own perspective. This state of mind is evidently none other than what previous chapters called the "Heavenly Reservoir" (2:36) and the "Numinous Reservoir" (5:16).

7   "Completeness" is *cheng* 成. See Glossary.

8   "In its very demise, to ascend through the remotest vistas" is *dengxia* 登假. See 5:11, note 9.

9   "Intent" renders *zhi* 志, which seems to make little sense. For this reason, most commentators substitute *wang* 忘, rendering, "Their minds forget." However, Fang Yizhi remarks: "This empty use of the word *zhi* is most extraordinary. There is no way to fathom it. They have nothing but this one intent, so their faces are tranquil."

tend to ten thousand generations, but not because he harbors any love for humankind. So he may take joy in clearing the way for things, but he is not being a "sage." He may have a certain intimacy with others, but he is not being "Humane." His timeliness is Heaven-like, but he is not being a "worthy man." Benefit and harm do not get through to him, but he is not being an "exemplary man." He may do what his designated role requires, ignoring his personal interests, but he is not being a "steadfast knight." He may lose his life without losing what is most genuine to him, but he is not being a "man devoted to service."[10] Xu Buxie, Wu Guang, Bo Yi, Shu Qi, Qi Zi, Xu Yu, Ji Tuo, and Shentu Di[11] served in the service of others, took comfort in the comfort of others, but failed to take comfort in their own comfort.

    The Genuine Human Beings of old seemed to do whatever was called for[12] but were not partisan to any one course.[13] They appeared to be in want but accepted no assistance. Taking part in all things, they were solitary but never rigid.[14] Spreading out everywhere, they were empty but never insub-

6:14

6:15

6:16

---

[10] The traditional reading of this passage, adopted by all commentators known to me, is along the following lines:

> Hence, he who delights in clearing the way for things is not a sage. He who favors his intimates is not Humane. He who is beholden to the seasons of Heaven is not a worthy. He who does not open himself to and comprehend both benefit and harm is not an exemplary man. He who works for fame and thereby loses himself is not a true knight. He who loses his life in the inauthentic is not really being served by others."

The present translation, though grammatically just barely possible, seems to accord better with the preceding and subsequent lines, and with Zhuangzi's thought as a whole. In particular, it should be noted that the traditional reading takes the last phrase to mean, "being served by others," but the historical martyrs for justice that follow are all described as "serving in the service of others," rather than being served by them, hence being consistent with a critique of "serving others." They "lost their life without losing what was most genuine to them" but thought they were thereby serving others. Zhuangzi's Genuine Human Being may live or die, but he will not die for an ideal; nor is "being served by others" (or for that matter, being a "worthy," an "exemplary man," a "steadfast knight") his desideratum.

[11] These are all legendary figures who sacrificed their lives in the service of loyalty to a ruler or an ideal of some sort.

[12] "Whatever was called for" is *yi*. See *Ren yi* in Glossary.

[13] The following few lines are among the most resolutely ambiguous in all world literature. To give the reader some sense of the overlapping possibilities, the notes will provide some of the alternate readings. For this line: "The Genuine Human Beings of old were towering without collapsing" or "The Genuine Human Beings of old fulfilled their responsibilities to others without being partisan to them."

[14] "Solitary" comes from reading *gu* 孤 for *gu* 觚 and reversing the order. Leaving the text as is, it would mean something like the following: "Firmly contoured but not rigid" or "Firm but not prickly."

6:17 stantial. Cheerful, they seemed to be enjoying themselves. Impelled along,[15] they did what they could not help doing. They let everything gather within
6:18 them but still it manifested outwardly to the world as their own countenance.[16] They gave it all away, but still it rested securely within them as their own Vir-
6:19 tuosity.[17] Leprous with symptoms,[18] they seemed just like everyone else. Haughty, nothing could control them. Unbreached, they seemed to prefer to
6:20 close themselves off. Oblivious, they would forget what they were saying.[19]

They took punishments as their own body, ritual as their wings, under-standing[20] as a temporary expedient, and Virtuosity as a sliding along. With punishments as their own body, they could kill or be killed gracefully. With rit-ual as their wings, they could get around in the world. Their understanding was a temporary expedient, arising only when the situation made it unavoid-able. Their Virtuosity was a sliding along, like strolling with other able-legged people through the village, so to speak.[21] And yet others thought they had
6:21 worked hard to get there.

Thus, what they liked was the oneness of things, but what they disliked was also the oneness of things.[22] Their oneness was the oneness, but their non-one-ness was also the oneness. In their oneness, they were followers of the Heavenly.
6:22 In their non-oneness, they were followers of the Human. This is what it is for neither the Heavenly nor the Human to win out over the other. And that is what
6:23 I call being both Genuine and Human, a Genuine Human Being.

---

15   Or "Steeply imposing."

16   Or "Pooling it all in, their personal presence yet somehow seemed to advance into the world" or "When they sequestered themselves away, their personal presence nonetheless seemed to advance into the world."

17   Or "When they joined with others, they nevertheless came securely to rest in their own Virtuosity."

18   Following Wang Fuzhi's reading of *li* 厲, leaving the character unsubstituted. Zhuangzi uses the same character unambiguously to refer to leprosy in Chapter 2 (2:21). Many commentators, however, suggest replacing this character with *guang* 廣, meaning "broad[-minded]."

19   Or "what they had said" or "what they were going to say."

20   "Understanding" is *zhi*. See Glossary.

21   There is perhaps a pun here, since the character for "village" here is also the personal name of Confucius. The joke might then be, picking up on the imagery from the previous chapter, something like the following: "making it with the still unpunished up to the level of Confucius."

22   Alternate readings: "Thus, their liking for things revealed their oneness, but their dis-liking for things also revealed their oneness"; "Thus, their liking of things was a oneness, but their disliking of things was also a oneness"; "Thus, when they had a liking for things, they were one with them, but when they had a dislike for things, they were also one with them"; "Thus, their liking was the oneness, but their disliking was also the oneness."

Life and death are fated, and that they come with the regularity of day and night is of Heaven—that which humans can do nothing about, simply the way things are. Merely because they look on Heaven as their father, people go on to offer it their love—how much more for that which towers even higher? Merely because they see their ruler as beyond themselves, people can even die without regret—how much more in the face of what is all the more genuinely [beyond]? 6:24

When the springs dry up, the fish have to cluster together on the shore, gasping on each other to keep damp and spitting on each other to stay wet. But that is no match for forgetting all about one another in the rivers and lakes. Rather than praising Yao and condemning Jie,[23] we'd be better off forgetting them both and transforming along our own courses. 6:25

The Great Clump burdens me with a physical form, labors me with life, eases me with old age, rests me with death. So it is precisely because I consider my life good that I consider my death good. You may hide a boat in a ravine or 6:26 a net in a swamp, thinking it is secure there. But in the middle of the night, a mighty one comes along and carries it away on his back, unbeknownst to you in your slumber. When the smaller is hidden within the larger, there remains 6:27 someplace into which it can escape. But if you hide the world in the world, so there is nowhere for anything to escape to, this is an arrangement, the vastest arrangement, that can sustain all things.

This human form is merely a circumstance that has been met with, just something stumbled into, but those who have become humans take delight in it nonetheless. Now the human form in its time undergoes ten thousand transformations, never stopping for an instant—so the joys it brings must be beyond calculation! Hence, the sage uses it to roam in that from which nothing ever 6:28 escapes, where all things are maintained. Early death, old age, the beginning, the end—this allows him to see each of them as good. People may try to model themselves on him. But how much better off are those who bind themselves equally to each and all of the ten thousand things, making themselves dependent[24] only on each transformation, on all transformation![25] 6:29

That Course has its own tendency and consistency, but without any deliberate activity or definite form. It can be transmitted but not received, attained 6:30 but not shown. Being its own root and its own foundation, it exists firmly even when heaven and earth are not yet there. It makes the spirits and the Lord-on- 6:31 High divine, generates both heaven and earth. It is above the summit without 6:32

---

23   Yao the premier sage-king has appeared several times already. Jie is his traditional antipode, the last emperor of the Xia dynasty, which ended in the sixteenth century B.C.E. He is a legendary symbol of tyranny, cruelty, and all-around wickedness, and his excesses were used to justify the Shang dynasty's overthrow of the Xia.

24   "Dependent" is *dài* 待 . See 1:8, 2:44, 2:45, 2:48, 4:9, 6:5, 7:15, and Glossary.

25   "On each transformation" and "on all transformtion" are two alternate interpretations of the same phrase, *yi hua* 一化 .

being high, beneath the nadir without being deep. It precedes heaven and
earth without being of long duration. It is elder to the earliest antiquity with-
6:33   out being old.

Xiwei got it and thereby put the measure around heaven and earth. Fuxi got
it and thereby inherited the matrix of vital energy. The Big Dipper got it and
thereby has remained undeflected since antiquity. The sun and moon got it
and thereby have continued on without cease since antiquity. Kanpi got it and
thereby inherited the power of Mt. Kunlun. Pingyi got it and thereby roams
the great rivers. Jian Wu got it and thereby dwells on the heights of Mt. Tai.
The Yellow Emperor got it and ascended the clouds of Heaven. Zhuan Xu got
it and thereby occupies the Dark Palace. Yu Qiang got it and thereby took his
place at the Northern Extremity. The Queen Mother of the West got it and
thereby took her seat on Mt. Shaoguang—no one knows her beginning or her
end. Pengzu got it and thereby remained alive all the way back from the time
of Shun Youyu down to the time of the Five Tyrants. Fu Yue got it and thereby
ministered to Wuding, who took possession of the world, rode upon the Dong-
wei galaxy, mounted upon the Qiwei constellation, and assumed his place arrayed among the stars. Born without father or mother, his death was an ascension into the distance,[26] going on until his body finally vanished entirely three
years later. All of which is to say that a single identity can never be designated
6:34   for the spirit.[27]

Nanbo Zikui said to Lady Ju, "You are old and yet your face is still that of a
child. How?"

Lady Ju said, "I have heard the Course."

Nanbo Zikui said, "May I learn this Course?"

Lady Ju said, "No, no! How could you? You are not the right person for the
job. Now, Puliang Yi had the innate powers of a sage, but not the Course of a
sage. I had the Course of a sage but no [student with] the innate powers of a
sage. So I wanted to teach him, thinking he would immediately become a sage.
Although it was not quite like that, it was still very easy to announce the
Course of a sage to one who already has the innate powers of a sage. After I
kept at him, with it for three days, he could oust the entire world from himself. After seven days more, he could likewise oust all *things*, and after another
6:35   seven, even *life*. Only when life was put outside himself could the dawn break
6:36   through him. Only with the breakthrough of dawn could he see the Singu-
6:37   larity. After seeing the Singularity, he could free himself of past and present.
Free of past and present, he could enter the unborn and undying. What kills
all the living does not die. What gives birth to all the living is not born. It is
something that sends all beings off and welcomes all beings in, destroys all and

---

26   *Dengxia.* See note 8 of this chapter.

27   The last three lines are added in accordance with the Cui edition, as recorded by Qian
Mu.

completes all.[28] Its name is the Tranquility of Turmoil. This Tranquil Turmoil! It is what reaches completion only through its turmoil." 6:38

Nanbo Zikui said, "Where did you learn of this?"

Lady Ju said, "I learned it from the son of Aided-by-Ink, who learned it from the grandson of Caught-in-Recitation, who learned it from Look-and-See, who learned it from Heard-in-a-Whisper, who learned it from In-Need-of-Labor, who learned it from There-in-the-Singing, who learned it from Dark-Oblivion, who learned it from Joined-in-the-Void, who learned it from Perhaps-a-Beginning. 6:39

Ziji, Ziyu, Zili, and Zilai were talking. One of them said, "Who can see nothingness as his own head, life as his own spine, and death as his own ass? Who knows the single body formed by life and death, existence and nonexistence? I will be his friend!" The four looked at one another and laughed, feeling complete concord, and became friends.

Suddenly, Ziyu took ill. Ziji went to see him. Ziyu said, "How great is the Creator of Things, making me all tangled up like this!" For his chin was tucked into his navel, his shoulders towered over the crown of his head, his ponytail pointed toward the sky, his five internal organs at the top of him, his thigh bones taking the place of his ribs, and his yin and yang energies in chaos. But his mind was relaxed and unbothered. He hobbled over to the well to get a look at his reflection. "Wow!" he said. "The Creator of Things has really gone and tangled me up!"

Ziji said, "Do you dislike it?"

Ziyu said, "Not at all. What is there to dislike? Perhaps he will transform my left arm into a rooster; thereby I'll be announcing the dawn. Perhaps he will transform my right arm into a crossbow pellet; thereby I'll be seeking out an owl to roast. Perhaps he will transform my ass into wheels and my spirit into a horse; thereby I'll be riding along—will I need any other vehicle? Anyway, getting it is a matter of the time coming, and losing it is just something else to follow along with. Content in the time and finding one's place in the process of following along, joy and sorrow are unable to seep in. This is what the ancients called 'the Dangle and Release.' We cannot release ourselves—being beings, we are always tied up by something. But it has long been the case that mere beings cannot overpower Heaven. What is there for me to dislike about it?" 6:40

Suddenly Zilai fell ill. Gasping and wheezing, on the verge of keeling over, he was surrounded by his weeping family. Zili, coming to visit him, said to them, "Ach! Away with you! Do not disturb his transformation!" Leaning across the windowsill, he said to the invalid, "How great is the Process of Creation-Transformation! What will it make you become; where will it send you? Will it make you into a mouse's liver? Or perhaps an insect's arm?" 6:41

Zilai said, "A child obeys his parents wherever they may send him—north, south, east, or west. Now, yin and yang are much more to a man than his par-

---

28 "Completes" is *cheng*. See Glossary. This includes the meanings that it "forms, comes to be, is accomplished and reaches perfection" only through turmoil.

ents. If they send me to my death and I disobey them, that would make me a traitor—what fault would it be of theirs? The Great Clump burdens me with a physical form, labors me with life, eases me with old age, and rests me with death. Hence it is precisely because I regard my life as good that I regard my death as good. Now, suppose a great master smith were casting metal. If the metal jumped up and said, 'I insist on being nothing but an Excaliber!' the smith would surely consider it to be an inauspicious chunk of metal. Now, if I, having happened to stumble into a human form, should insist, 'Only a human! Only a human!' Creation-Transformation would certainly consider me an in-
6:42   auspicious chunk of person. So now I look upon all heaven and earth as a great
6:43   furnace, and Creation-Transformation as a great blacksmith—where could I go
6:44   that would not be all right? All at once I fall asleep. With a start I awaken."

Zisanghu, Mengzifan, and Ziqinzhang came together in friendship, saying, "Who can be together in their very not being together, do things for one another by not doing things for one another? Who can climb up upon the Heavens, roam-
6:45   ing on the mists, twisting and turning round and round without limit, living their lives in mutual forgetfulness, never coming to an end?" The three of them looked at one another and burst out laughing, feeling complete concord, and thus did they become friends. After a short silence, without warning, Zisanghu fell down dead. Before his burial, Confucius got the news and sent Zigong to pay his respects. There he found them, one of them composing music, the other plucking the zither, and finally both of them singing together in harmony:

> "Hey Sanghu, hey Sanghu!
> Come on back, why don't you?
> Hey Sanghu, hey Sanghu!
> Come on back, why don't you?
> You've returned to what we are really,
> While we're still humans—wow, yippee!"

Zigong rushed forward and said, "May I venture to ask, is it ritually proper to sing at a corpse like that?"

The two of them looked at each other and laughed, saying, "What does this
6:46   fellow understand about the real point of ritual?"

Zigong returned and reported this to Confucius, asking, "What kind of people are these? They do not cultivate their characters in the least, and they treat their bodies as external to themselves, singing at a corpse without the least change of expression. I don't know what to call them. What sort of people are they?"

Confucius said, "These are men who roam outside the lines. I, on the other hand, do my roaming inside the lines. The twain can never meet. It was vulgar of me to send you to mourn for such a person. For the previous while, he had been chumming around as a human with the Creator of Things, and now

he roams in the single vital energy of Heaven and Earth. Men such as these   6:47
look upon life as a dangling wart or swollen pimple, and on death as its dropping off, its bursting and draining. Being such, what would they understand
about which is life and which is death, what comes before and what comes after? Depending on all their diverse borrowings, they yet lodge securely in the
one and only selfsame body. They forget all about their livers and gallbladders,
cast away their eyes and ears, reversing and returning, ending and beginning,
knowing no start or finish. Oblivious, they drift uncommitted beyond the dust
and grime, far-flung and unfettered in the great work of doing nothing in particular. Why would they do something as stupid as practicing conventional rituals to impress the eyes and ears of the common crowd?"

Zigong said, "Since you know this, Master, of which zone do you consider
yourself a citizen?"

Confucius said, "As for myself, I am a victim of Heaven. But that is something you and I may share."

Zigong said, "Please tell me more."

Confucius said, "Fish come together in water, and human beings come together in the Course. Those who meet each other in the water do so by dart-
ing through the ponds, thus finding their nourishment and support. Those who
meet each other in the Course do so by not being bothered to serve any one
particular goal, thereby allowing the flow of their lives to settle into stability.
Thus it is said, fish forget one another in the rivers and lakes, and human beings forget one another in the arts of the Course."

Zigong said, "But please explain to me about these freakish people."

Confucius said, "They are freakish to humans but normal to Heaven. So it
is said, he who to Heaven is a petty man is to the people an exemplary man,
while he who to Heaven is an exemplary man is to the people a petty man."

Yan Hui went to question Confucius. "When his mother died, Mengsun Cai
wailed but shed no tears, unsaddened in the depths of his heart, observing the
mourning but without real sorrow. Lacking tears, inner sadness, and real grief,
he nonetheless gained a reputation throughout Lu as an exemplary mourner.
Is it really possible to have a reputation that is utterly at odds with reality? I have
always found it very strange."

Confucius said, "Mengsun Cai has gone to the very end of this matter, beyond merely understanding it. For when you try to simplify things for yourself
but find it impossible to do so, things have already been simplified for you. This   6:48
Mr. Mengsun understands nothing about why he lives or why he dies. His ignorance applies equally to what went before and what is yet to come. Having already transformed into some particular being, he takes it as no more
than a waiting for the next transformation into the unknown, nothing more.
When he's in the process of transforming, what could he know about not transforming? When he's no longer transforming, what could he know about whatever transformations he's already been through? You and I, conversely, are

dreamers who have not yet begun to awaken. As for him, his physical form may meet with shocks but this does not harm his mind. His life is to him but a morning's lodging, so he does no real dying. This Mr. Mengsun alone has awakened.

6:49   Others cry, so he cries too. And that is the only reason he does so.

6:50   "You temporarily get involved in something or other and proceed to call it 'myself'—but how can we know if what we call 'self' has any 'self' to it? You dream you are a bird and find yourself soaring in the heavens, you dream you are a fish and find yourself submerged in the depths. I cannot even know if what I'm saying now is a dream or not. An upsurge of pleasure does not reach the smile it inspires; a burst of laughter does not reach the jest that evoked it.[29] But when you rest securely in your place in the sequence, however things are arranged, and yet separate each passing transformation from the rest, then you

6:51   enter into the clear oneness of Heaven."

Yierzi went to see Xu You. Xu You asked him, "How did Yao instruct you?"

Yierzi said, "He told me to submit wholeheartedly to Humanity and Responsibility and to speak clearly of right and wrong."

Xu You said, "Then what on earth did you come here for? Yao has already tattooed your face with Humanity and Responsibility and de-nosed you with right and wrong. How can you ever roam in the far-flung and unconstrained paths of wild, unbound twirling and tumbling?"

Yierzi said, "Nonetheless, I'd like to roam at least around its outskirts."

Xu You said, "Not possible. The blind have no way to take part in the fineness of a lovely face, and the sightless have no way to take part in the marvel of vividly embroidered garments."

Yierzi said, "But Wuzhuang lost his beauty, Juliang lost his strength, the Yellow Emperor lost his wisdom,[30] all from being knocked about in the great smelting and hammering. How do you know the Creator of Things will not wipe away my tattoo and restore my nose, making me intact to follow you?"

Xu You said, "Ah! It is indeed unknowable. I will speak to you of the broad outlines then. My teacher! My teacher! He destroys all things, but he is not being responsible and just. His bounty reaches all things, but he is not being humane and kind.[31] He is an elder to the remotest antiquity, but without being

---

49   29   "Jest" comes from reading *pai* 俳 for *pai* 排, the latter being perhaps mistakenly transposed from the following line. Leaving the character unsubstituted would yield, "When you stumble into a pleasant situation, there is no time even to smile, and when a smile bursts forth there is no time to arrange it in some particular way," adopting Chen Shouchang's reading. Others take the *buji* 不及 (does not reach) in the sense of "not as good as," which yields something like, "Just going wherever you please is not as good as laughing, and offering a laugh is not as good as just taking your place in the sequence of things."

30   "Wisdom" is *zhi*. See Glossary.

31   "Humane and kind" is *ren*. "Responsible and just" is *yi*. See Glossary.

old. He covers and supports heaven and earth and carves out all forms, but without being skillful. It is all the play of his wandering, nothing more." 6:52

Yan Hui said, "I am making progress."
Confucius said, "What do you mean?"
Yan Hui said, "I have forgotten Humanity and Responsibility."[32]
Confucius said, "That's good, but you're still not there." 6:53
Another day he came again and said, "I am making progress."
"What do you mean?"
"I have forgotten ritual and music."
Confucius said, "That's good, but you're still not there."
He returned another day and said yet again, "I am making progress."
"What do you mean?"
Yan Hui said, "I just sit and forget."
Confucius, jolted as if kicked, said, "What do you mean, you sit and forget?"
Yan Hui said, "It's a dropping away of my limbs and torso, a chasing off of my sensory acuity, which disperses my physical form and ousts my understanding[33] until I am the same as the Transforming Openness.[34] This is what I call just sitting and forgetting."
Confucius said, "The same as it? But then you are free of all preference! 6:54
Transforming? But then you are free of all constancy! You truly are a worthy 6:55
man! I beg to be accepted as your disciple." 6:56

Ziyu and Zisang were friends. After ten days of freezing rain, Ziyu said to himself, "Zisang must be in distress." He packed up some rice to ease his friend's hunger. When he got to Zisang's gate, he heard a sound somewhere between singing and weeping, accompanied by the strum of a zither, forming the words: "Father? Mother? Heaven? Man?" Unable to sustain the sound, the voice collapsed brokenly through the lyric.
Ziyu entered and said, "Why do you sing like this?"
Zisang said, "I have been thinking about what could have caused me to reach this extreme state, and I could find no answer. My mother and father would surely never wish to impoverish me like this. Heaven covers all equally, earth supports all equally, so how could heaven and earth be so partial as to single me out for impoverishment? I search for some doer of it all but cannot find anything—and yet here I am in this extreme state all the same. This must be what is called Fate, eh?" 6:57

---

[32] *Ren yi.* See Glossary.

[33] "Understanding" is *zhi.* See Glossary.

[34] Reading *huatong* 化通 for *datong* 大通 ("Great Openness"), as in the parallel passage in *Huainanzi,* "Daoyingxun."

CHAPTER SEVEN
Sovereign Responses for Ruling Powers[1]

Nie Que asked Wang Ni four questions, and the answer to each was the same: "Don't know."[2] This sent Nie Que into leaps of ecstasy. He went to tell Puyizi[3] about it. Puyizi said, "So now you finally *know*[4] this? But the man of the Youyu[5] clan is no match for the man of the Tai clan. A Youyu still harbors Humanity in his breast, with which he tries to constrain other human beings. He may be able to win people over that way, but in doing so he never gets beyond *criticizing* people, considering them wrong. A Tai, on the other hand, lies down to sleep without hurry and wakes without cares. Sometimes he thinks he's a horse, sometimes he thinks he's an ox. Such understanding[6] is truly reliable, such Virtuosity deeply genuine. For they never involve him in criticizing other human beings, in considering them wrong."

7:1

Jian Wu went to see crazy Jieyu, who said to him, "What did Ri Zhong Shi[7] tell you?"

Jian Wu said, "He told me that if a ruler can produce regulations, standards, judgments, and measures derived from the example of his own person, none will dare disobey him and all will be reformed by him."

---

[1] The title of this chapter is usually interpreted as something like "Responses to Emperors and Sovereigns," parsing its three characters *ying di wang* 應帝王 as 1–2 rather than 2–1. All the other Inner Chapters that parse unambiguously divide as 2–1. The two ambiguous cases are Chapters 2 and 6, and a strong argument can be made for a 2–1 parsing of the title of Chapter 6 ("The Great Source *as* Teacher," as contrasted to "the taking of the mind as teacher," which is satirized by Zhuangzi earlier). While I have myself adopted a 1–2 parsing of the title of Chapter 2, I believe it involves a deliberate punning (meaning, "an assessment that equalizes beings" and also "an equalizing of the assessments made by beings"), which I've tried to preserve by other means. The same may be said for this title. It consists of *kingly* responses to questions *about* ruling, responses which are suitable *for* rulers both in the sense of suitable for rulers to use and suitable to use in dealing with rulers and ruling. It is perhaps significant that *di* 帝 is a term for supreme power in both the political and religious realms, which may explain why the story of the Zhuangzian response to Jixian the shaman is also included here. Wu Yi has also suggested the possibility of separating the usually combined *di* (emperor) and *wang* (king) in this title (*Zhuangzi neipian jieyi*, p. 276).

[2] Cf. 2:39 and Chapter 22.

[3] "Master Reedcoat," said by some commentators to be Nie Que's teacher. Both figures are purported to have lived during the time of the sage-emperor Shun.

[4] "Know" is *zhi* 知. See Glossary.

[5] The clan name of the sage-emperor Shun.

[6] "Understanding" is *zhi*. See Glossary.

[7] The name "Ri Zhong Shi" means something like "Noontide Beginning."

Jieyu said, "That is sham Virtuosity. To rule the world in this way is like trying to carve a river out of the ocean, or asking a mosquito to carry a mountain on its back. For when a sage rules, does he rule anything outside himself? He goes forth only after rectifying himself, just making sure that he is capable of his own task. A bird avoids the harm of arrows and nets by flying high, and a mouse burrows in the depths beneath the shrines and graves to avoid poisons and traps. Do you lack the wisdom[8] of these two little creatures?"

7:2

7:3

Tian Gen[9] roamed along the sunny slopes of Mt. Yin, until he came upon a nameless man on the banks of the Liao River. He said to him, "How is the world to be managed?"

The nameless man said, "Away with you, you boor! What a dreary question! I was just about to go chum around as a human being with the Creator of Things. When I get tired of that, I'll ride off on a bird formed from the unkempt wisps of the air, out beyond the six extremities of the known world, roaming in the homeland of nothing at all, thereby taking my place in the borderless wilds. Why do you come here to bother my mind with this business about ordering the world?"

But Tian Gen asked the same question again. The nameless man then said, "Let your mind roam in the flavorless, blend your vital energy with the boundless silence, follow the rightness of the way each thing already is without allowing yourself the least bias. Then the world will be in order."

7:4

Yang Ziju went to see Lao Dan, saying, "Here is a man, ambitious and quick, aggressively proactive, with a profound comprehension of things and a capacious intelligence, who studies the Course without fatigue. Can such a man be compared to a clear-sighted sovereign?"

Lao Dan said, "Compared to a sage, he is a petty official or diviner bound to his craft, laboring his own body and terrorizing his own mind. The beautiful patterns of the tiger and the leopard bring on the hunters that kill them; the monkey's grace and the dog's rat catching bring on the leashes that bind them. Can these be compared to a clear-sighted sovereign?"

Yang Ziju, jolted as if kicked, said, "I beg to ask about how a clear-sighted sovereign governs."

Lao Dan said, "When a clear-sighted sovereign rules, his achievements cover all the world, but they seem not to come from himself. He transforms all things, and yet the people do not rely upon him. There is something unnameable about him that allows all creatures to delight in themselves. He establishes his footing in the unfathomable and roams where nothing at all exists."

7:5

There was a shaman in Zheng named Jixian who could discern whether people would live or die, survive or perish. He knew how long their lives would be and

---

8 "Wisdom" is *zhi*. See Glossary.

9 The name "Tian Gen" means something like "Heavenly Root."

what turns their fortunes would take, giving the exact year, month, week, and date for each event like some kind of god. When the people of Zheng caught sight of him, they would turn and run. Liezi went to see him, and his mind became quite intoxicated. He returned and told Huzi about it, saying, "I used to think your Course was the ultimate, but now I see that there is something beyond it."

Huzi said, "I have only finished showing you its outward ornament, not yet its inner reality. Have you really mastered this Course? A multitude of hens 7:6 with no rooster can produce no chicks. You use the Course to browbeat the world, insisting that people believe in it. Because you try to control others, you have allowed yourself to be controlled. That is why this man was able to read 7:7 your fortune on your face. Bring him here, and I will show myself to him."

The next day, Liezi brought the shaman to see Huzi. He came out and said to Liezi, "Alas! Your master is as good as dead! That is not a living being in there! He has at most a few weeks left. I saw something very strange in him, something resembling wet ashes."

Liezi went in, his collar drenched with tears, and reported these words to Huzi. Huzi said, "Just now I showed him the patterns of the earth, sprouting forth without any strenuous rumblings and without straightening themselves 7:8 out.[10] He must have seen in me the incipient impulse of the Virtuosity that blocks everything out. Try bringing him again."

The next day, Liezi brought the shaman once more. He came out and said, "Your master is lucky to have met me! He's recovering; there are healthy signs of life! I could see his blockage moving into balance."

Liezi went in and reported this to Huzi, who said, "Just now I showed him Heaven's soil. Impervious to both names and realities, renown and profit, the incipient impulse nonetheless comes forth from the heels. He must have seen in me the incipient impulse of all that flourishes.[11] Try bringing him again."

The next day, he brought the shaman yet again to see Huzi. He came out and told Liezi, "Your master is an incoherent mess, I have no way to read his face. Have him get himself together, then I'll come back to do a reading."

Liezi went in and reported this to Huzi, who said, "Just now I showed him the vast gushing surge[12] in which no one thing wins out. He must have seen

---

10   "Straighten out" is *zheng* 正. See Glossary.

11   Literally, "of all that does well" or "of goodness." Cf. Lu Huiqing's comment at 7:10 of the "Commentaries" section.

12   "The vast gushing surge" is *chong* 沖. The word means "to flush something out with a surge of water" but is also used to denote the apparently derivative meanings of both "emptiness" (open space) and "harmony." One may combine these ideas into the image of a cleansing flush of water that empties and that restores harmony by washing away all one-sided cloggings, that blends all the elements by allowing fluid interconnections between them. The "water" imagery is surely relevant in the present context.

in me the incipient impulse that balances all energies. The frothing of a salamander's[13] swirl is the reservoir. The frothing of still water is the reservoir. The
frothing of flowing water is the reservoir. The reservoir has nine names, nine
aspects, and I have shown him three of them.[14] Try bringing him again."   7:9

The next day, Liezi brought him to see Huzi again. But before the shaman
had even come to a halt before him, he lost control of himself and bolted out
the door. Huzi said, "Go after him!" But Liezi could not catch up with him.
He returned and reported to Huzi, "He's gone! I cannot catch him!"

Huzi said, "Just now I showed him what I am when not yet emerged from my
source—something empty and serpentine in its twistings, admitting of no understanding of who or what. So he saw it as something endlessly collapsing and
scattering, something flowing away with every wave. This is why he fled."   7:10

That was when Liezi realized he had not yet learned anything. He returned
to his home and did not emerge for three years, cooking for his wife, feeding the
pigs as if he were serving guests, remaining remote from all endeavors and letting all the chiseled carvings of his character return to an unhewn blockishness.
Solitary like a clump of soil, he planted his physical form there in its place, a
mass of chaos and confusion. And that is how he remained to the end of his days.   7:11

> Not doing, not being[15] a corpse presiding over your good name;
> Not doing, not being a repository of plans and schemes;
> Not doing, not being the one in charge of what has to happen;
> Not doing, not being ruled by your own understanding;[16]   7:12

---

[13] There has been much debate about what creature is meant here. Sima Biao suggests
a "whale," and some commentators go the other way and suggest a swarm of small guppies.
It is surely significant that Zhuangzi here chooses a word that can mean *either* an enormous
whale *or* very small fish. "Salamander" is the literal meaning of the character used, but it
should be remembered that this most likely refers to the "giant salamander" found in China
(*Andrias davidianus*), which can reportedly grow to six feet in length. The resonance of this
image with the opening story in Chapter 1 of the enormous fish Kun should be noted; the
salamander is an amphibian, transforming from an aquatic to a terrestrial creature in the
course of its life, and it also has the capacity to regenerate lost limbs (cf. the lost feet in Chapter 5)—a fitting Zhuangzian symbol.

[14] The *Liezi* gives all "nine names of the reservoir": the salamander's swirl, still water,
flowing water, gushing water, dripping water, pouring water, stagnant water, rippling water,
and irrigating water.

[15] This translation is an attempt to capture the embedded pun on the crucial Daoist term
wuwei 無為 ("nondoing," i.e., absence of deliberate activity) in each of these phrases.

[16] "Understanding" is *zhi*. See Glossary. Alternately, this sentence can be rendered as
follows: "Not doing, not being the proprietor of wisdom." But the current reading, though it
strains the grammar of the parallelism a little, is consistent with Zhuangzi's critiques of taking the mind as teacher (2:12, 4:8) or the giving of precedence to "life" over "knowing" as
the "ruler" (*zhu*, as here) in the opening of Chapter 3 (3:2).

In this way, wholeheartedly embody the endlessness and roam where there is no sign, fully realize whatever is received from Heaven, but without thinking anything has been gained thereby.

7:13   It is just being empty, nothing more.

The Consummate Person uses his mind like a mirror, rejecting nothing, welcoming nothing: responding but not storing. Thus he can handle all things

7:14   without harm.

The emperor of the southern sea was called Swoosh. The emperor of the northern sea was called Oblivion. The emperor of the middle was called Chaos. Swoosh and Oblivion would sometimes meet in the territory of Chaos, who always attended to[17] them quite well. They decided to repay Chaos for his virtue.[18] "All men have seven holes in them, by means of which they see, hear, eat, and breathe," they said. "But this one alone has none. Let's drill him some."

7:15   So each day they drilled another hole. After seven days, Chaos was dead.

---

17   "Attended to" is *dai* 待. See 1:8, 2:44, 2:45, 2:48, 4:9, 6:5, 6:29, and Glossary.

18   "Virtue" is *de* 德, "Virtuosity." See Glossary.

Selections from

THE OUTER CHAPTERS

CHAPTER EIGHT
Webbed Toes

A web of flesh joining the toes together, or an extra finger branching off from the hand—they might come from the inborn nature of a person, but they are still extraneous to that person's Virtuosity. A "dangling wart or swollen pimple"[1] may emerge from a person's physical body, but it would still be extraneous to that body's inborn nature. If you are crafty enough in manipulating Humanity and Responsibility, you may be able to correlate them to the five internal organs, but this is not the true and unskewed expression[2] of the Course and its Virtuosity. For to web the toes together is to add useless flesh; to branch something off from the hand is to plant a useless finger, and when your craftiness webs or grafts something extra to the uncontrived condition of the five organs, it makes for perverse and distorted applications of Humanity and Responsibility, and for crafty uses of the powers of seeing and hearing. Webbing something extraneous to the power of seeing disrupts the Five Colors, and corrupts patterns and forms—is not the flashiness of the blue and yellow embroideries on the ceremonial garments an example? But that is what the likes of Li Zhu[3] really accomplish. Excessively sharp hearing disrupts the Five Tones and corrupts the Six Modes—are not the sounds of the "Yellow Bell" and "Great Tube" modes in the bells, chimes, strings, and woodwinds an example? But that is what the likes of Master Kuang[4] really accomplish. Branching extensions of Humanity and Responsibility uproot Virtuosity and obstruct the inborn nature in exchange for a good name—is not the trumpeting and drumming forth of all the world in pursuit of some unreachable standard an example? But that is what the likes of Zeng and Shi[5] really accomplish. Excess webbings of disputational acumen lead to the manipulation of verbal phrases, as if piling bricks or twining cords, sending the mind wandering around amid "hard" and "white," "same" and "different"—are not all the useless discussions

---

[1] The expression appears in the Inner Chapters (just after 6:47), to which this is perhaps an allusion.

[2] "True and unskewed" is *zheng* 正. See 1:4, 1:8, 2:39, 2:44, and Glossary.

[3] A paragon of sharp eyesight.

[4] A paragon of musical skill. See 2:28.

[5] Paragons of moral virtue.

with their wearying stagger toward honor an example? But that is exactly what the likes of Yang Zhu and Mozi[6] really accomplish.

All of these describe a course of excess webbings and side branchings, not at all "the world's most perfectly true and unskewed Course." The truly true[7] and unskewed way is just not to lose the uncontrived condition of one's inborn nature and the allotment of one's life. In this, what is joined is not so because of extra webbing and what is branched is not so because of additions. The long is not excessive and the short is not deficient. The duck's neck may be short, but lengthening it would surely vex him; the swan's neck may be long, but cutting it short would surely sorrow her. What is long in its inborn nature is not to be cut short, and what is short in its inborn nature is not to be lengthened. For there is nothing there that needs to be excised or worried over. So I have to surmise that Humanity and Responsibility are not the uncontrived condition of man! Otherwise, why are those "Humane Men" so wracked with worries?

Put it this way: if the toes are webbed together, cutting them loose will draw tears, and if the extra finger branches off from the hand, uprooting it will cause weeping. Whether something is added or something is taken away, the sorrow is the same. These days the Humane Men gaze wide-eyed into the distance worrying about all the world's troubles, while the inhumane men mutilate the uncontrived condition of their inborn nature and the allotment of life by gluttonously seeking wealth and rank. That is why I think Humanity and Responsibility are not the uncontrived condition of man!

From the Three Dynasties on down, what a racket and rumpus the world has become! For any rectification that requires hooks, ropes, compass, or T-square is really a hacking up of the inborn nature. Any consolidation that requires ropes, cords, or glues is really an invasive attack on Virtuosity. And bending and scraping before ritual and music, warmly eulogizing Humanity and Responsibility "to comfort the hearts of everyone in this world," all that is really just a way of destroying the normal and sustainable state of things.[8] The normal and sustainable state of things is to curve without needing a hook, to be straight without needing a carpenter's line, to be round without needing a compass, to be angled without needing a T-square, to be attached without needing glue, and to be bound together without needing cords. For all creatures in the world spring to life as if lured forth, not knowing how they are born. Obliviously they get hold of it somehow, without knowing how they do so. In this, past and present are alike, for this is something that can never be lacking. So what is the use of throwing Humanity and Responsibility into the midst of

---

6   Yang Zhu is traditionally considered an advocate of extreme egoism, and Mozi (founder of the Mohists; See Introduction and 2:15) an advocate of extreme altruism. Here, both are taken as paragons of philosophical disputation.

7   "The truly true and unskewed" is *zhengzhengzhe* 正正者. For *zheng*, see Glossary.

8   "Normal and sustainable state of things" is *chang ran* 常然. For *chang*, see Glossary.

the Course and its Virtuosity, trying to fasten everything together as if with glue and knotted cords? All it does is cast the world into confusion.

Now a small confusion is easily remedied, but a great confusion can alter the inborn nature. How do we know this? Ever since that Mr. Yu[9] started waving his Humanity and Responsibility around to stir up the world, everyone has spurred his allotment of life to a gallop after these ideals — do they not end up altering their inborn nature with all this Humanity and Responsibility?

Let me try to describe it. Since the time of the Three Dynasties on down, everyone in the world has altered his inborn nature for the sake of some *thing*. The petty man sacrifices himself for profit, the knight sacrifices himself for fame, the noble sacrifices himself for his clan, and the sage sacrifices himself for the world. Though the goal to which each devotes himself may differ, along with the reputations gained, all of them are the same in harming their inborn natures by sacrificing themselves to some *thing*.

Zang and Gu were herding sheep, and both of them lost their herds. Asked for the reason, Zang said he was busy studying his books, while Gu said he was busy gambling with his dice. Though they devoted themselves to different goals, they were alike in losing their sheep. Now, Bo Yi[10] died in pursuit of fame at the foot of Mt. Shouyang, while Robber Zhi[11] died in pursuit of profit at the top of Mt. Dongling. They died for different things, but they were alike in damaging their lives and harming their inborn natures. So why must we say that Bo Yi was right and Robber Zhi was wrong? Everyone in the world is sacrificing himself for something or other. Those who do so for Humanity and Responsibility are praised by the vulgar as exemplary men, while those who do so for wealth are condemned as petty men. But they are all alike in sacrificing themselves. So are there really any such things as "exemplary men" and "petty men"? In that they damage their lives and harm their inborn natures, Robber Zhi is no different from Bo Yi. Why should one be praised and the other condemned?

So to subordinate your inborn nature to Humanity and Responsibility, even if you succeed like Zeng and Shi, is not what I call good. To subordinate your inborn nature to the Five Flavors, even if you succeed like Yu Er,[12] is not what I call good. To subordinate your inborn nature to the Five Tones, even if you

---

[9] An irreverent way of referring to the ancient sage-emperor Shun, a Confucian paragon of perfect governance.

[10] Another Confucian paragon of virtue, who, along with his brother Shu Qi, starved himself to death rather than eat the rice of the Zhou dynasty, of whose violent revolution he disapproved.

[11] A stock example of extreme evil and lawlessness; see also Chapter 10. Robber Zhi is also defended in Chapter 29 of the version of the *Zhuangzi* bearing his name (not included in this volume).

[12] A paragon of culinary discernment.

succeed like Master Kuang, is not what I call acute hearing. To subordinate your inborn nature to the Five Colors, even if you succeed like Li Zhu, is not what I call acute vision. What I call good is not Humanity and Responsibility, but just being good at your own Virtuosity. What I call good is certainly not what these people call Humanity and Responsibility! It is just fully allowing the uncontrived condition of your inborn nature and allotment of life to play itself out. What I call sharp hearing is not hearing others, but rather truly hearing yourself, nothing more. What I call sharp vision is not seeing others, but rather truly seeing yourself, nothing more. For to see others without seeing yourself, to gain some external *thing* without finding yourself, is to attain the success of others without attaining your own success, "to take comfort in the comfort of others but not in your own comfort."[13] In taking their comfort in something external to themselves, Robber Zhi and Bo Yi are alike. Both perverted and distorted themselves. As for me, since I am not entirely shameless in the face of the Course and its Virtuosity, I venture to engage in neither the lofty deeds of Humanity and Responsibility nor in the debased practices of perversity and excess.[14]

CHAPTER NINE
Horse Hooves

Here are the horses, with their hooves to tramp over frost and snow and their coats to keep out the wind and cold. Chomping the grass and drinking the waters, prancing and jumping over the terrain—this is the true inborn nature of horses. Even if given fancy terraces and great halls, they would have no use for them. Then along comes Bo Le, saying, "I am good at managing horses!" He proceeds to brand them, shave them, clip them, bridle them, fetter them with crupper and martingale, pen them in stable and stall—until about a quarter of the horses have dropped dead. Then he starves them, parches them, trots them, gallops them, lines them up neck to neck or nose to tail, tormented by

---

[13] Cf. 6:14–15, to which this is perhaps an allusion.

[14] The author of this chapter here rejects both so-called good and so-called evil in favor of a "neither/nor" position between them. This is typical of the "primitivist" author of Chapters 8 through 11 and builds on a particular reading of the *Daodejing*, which this author often quotes. The original human nature is here regarded as prior to the distinction between good and evil but ultimately, if left to itself and undisturbed by interfering "ideals" of goodness, is a higher source of Good. See Chapter 9 for a fuller description of this author's conception of "the inborn nature and uncontrived condition." This definitiveness of this particular nature is to be contrasted to the "lack of fixed identity" evoked by the Inner Chapters, and the idea of "neither good nor evil" is to be compared to the "both 'good' and 'evil'" formulation set forth at the start of Chapter 3 (3:3).

bit and rein in front and by whip and spur behind. By then over *half* of the horses have dropped dead.

The potter says, "I'm good at managing clay! I round it until it matches the compass, square it until it matches the T-square." The carpenter says, "I'm good at managing wood! I curve it until it matches the arc, straighten it until it corresponds to the line." Do you suppose the inborn nature of the clay or the wood wants to match a compass, T-square, arc, or line? And yet somehow or other, generation after generation bursts into songs of praise: "Bo Le is so good at managing horses! The potter and carpenter are so good at managing clay and wood!" And this is the same error made by those who "govern," who "manage" the world.

In my opinion, someone who was really good at managing the world would not go about it like that. For the people too have their own constant inborn nature. To be clothed by their own weaving, fed by their own plowing—this is what is called their shared Virtuosity. All as one, without faction—I call that simply the way Heaven has cast them forth. Thus, in the age of perfect Virtuosity their actions were solid and full but their gaze was distant and blank.[1] For in those days, there were no paths or trails through the mountains, no boats or bridges over the ponds; all creatures lived together, merging their territories into one another. The birds and beasts clustered with each other, the grasses and trees grew unhampered, so one could tie a cord to a bird or beast and take a stroll with it or bend down a branch to peep into a bird's nest. Indeed, in those days of perfect Virtuosity, the people lived together with the birds and beasts, bunched together with all things. What did they know about "exemplary men" and "petty men"? All the same in knowing nothing, their undivided Virtuosity never left them. They were all the same in wanting nothing: that is what it means to be undyed and unhewn. It was by being left undyed and unhewn that the inborn nature of the people reached its full realization.

Then along came the sages. Limping and staggering after Humanity, straining on tiptoe after Responsibility, they filled everyone in the world with self-doubt. Lasciviously slobbering over music, fastidiously obsessing over ritual, they got everyone in the world to take sides. For unless the undyed and unhewn are mutilated, what can be made into libation goblets? Unless the white jade is broken, what can be made into the ritual scepters and batons? And unless you drop the Course and its Virtuosity, how can you take up Humanity and Responsibility?[2] Unless our inborn nature and our uncontrived condition are

---

[1] Tentative reading of a mysterious description, literally, "Their steps full-full, their gaze summit-summit." Alternately, taking 蹎 for 顛 and reversing these two sentences and criss-crossing their predicates, we might get, "Their vision was packed to capacity, while their steps seemed teetering and precarious." This would be a description of tentative, directionless movement through the untamed, animal-crammed environment. For another depiction of the apparently cautious tentativeness of the Daoist's motions, compare *Daodejing* 15.

[2] Cf. *Daodejing* 18.

dismembered, what use will there be for ritual and music? Unless the Five Colors are in chaos, what can be formed into designs and decorations? Unless the Five Tones are in chaos, what can be forced into step with the Six Modes? The mutilation of the unhewn raw material to make valued vessels is the crime of the skilled carpenter. The destruction of the Course and its Virtuosity to make Humanity and Responsibility is the fault of the sages.

Horses dwelling out on the plains chomp the grasses and drink the waters there. When pleased, they twine and rub their necks together. When angry, they turn their backs and kick. This is the extent of a horse's knowledge.[3] If you put yokes and poles on their necks and level them down with crossbars and shafts, they will come to know a bit more: how to split the shafts, wriggle out of the yokes, butt the hood, spit out the bit, and gnaw through the reins. So it is really Bo Le's fault that the horses' knowledge reaches the point of making criminals of them.

Likewise, in the days of Hexu, the people stayed at home without knowing what they were doing, ventured out without knowing where they were going. Filling their mouths they were merry; drumming their bellies they amused themselves. This was the extent of the people's abilities. Then along came the sage, bending and twisting over ritual and music to reform the bodies of the world, dangling Humanity and Responsibility overhead "to comfort the hearts of everyone in the world." Only then did the people begin groping on tiptoe in their eagerness for knowledge. From there it was inevitable that they would end up struggling for profit and advantage above all. And this, all this, is really the fault of the sages.

CHAPTER TEN
Breaking into Trunks

To protect your trunks, your sacks, your cabinets from thieves who would break into them, rifle through them, bust them open, no doubt you will bind them with seals and ropes, secure them with latches and locks. This is what the conventional world calls wisdom.[1] But when a great thief arrives, he will take the cabinet on his back, haul off the trunk, shoulder the sack, and make off with them—fearing nothing more than that the seals, ropes, latches, and locks are

---

[3]   "Knowledge" is *zhi* 知. See Glossary.

[1]   "Wisdom" throughout this chapter translates *zhi* 知, the same character usually translated as "knowing consciousness," "intelligence," "understanding," "cleverness," and so on, in the Inner Chapters. Here, its association with the sages tilts the implication toward "wisdom." See Glossary. In the final paragraph of the chapter, the same character is used as a verb, translated simply as "know."

not secure *enough*. So this thing you've been calling "wisdom"—is it anything more than the piling up of loot for the greater thieves?

Let me try to explain this further. Is there anything at all that the conventional world calls wisdom that is not really just piling up loot for the great thieves? Are there any so-called sages who are not just guards in the service of the great thieves? How do I know this is so? The state of Qi was in olden days so densely populated that one could peer over to the neighboring village and hear its dogs and chickens. The territory reached by Qi's fishing nets and plows exceeded two thousand square miles. And in all the shrines and temples, in every province and hamlet and town, there was no corner that was not regulated by the rules of the sages. Then one day, Tian Chengzi killed the ruler of Qi and took his state. But what he stole was not only the state; with it, he appropriated the laws and regulations devised by the sagely wisdom. So although Tian Chengzi may have been called a thief, he lived as securely as the sage-kings Yao and Shun. Smaller states dared not criticize him and larger states dared not attack him, and his family held on to the throne of Qi for twelve generations. Did he not then steal, along with the state of Qi, the rules of sagely wisdom by which to protect his thieving self?

Let me say more about this. Is there anything that worldly convention calls "perfect wisdom" which is not in reality the piling up of loot for the great thieves? Are there any so-called perfect sages who are not really bodyguards of the great thieves? How do I know this is so? In olden days, Guan Longfeng was beheaded, Bi Gan had his heart torn out, Chang Hong got drawn and quartered by chariots, Wu Zixu was tossed into the river to rot. The worthiness of these four could not save them from execution [under the authority granted by "sagely law"].

Once, Robber Zhi's disciple asked him, "Do robbers also have the Course?"

Zhi said, "Where can one go without the Course? To guess where the treasure is hidden is Sagacity. To go in first is Courage. To be the last to leave is Responsibility. To judge whether a job can succeed or not is Wisdom. To distribute the loot equally is Humanity. No one can become a great robber without these five virtues!"

From this we can see that, while it is true that the good man cannot stand without the Course of the sage, Robber Zhi could not operate without it either. But since there are more bad men than good men in the world, the sage benefits the world little and harms the world much. Hence, it is said, "When the lips are gone, the teeth get cold. The wine of Lu ran thin, and so Handan was besieged."[2]

---

[2] King Xuan of Chu called Duke Gong of Lu to court. The latter arrived late and with offensively thin wine. A dispute ensued, leading to Chu's attack on Lu. Handan was the capital of the state of Zhao, an ally of Chu. With the Chu armies occupied in attacking Lu, Handan was left open to an attack from King Hui of the state of Liang.

When a sage is born, great robbers arise. So it is only when you destroy the sages and pardon all the thieves and robbers that the world can be properly ordered. When the streams dry up, the valley becomes empty; when the hills are leveled, the reservoirs are filled; and once the sages die, great robbers will no longer arise. Then the world will be at peace and without trouble. If the sages do not die, great robbers will never stop coming.

To try to govern the world by doubling the number of sages would merely double the profits of the great robbers. If you create pounds and ounces to measure them with, they'll steal the pounds and ounces and rob with them as well. If you make scales and balances to regulate them with, they'll steal the balances and rob with them as well. If you create tallies and seals to enforce their reliability, they'll steal the tallies and seals and rob with them as well. And if you create Humanity and Responsibility to regulate them with, why, they'll just steal the Humanity and Responsibility and rob with them as well.

How do I know this is so? He who steals a belt buckle is executed, but he who steals a state is made a feudal lord. Humanity and Responsibility are always among the properties found in the homes of the feudal lords. Have they not also stolen Humanity, Responsibility, Sagacity, and Wisdom?

So as long as the great robbers continue to go scot-free—as long as these feudal lords continue to be exalted—they will keep stealing Humanity and Responsibility, together with the weights, measures, scales, balances, tallies, and seals that ensure their advantage, even if you reward them with high rank for refraining or threaten them with execution for persisting. Doubling the profits of the Robber Zhis of the world to the point where they can never be stopped— it is all the fault of the sages!

Hence, it is said, "The fish should not leave the deep pool, and a nation's sharp weapons should not be displayed to the people."[3] The sages are the sharpest of all the world's weapons and should not be displayed. Hence, only when sagacity is destroyed and wisdom abandoned will the great robbers disappear.[4] Smash the jades and crush the pearls, and the small robbers will not arise. Burn the tallies and shred the seals, and the people will become plain and straight. Break the measures and split the scales, and the people will no longer bicker and fight. Only when we decimate the sagely laws throughout the world will the people be able to listen to reason. Only when we uproot and scramble the Six Modes, smelt down the flutes and zithers, and plug up the ears of Master Kuang will the people of the world be able to hang on to their keen hearing. Only when we destroy patterns and ornaments, scatter the Five Colors, and glue up Li Zhu's eyes will the people of the world be able to hang on to their keen vision. Only when we destroy the hooks and rope levels, abandon the compasses and T-squares, and break Carpenter Chui's fingers will the

---

3   *Daodejing* 36.

4   Cf. *Daodejing* 19.

people of the world be able to retain their own skills. Hence, it is said, "Great skill seems like clumsiness."[5] Only when we cut away the virtuous practices of Zeng and Shi, restrain the mouths of Yang and Mo, and cast away Humanity and Responsibility will the Virtuosity of the people of the world find its oblivious unity.

When everyone keeps their keen vision to themselves, the world will no longer be distorted. When everyone keeps their keen hearing to themselves, the world will no longer be fettered. When everyone keeps their wisdom to themselves, the world will no longer be confused. When everyone keeps their Virtuosity to themselves, the world will no longer be awry. Zeng, Shi, Yang, Mo, Master Kuang, Carpenter Chui, and Li Zhu all set their Virtuosities outside themselves, using their radiance to disorder the world. But these are things for which standards are of no use.

Have you never heard about the age of perfect Virtuosity? In the olden days of Rongcheng, Dating, Bohuang, Zhongyang, Lilu, Lixu, Xuanyuan, Hexu, Zuntu, Zhurong, Fuxi, and Shennong,[6] the people knotted ropes as their only records, delighted in their food and clothes, and enjoyed their own customs and dwellings. Neighboring countries could see one another in the distance, their dog barks and cock crows were audible to one another, but all their lives the people had no occasion to travel from one to the other.[7] This was the time of perfect order. But nowadays, it has gotten to the point where they make the people crane their necks and stand on tiptoe, saying, "In such and such a place there is a worthy man!" They pack their provisions and head out to find him, abandoning their own parents and dropping their service to their own rulers, their footprints littering the territories of various feudal lords and their carriage tracks crisscrossing for thousands of miles. This is all the fault of the love of wisdom shown by those above them. If those above sincerely love wisdom but lack the Course, it throws the world into disorder.

How do we know this is so? Much wisdom[8] in the use of crossbows and arrows, traps and nets, plots and schemes, throws the birds of the sky into disorder. Much wisdom in the use of hooks, bait, nets, poles, and lures throws the fish of the waters into disorder. Much wisdom in the use of traps, nets, snares, and lattices throws the beast of the woodlands into disorder. And wisdom turns into cunning, like a kind of gradual poisoning, rigidifying and unmooring "hard" and "white," disjoining and muddying "sameness" and "difference," and ends up casting the people into a muddle of disputation. Thus it is that each and every great disorder of the world is caused by the love of wisdom.

---

5   *Daodejing* 45.

6   According to Sima Biao, these twelve are all ancient sage-emperors.

7   See *Daodejing* 80.

8   "Wisdom" is *zhi* 知. See Glossary.

Everyone in the world knows how to raise questions about what they don't know, but none know how to raise questions about what they already know.[9] Everyone understands enough to reject what they consider bad, but not enough to reject what they consider good. This is the reason for the great disorder, which violates the brightness of the sun and moon above and melts away the vital essence of the mountains and rivers below, toppling the ordered succession of the four seasons in between. All creatures, down to the smallest wriggling and fluttering insects, have thus lost touch with their inborn natures. How profoundly the love of wisdom disrupts the world! Abandoning the seedlike impulse within them, they instead insist on laborious subservience. Letting go of the peaceful blandness of the purposeless, they instead delight in ideas and plans full of jibber jabber. And how this jibbering and jabbering has already disordered the world!

CHAPTER FOURTEEN
The Turnings of Heaven (Selections)

[. . . .]

Dang, the Great Overseer of Shang, asked Zhuangzi about Humanity.

"Tigers and wolves are humane," Zhuangzi said.

"What do you mean?"

"The parents and children among them have affection for one another— can you say they're being inhumane?"

"But I am asking about *perfect* Humanity."

"Perfect Humanity involves no affection."

"I have heard that without affection there is no love, and without love there is no filial piety. Surely perfect Humanity cannot be lacking in filial piety!"

"Not so," Zhuangzi said. "Perfect Humanity is a lofty thing; it is quite impossible to talk about it in terms of filiality. And by this I don't mean it goes beyond filiality, but just the contrary: it does not even reach filiality. When a traveler to the south reaches the city of Ying, he may turn around to gaze northward, but he will never be able to see Mt. Ming in the north. It is just too far away. Now, they say it is easier to be filial out of respect than out of love. And it is easier to be filial out of love than to forget your parents. It is easier to forget your parents than to get them to forget you. It is easier to get them to forget you than to forget the whole world. It is easier to forget the whole world than to get the whole world to forget you. The Virtuosity that leaves behind even Yao and Shun, not taking any deliberate action, bestows its nourishing bounty on ten thousand generations, but the world is never aware of it. How could this be matched by those who just go around mouthing off and sighing about Humanity and filiality? For filiality and fraternity, Humanity and Re-

---

9 "Know" is *zhi* 知. See Glossary.

sponsibility, loyalty and faithfulness, resoluteness and integrity are all just ways of forcing yourself to labor your own Virtuosity. They merit no special esteem. Hence, it is said, 'The noblest are those who scorn even the highest rank of the nation; the wealthiest are those who abandon even the greatest riches in the nation; the most ambitious discard even fame and honor.' This is how the Course remains unspoiled."

Cheng of Northgate said to the Yellow Emperor, "When I heard you perform the Xianchi music in the wilds of Dongting, I was at first terrified. As it continued, I started to feel exhausted, and by the end I was in a state of total confusion—cast into chaos, speechless, unable to get a hold of myself!"

The emperor said, "I should think you would! I performed it with the Human in me but attuned it to the Heavenly, advancing it with the trappings of Ritual and Responsibility, but rooting it in the Great Clarity. For perfect music —which is perfect joy—must start out by resonating with human affairs but also flowing along the guideline of the Heavenly.[1] It must run its course through all the Five Virtues but still accord with what is unforced in things. Only then can it concordantly adjust the four seasons within it, bringing all things into its great harmony. The four seasons arrive one after the other, and the ten thousand things are produced accordingly—now flourishing, now declining, now peaceful, now warlike, all grouping into their own regularities. Sometimes clear, sometimes turbid, yin and yang adjust to each other, forming a harmony. The sound then flows and radiates, stirring the hibernating insects to life. I startle them up with sudden thunder and lightning, without overture or conclusion, without head or tail, now dead, now alive, now rising, now falling. Endlessly sustainable, it yet has no predictable consistency. That is what terrified you.

"I continued to play it as a harmony of yin and yang, brightened with the light of the sun and moon. The sound could then expand or contract, could soften or harden freely. It transformed with a leveling unity but was controlled by no constant precedent. Coming to a valley, it perfectly filled the valley; coming to a pit, it perfectly filled the pit. Fitting any opening, it yet maintained its spirit, taking on the measure of each thing it encountered. The sound undulated and lilted, giving an impression of loftiness and light, thus leaving the ghosts and spirits holding to their darkness, the heavenly bodies moving along in their proper proportions. I halted it in the limited but also let it flow with the unstoppable. You tried to find a way to conceive it but could not grasp it; you looked for it but could not see it; you chased after it but could not catch it. All at once you were standing in the midst of the Course that opens out in all directions, leaning against a withered tree and inadvertently singing along. Your eye and mind were exhausted in their quest to see it, your strength frustrated in its attempt to catch it. But since your self could not catch up with it, your

---

[1]   "The guideline of the Heavenly" is *tianli* 天理. Cf. 3:5, and see *li* in Glossary.

body filled the expanses of space, following along with all its serpentine changes. This is why you felt exhausted.

"I went on to play it with tireless sounds, adjusting it to the unforced mandates of things.[2] Hence, the tones, springing up in clumps, mingled and chased each other, forests of sounds that nonetheless took no identifiable form, spreading into activity but without pulling one another along—dark, obscure, ultimately noiseless. The music sprang into motion from no specifiable place, rooted in the recesses of oblivion. Some would call it death, some would call it life, some would call it fruit, some would call it flower—moving, flowing, scattering, escaping, controlled by no constant tone. The world is cast into doubt by it and can only query the sage. The sage is one who understands the uncontrived inclinations of things and allows them to accomplish their own mandates. His Heavenly Impulse is undisplayed although all his bodily organs are intact. This is called the Heavenly Music, the Heavenly Joy. Wordless, the heart finds its delight there. This is why the man of the Youyan clan[3] praised it, saying: 'Listening for it, I hear no sound; looking for it, I see no shape. It fills heaven and earth, encompassing the world's outermost limits.' You wanted to listen but could find no place to receive it, nowhere to make contact with it. This is why you were confused.

"Music, joy, begins as terror, and so it always comes first as a calamity. I follow that up by making it exhausting, for that is what allows one to vanish into it. Then I finish it off with confusion, for that brings foolishness. It is through your foolishness that it takes you on its course. It is then the coursing of the Course that carries you along, keeping you right there with it wherever it may go."

[. . . .]

CHAPTER SEVENTEEN
Autumn Floods

The time of the autumn floods had come, and all the streams were pouring into the great river. The expanse of its unobstructed flow was so great that a horse on the other bank could not be distinguished from a cow. The River God was overjoyed, delighting in his own powers, believing all the world's beauty now to be encompassed within himself. Flowing eastward, he arrived at the Northern Sea. Casting his gaze toward the east, he saw no end to the waters. It was then that his face began twisting and turning, a whirlpool of features, in his attempt to take the sea in his sights. He addressed Ruo of the Northern Sea with a sigh: "There is a saying in the outlands: 'He who hears the Course a

---

[2] "The unforced mandates of things" is *ziran zhi ming* 自然之命 . For *ming*, see Glossary.

[3] The sage-emperor Shennong.

mere hundred times believes no one can compare with him.' This describes me perfectly. When I first heard that there are those who belittle the erudition of Confucius and the conscientiousness of Bo Yi,[1] I didn't believe it. But now I have seen your vastness with my own eyes. If I had never come here to your gate I might have become a laughingstock to the masters of the Great Method!"

Ruo of the Northern Sea said, "You cannot discuss the sea with a well turtle, for he is limited in space. You cannot discuss ice and snow with a summer insect, for he is fixed in his own time. And you cannot discuss the Course with a nook-and-corner scholar, for he is bound by his doctrines. Now that you have emerged from your dusty banks and had a look at the great ocean, you finally realize how hideous you are! Only now can you understand anything about the Great Guideline.[2]

"There is no body of water in the world larger than the ocean. All the rivers revert to it ceaselessly, yet it is not filled. It leaks away at Weilu continuously, yet it is not emptied. Unchanging in both spring and autumn, it is unaffected by either floods or droughts. Its superiority to all the streams and rivers is beyond calculation, but I have never for this reason thought much of myself. For if I compare myself to all the creatures taking shape between heaven and earth and receiving vital energy from the yin and yang, I see that my position between heaven and earth is like that of a small stone or a tiny weed on a vast mountain. Having this insight into my insignificance, what conceit could I have? For are not the four seas, calculated against the space between heaven and earth, like a swirling hollow on the surface of a vast lake? Is not the Middle Kingdom, calculated against all the known world, like a single grain of rice lost in a granary? We number the types of creatures at ten thousand, and man is but one of them. And even in the nine regions crowded with humans, where they are able to grow their crops and ride their boats and carriages, a single person is just one among the throng. Among the ten thousand things, is not the human realm like the tip of a hair on the body of a horse? What the Five Emperors unified, what the Three Hegemons fought for, what the humane men worry themselves about, what the diligent knights labor themselves for, is nothing more than this. Bo Yi was considered worthy of fame for renouncing no more than this; Confucius was considered erudite for talking about no more than this—such was their conceit! Does it not resemble your previous conceit over your waters?"

The River God said, "Then I should consider heaven and earth large, and the tip of an autumn hair small—is that right?"

Ruo of the Northern Sea said, "Not at all. For there is no end to the comparative measuring of things, no stop to the changing times, no constancy to

---

[1] "Conscientiousness" is *yi* 義, elsewhere translated, when paired with *ren* 仁 (Humanity), as "Responsibility." See Glossary. For Bo Yi, see Chapter 6, note 11.

[2] "Guideline" is *li* 理. See Glossary.

the ways things can be divided up, no fixity to their ends and beginnings. Thus, when a person of great wisdom contemplates both the far and the near, he does not find what is small to be too little nor what is great to be too much, for he knows that comparative measurings are endless. Witnessing the totality of ancient and modern times, he does not find the lofty and distant to be dispiritingly great nor the cramped and nearby to be in need of improvement, for he knows that the temporal changes of things are endless. Understanding their fillings and emptyings, he can gain them without joy and lose them without sorrow, for he knows that there is no single constant way of dividing them up. Comprehending their juttings and flattenings, he does not rejoice in finding himself alive nor bemoan his death, for he knows that there can be no fixity to their endings and beginnings.

"What man knows is far less than what he does not know. The time he exists is insignificant compared to the time he does not exist. It is because he tries to exhaust this vastness with this meagerness that he bewilders and frustrates himself. From this point of view, how can we know that the tip of a hair can delimit the ultimate measure of smallness, or heaven and earth the fullest expanse of vastness?"

The River God said, "The debaters of the world say, 'The most minute and subtle has no physical form, and the largest and coarsest is unencompassable.' Is this correct?"

Ruo of the Northern Sea said, "Looking at the large from the viewpoint of the small, it appears inexhaustible. Looking at the small from the viewpoint of the large, it appears indistinct. The subtle is the minutest of the small, and the limiting circumference is the vastest of the large. So it is sometimes convenient to differentiate between them, as determined by the situation. But both the subtle and the coarse are limited to the realm of things with definite form. What has no form can be distinguished by no quantities; what cannot be encompassed can be exhausted by no quantities. What can be discussed in words is just the coarser aspect of things; what can be reached by thought is just the subtler aspect of things. But what words cannot describe and thought cannot reach cannot be determined as either coarse or subtle.

"So the conduct of the Great Man harms no one, but he places no special value on humanity and kindness. His actions are not motivated by profit, but he does not despise those who slavishly subordinate themselves to it. He does not fight over wealth, but he places no special value on yielding and refusing it. He doesn't depend on others, but he places no special value on self-sufficiency. He does not despise the greedy and corrupt, and though his own conduct is unconventional, he places no special value on eccentricity and uniqueness. His actions do [not] follow the crowd, but he does not despise the obsequious flatterers. All the honors and stipends in the world are not enough to goad him into doing anything, and all its punishments and condemnation are not enough to cause him shame, for he knows that right and wrong cannot be definitively divided, and that no border can be fixed between great and small. I have heard it said, 'The man of the Course has no reputation; perfect Virtuosity achieves nothing; the Great Man has no fixed identity.'[3] For he holds perfectly to the differing allotment of things."

The River God said, "From within things or without, where is the standard that can divide the more from the less valuable, the great from the small?"

Ruo of the Northern Sea said, "From the point of view of the Course, no thing is more valuable than any other. But from the point of view of itself, each thing is itself worth more and all the others are worth less. And from the point of view of convention, the value of things is not determined by themselves.

"From the point of view of their differences, if we consider something big because it is bigger than something else, no thing is not big. If we consider it small because it is smaller than something else, no thing is not small. When you can understand the sense in which heaven and earth are just like a grain of rice and the tip of a hair is just like a mountain range, you have grasped the principle of their differences. If we consider something to be worthy because it has some positive effectiveness, there is no thing that is not worthy. If we consider it to be unworthy because there is some positive effectiveness it lacks, there is no thing that is not unworthy. When you understand the sense in which east and west are opposed to each other and yet indispensable to each other, you have clarified the allotments of their positive effects. From the point of view of the inclinations of various beings, if we consider something right because someone considers it right, then no thing is not right. If we consider it wrong because someone considers it wrong, then no thing is not wrong. When you understand the sense in which Yao and Jie each considers himself right and the other wrong, you have grasped the operation of their inclinations. In olden times, Yao yielded the throne to Shun and Shun became a true emperor, but Kuai yielded the throne to Zhi and Zhi was destroyed. Tang and Wu fought for the throne and became rulers, but Bo Gong fought for the throne and perished. From this point of view, the propriety of struggle or of yielding, the conduct of a Yao or a Jie, is given different values at different times, none of which can be taken as a constant. Pillars and cross beams can be used to ram down a wall, but not to plug a hole, for this requires a different kind of tool. A great stallion can gallop a thousand miles in a day, but it cannot catch mice as well as a cat, for that requires a different kind of skill. Kites and owls can catch a flea or discern the tip of a hair on a dark night, but in the daytime they are blinded and cannot even make out a mountain range, for that requires a different inborn nature. So if someone says, 'Why don't we make only rightness our master and eliminate wrongness, make only order our master and eliminate chaos?' this is someone who has not yet understood how heaven and earth fit together[4] and the way the ten thousand things really are. That would be like taking Heaven alone as your master

---

[3] Cf. 1:8.

[4] "How [they] fit together" is *li*. See Glossary.

and eliminating earth, or taking yin alone as your master and eliminating yang—an obvious impossibility. If someone nonetheless insists on talking this way, he is either a fool or a swindler. The rulers of the Three Dynasties sometimes yielded their thrones and sometimes passed them on to their sons; those who did either at the wrong time, contravening the current conventions, were called usurpers, while those who did either at the right time, in accord with current conventions, were called righteous men. Silence, River God, silence! How could you know which gateways lead to worthiness and which to worthlessness, or which allegiances make one the greater or the lesser?"

The River God said, "But then what should I do? What should I not do? How shall I decide what to accept, what to reject, what to pursue, what to avoid?"

Ruo of the Northern Sea said, "From the point of view of the Course, the reciprocal overflowings of things are such that nothing can be definitively called worthy or unworthy. So do not restrict your will, but expansively limp and stagger along with the Course. The fading and blooming of things is such that nothing can be definitively called greater or lesser. So do not unify your conduct, but be uneven and varied along with the Course. Severe, like the ruler of a state—such is its unbiased Virtuosity. Giving forth continuously, like a festival centered around its shrine—such are its unbiased blessings. Extensive, like the endlessness of the four directions—such is its limitlessness. Methodless, in no definite location, it embraces all things, giving special protection to none. Leveling all things into one, what is long or short? The Course has no end or beginning, while creatures are born and die, coming to no reliable completion. Now empty, now full, things do not remain positioned in any one fixed form. The years cannot be held on to; time cannot be stopped. Waxing and waning, filling and emptying, each end is succeeded by a new beginning. This is a way of describing the method by which they are in the greatest sense just right for their position,[5] the way all things fit together.[6] The becoming of things is like a galloping horse, transforming with each movement, altering at each moment. What should you do? What should you not do? You will in any case be spontaneously transforming!"

The River God said, "In that case, what value is there in the Course?"

Ruo of the Northern Sea said, "When you understand the Course, you will be able to see through to the way things fit together, and then you will certainly understand what is appropriate to each changing situation. This will keep you from harming yourself with things. A man of perfect Virtuosity can enter fire without feeling hot, enter water without drowning. Neither heat nor cold can harm him; the birds and animals do not impinge upon him. This is not to say that he treats these things lightly, but rather precisely that he discerns where there is danger, remains calm in both good and bad fortune, is

---

[5] "Just right for their position" is *yi* 義. See Glossary.

[6] "The way [they] fit together" is *li*. See Glossary.

cautious about what he flees and what he approaches. Thus, nothing can harm him. Hence it is said, the Heavenly is internal while the Human is external, and Virtuosity resides in the Heavenly. He who knows which activities are of the Heavenly and which are of the Human roots himself in the Heavenly and positions himself comfortably in whatever he attains from it. Advancing and retreating, shrinking and expanding according to the time, he returns always to the most constrained but can thereby be described as reaching the expanse of the ultimate."

The River God said, "What do you mean by the Heavenly and what by the Human?"

Ruo of the Northern Sea said, "That cows and horses have four legs is the Heavenly. The bridle around the horse's head and the ring through the cow's nose are the Human.[7] Hence, it is said, 'Do not use the Human to destroy the Heavenly, do not use the purposive to destroy the fated, do not sacrifice what you have attained [from Heaven] for the sake of mere names.' Hold onto this carefully, for then you can return to what is genuine in you."

The unipede envied the millipede, the millipede envied the snake, the snake envied the wind, the wind envied the eye, and the eye envied the mind. The unipede said to the millipede, "Hopping around on my single leg, I manage to get from place to place, but it requires all my skill. And yet you are some-how able to manage ten thousand legs at the same time. How do you do it?"

The millipede said, "It's not like that. Haven't you ever seen a person spit? He gives a hock and all at once the big globules come flying forth like innu-merable pearls and the little droplets go spreading out like mist, raining down in a tangle. In my case, all I do is set my Heavenly Impulse into action—I have no idea how it's done!"

The millipede said to the snake, "I can move along on all these feet of mine, but it is still no match for the way you do it with no feet at all. But how?"

The snake said, "How could the motions of the Heavenly Impulse be al-tered? What use would I have for feet?"

The snake said to the wind, "I move along by putting my spine and flanks into action—at least there seems to be something there doing it. But you come whooshing up from the Northern Sea and all at once you are whooshing off into the Southern Sea, as if there is nothing there doing it at all. How do you do it?"

The wind said, "True, I can whoosh up from the Northern Sea and just as

---

[7]   It is worth noting the stark difference between this passage and the position put forth in the Inner Chapters, which makes the distinction between the Heavenly and the Human only to overturn it into unknowability (6:5) and even provisionally is only willing to say that neither should overpower the other (6:23). Here, on the contrary, the Heavenly definitively means the natural, while the Human means the deliberate and artificial; the two terms have definite contents, these can be unproblematically known, and "Virtuosity resides in the Heavenly." Compare Chapters 8 and 9, which also offer a fixed definition of the content of the Heavenly inborn nature.

suddenly into the Southern Sea, but whoever so much as points a finger or raises a foot at me immediately defeats me. Nonetheless, I alone am capable of snapping massive trees in two and tossing whole houses into the sky. I use all my small defeats to make one great victory. But the really great victory of this kind is something accomplished only by the sage."

When Confucius traveled to Kuang, the people of Song surrounded him in multiple ranks, and yet he went on singing and strumming his strings without pause. Zilu, going in to see him, asked, "How can you be so happy, Master?"

Confucius said, "Come, I will tell you. I've been trying to avoid failure for such a long time, and yet here it is—that is fate. I've been seeking success for so long, and yet it still eludes me—that's due to the times we live in. In the days of Yao and Shun, no one in the world was a failure, but this was not gained due to any wisdom[8] on their parts. In the days of Jie and Zhou, no one in the world was a success, but this was not because of any failure of their wisdom. It was just the circumstantial tendencies of the times that made it so. To travel over water without fearing the sharks and dragons is the courage of the fisherman. To travel over land without fearing rhinos and tigers is the courage of the hunter. To view death as no different from life even when the blades are clanging in front of one's face is the courage of the warrior. And to know that success depends on fate and failure on the times, to face great calamities without fear, this is the courage of the sage. Relax, Zilu! My fate is already sealed."

A short while later, a soldier came in with a message saying, "We surrounded you because we thought you were Yang Huo. Since we have realized our mistake, we ask leave to yield way to you and withdraw."

Gongsun Long said to Prince Mou of Wei, "When I was young, I studied the Course of the former kings; when grown, I came to understand the practice of Humanity and Responsibility. I could combine the same and the different, separate 'hard' and 'white,' make the not-so appear so and the unacceptable appear acceptable. I had confounded the wisdom of all the philosophers and stopped the mouths of all the debaters. I thought I already understood everything. But now that I have heard Zhuangzi's words, I am bewildered and lost in their strangeness. Does his rhetorical skill surpass mine? Is my knowledge unequal to his? At this point, I barely know how to open my beak! Please explain this to me!"

Prince Mou leaned against his low table, breathing deeply, then looked up at the skies and laughed. "Have you never heard the story about the frog in the sunken well? He said to the tortoise of the Eastern Ocean, 'How happy I am! I jump about on the railings and beams of the well and rest on the ledges left by missing tiles along its walls. When I splash into the water, it supports my armpits and holds up my chin, and when I tread in the mud, it submerges my feet up to the ankles. The surrounding crabs and tadpoles are certainly no match for me! For to have such mastery over one whole puddle of water like

---

8   "Wisdom" is *zhi* 知. See Glossary.

this, possessing all the joy of this sunken well—that is perfection! Why don't you come in and have a look sometime?' But before the tortoise could even get his left foot in, his right knee was stuck in the opening. So he pulled himself back out and told the frog about the ocean:

"'Its vastness exceeds a distance of a thousand miles; its depth is beyond the measure of a thousand fathoms. In Yu's time the lands were flooded for nine years, but its waters did not rise. In Tang's day there were seven droughts in eight years, but its shores did not recede. Unpushed and unpulled by either a moment or an aeon, unreceded and unadvanced by either little or much—that is the great joy of the Eastern Ocean!'

"When the well-frog heard this, he was cast into uncontainable astonishment, shrinking into utter discouragement. Now, for the intellect,[9] which doesn't know how to handle even the ultimate reaches of affirmations and negations, to contemplate the words of Zhuangzi—that is like a mosquito trying to carry a mountain on its back, or an inchworm trying to scurry across the Yellow River. It cannot be done. Your intellect, not knowing how to make sense of these most wondrous words of his, instead taking delight in its own momentary gains—is it not a frog trapped in the sunken well of right and wrong? As for him, he is no sooner traipsing across the Yellow Springs than he is climbing through the blue of the heavens, free of both south and north, unobstructed and released in all the four directions, submerged in the unfathomable depths. Devoid of both east and west, he begins anew in the dark obscurity and returns to the Great Openness. For you to rigidly seek him out with your acute discernment, searching for him with disputations, why, that's just like trying to survey heaven through a tube, or to measure the depth of the earth with an awl. Isn't it just too small? You'd best simply forget about it and go your way. Haven't you heard about how Yuzi of Shouling tried to learn the walking style of Handan? Before he was able to master this local skill, he had forgotten his original gait and had to return home on his hands and knees. If you don't get out of here, you might lose your original skills and be left without a career!"

Gongsun Long, unable to close his mouth or retract his tongue, broke into a run and bolted away.

Zhuangzi was once fishing beside the Pu River when two emissaries brought him a message from the King of Chu: "The king would like to trouble you with the control of all his realm." Zhuangzi, holding fast to his fishing pole, without so much as turning his head, said, "I have heard there is a sacred turtle in Chu, already dead for three thousand years, which the king keeps in a bamboo chest high in his shrine. Do you think this turtle would prefer to be dead and having his carcass exalted or alive and dragging his backside through the mud?" The emissaries said, "Alive and dragging his backside through the mud." Zhuangzi said, "Get out of here! I too will drag my backside through the mud!"

---

[9] "Intellect" is *zhi*. See Glossary.

When Huizi was prime minister of Liang, Zhuangzi went to see him. Someone said to Huizi, "Zhuangzi is coming; he wants to take your place as prime minister." Huizi was terrified and ordered a search for Zhuangzi throughout the land for three days and three nights. Zhuangzi, when he got there, said to him, "In the south there is a bird called 'Yuanchu'—have you heard about it? This bird rises from the Southern Sea and flies to the Northern Sea, resting only on the sterculia tree, eating only the fruit of the bamboo, and drinking only from the sweetest springs. An owl who had found a rotten mouse carcass saw Yuanchu passing overhead and screeched, 'Shoo! Shoo!' Now you—are you trying to shoo me away from your state of Liang?"[10]

Zhuangzi and Huizi were strolling along the bridge over the Hao River. Zhuangzi said, "The minnows swim about so freely, following the openings wherever they take them. Such is the happiness of fish."

Huizi said, "You are not a fish, so whence do you know the happiness of fish?"

Zhuangzi said, "You are not I, so whence do you know I don't know the happiness of fish?"

Huizi said, "I am not you, to be sure, so I don't know what it is to be you. But by the same token, since you are certainly not a fish, my point about your inability to know the happiness of fish stands intact."

Zhuangzi said, "Let's go back to the starting point. You said, '*Whence* do you know the happiness of fish?' Since your question was premised on your knowing that I know it, I must have known it from here, up above the Hao River."[11]

---

[10]   Note the rhetorical similarity of this passage to the beginning of Chapter 1.

[11]   In other words, *your* initial question showed your acceptance of the principle that one *does* know what another experiences, since the question itself could only have been in response to your knowledge that I think I know the happiness of fish. So if you are able even to reject my claim, it is established. To just the extent that it is questionable, it is defensible. Just as my refutation of your objection implicitly accepted its premise, your objection of my initial claim implicitly demonstrated it. So you know my feeling that I know the feeling of fish from your position over there, without having to be here in my mind; in the same way, I know the feeling of the fish from over here, talking to you above the river, not down there in it. As a further wrinkle, Zhuangzi is saying, "I know their enjoyment down there from our enjoyment up here"—a friendly metajoke suggesting that the debate itself is an enjoyment, and thus in a deeper sense there is no disagreement—which also resolves the apparent refutation (you are not really disagreeing, we are agreeing to enjoy arguing) while also preserving it (without the argument and refutation there would be no enjoyment). As in the case of Zhuangzi and the butterfly, which surely "count as two distinct identities" (2:49), and the Inner Chapters generally, Zhuangzi's notion of oneness depends on the multiplicity of distinct identities and viewpoints, not on collapsing them into literal unity. It is just that each perspective, precisely by dwelling in its own perspective, necessarily posits other perspectives as part of *its own* experience. Throughout this passage, *zhi* is translated "to know." See Glossary.

CHAPTER NINETEEN
Fathoming Life

Those who fathom the real character of the life in us do not labor themselves over the aspects of life that deliberate activity can do nothing about. Those who fathom the real character of fate do not labor themselves over what understanding[1] cannot alter. Although the nourishing of the body requires external things, some fail to nourish their bodies even with more than enough things. Although the continuance of life requires that the body is not dismembered, some bodies lose the life in them even when still intact. When life comes, it cannot be refused, and when it departs, it cannot be detained. How sad it is that the people of the world think that nourishing the body is enough to preserve the life in them! But in the final analysis, a nourished body is not sufficient for the preservation of this life—so what in the world could be really worth doing? Though nothing is really worth doing, it is impossible not to do something or other, so our activity itself is simply one more thing that cannot be avoided.

But to liberate your body from always having to be doing something, there is nothing more effective than letting go of the world. When you let go of the world, you are free of entanglements. Free of entanglements, you are balanced and untilting. Balanced and untilting, you are reborn along with each presence that confronts you. With such rebirth, you have done about all that can be done.

Why then is it worthwhile to let go of your concerns and forget all about life? Because when concerns are let go of, the body is no longer labored. When life is forgotten, the seminal quintessence of vitality remains undamaged. When the body is intact and the seminal quintessence of vitality restored, you are one with Heaven. Heaven and earth are the parents of all things. When they come together, a substantial body is formed. When that disperses, a new beginning takes shape. With both body and the seminal vitality intact, you can then convey yourself onward. Making the quintessence of vitality still more concentrated and quintessential, you return to the source, thereby assisting in the operations of Heaven.

Liezi said to Guanyin, the guard of the pass, "The Consummate Person can walk under water without suffocating, tread on fire without getting scorched, move over the face of all things without trembling. How does he reach such a state?"

Guanyin said, "By preserving his pure vital energy—not through understanding,[2] skill, resoluteness, or courage. Stay awhile—I will tell you about it!

---

[1] "Understanding" is *zhi* 知. See Glossary.

[2] "Understanding" is *zhi*. See Glossary.

Whatever has an appearance, an image, a sound, or a color is a *being*. How can any being be much different from any other being? How could any of them have what it takes to be the first? For they themselves are nothing more than colors and forms. Hence, there must be a beginning of beings in the formlessness and an end of beings in the unchanging. How could those who find this, and realize it fully, be brought to a halt by any mere being? They will rather find their place without overflowing the proper measure and yet hide themselves away in the proportions of the endless, roaming through that in which all beings end and begin. They unify their inborn nature, nourish their vital energy, and merge their virtuosities, thereby opening into the place from which all beings are created. Someone like this keeps the Heavenly in him intact and the spirit in him free of gaps, so there is nowhere through which mere beings can get at him.

"When a drunken man falls from a cart, he may be hurt but he will not be killed. His bones and joints are no different from those of other men, but the degree of harm done by the fall differs radically, for the spiritual in him forms one intact whole. Having been unaware that he was riding, he is now unaware that he is falling. The frights and shocks of life and death have no way to enter his breast, so he is unflinching no matter how things may clash with him. Finding wholeness in liquor he reaches such a state—imagine then someone who finds his wholeness in the Heavenly. The sage submerges himself in the Heavenly, and that is why nothing can harm him.

"A seeker of revenge does not go so far as to smash his enemy's weapon, and even the most ill-tempered person bears no grudge against a loose tile that happens to plunk down on his head. This reveals to us a way in which all the world can become peaceful and balanced. It is through this Course that freedom from the chaos of war and the cruelties of killing can be reached. Do not develop the Heavenly of man, but the Heavenly of Heaven. Developing the Heavenly empowers life; developing the Human plunders it. Insatiably partake of the Heavenly, but do not neglect the Human either—then even the ordinary people around you will soon come to live by what is genuine in them."

When Confucius was traveling through the forests of Chu, he came upon a hunchback who was catching cicadas with a glue-tipped stick as if plucking them up with his hand. Confucius said, "How skillful you are! Or do you have a course?"

The old man said, "I have a course. For five or six months, I practiced piling one pellet on top of another. When I could make a stack of two without it toppling over, already I would lose only very few cicadas. When I could make a stack of three, I could catch nine out of ten. By the time I was able to balance a stack of five, I could catch the cicadas as if plucking them up with my hand. I settle my body like a twisted old stump, holding my arm still like the branch of a withered tree. Although heaven and earth are vast and the ten thousand things numerous, I am aware of nothing but cicada wings. Motionless, neither turning nor leaning, I would not trade away a single cicada wing for all of creation. How could I fail to catch them, no matter what I do?"

Confucius turned to his disciples and said, "Using his will undividedly, the spiritual in him converges and solidifies—such would perhaps be a description of this hunchbacked gentleman here!"

Yan Hui said to Confucius, "When I was crossing the gulf of Shangshen, I came across a ferryman who sailed his boat with the grace of a spirit. I asked him if such helmsmanship could be learned. He said, 'Yes. It is a good swimmer who can usually do it. If he can swim underwater, he can operate a boat even if he has never seen one before.' I asked him to explain this, but he refused. What did he mean?"

Confucius said, "A good swimmer can usually do it because he has forgotten the existence of the water. One who can swim underwater can operate a boat even if he's never seen one before because to him a deep pool is no different from a gentle hill, and a capsizing boat just like an overturning cart. Even if his vessel is tossed and flipped in all directions, it doesn't get to him, so he is relaxed and leisurely wherever he sails. When a man shoots an arrow to win a tile he is skillful. But if he is trying to win a silver buckle he starts getting nervous. And if he's competing for gold he almost loses his mind. His native skill is the same in each case, but because he has something to lose, he overvalues the external. Whenever the external is prized, the internal gets clumsy."

Tian Kaizhi was having an audience with Duke Wei of Zhou. The duke said, "I have heard that Zhu Shen is quite learned on the subject of the life in us. You, my dear sir, have spent some time with Zhu Shen—what did you hear from him about this topic?"

Tian Kaizhi said, "All I did there was tend to the outer courtyard, broom in hand; what could I have heard from the master?"

The duke said, "No need to be so modest! I want to hear what you have to say."

Tian Kaizhi said, "What I heard from the master was this: 'One who is skillful in nurturing the life within us goes about it just as if he were herding sheep. He just whips forward the ones he sees lagging behind."

Duke Wei asked, "What does this mean?"

Tian Kaizhi said, "In the state of Lu there was a man named Shan Bao who lived among the rocky cliffs and drank only water, completely isolating himself from the struggles for profit of the ordinary folk. He went on like this for seventy years and still had the physical glow of a young child. But then one day he had the bad luck of encountering a hungry tiger, which promptly killed and ate him. On the other hand, there was a man named Zhang Yi who rushed off to pay a visit to every rich family and fancy mansion he could find. He went on like this for forty years, and then he developed a fever from within that killed him off. Bao nurtured the internal and a tiger ate his external form; Yi nurtured the external and an illness attacked him from within. Both of these men failed to whip forward the one that was lagging behind."

Confucius said, "Do not go inside and hide yourself. Do not go out and make a show of yourself. Plant yourself firmly in the middle. One who can do all three of these will surely attain the greatest renown. When planning a journey on a dangerous road, hearing that even one in ten men are killed, fathers will take the utmost precautions with their sons, and brothers with their brothers, not daring to depart unless they have a large armed escort. Is this not wise? But these same men do not understand that they should take similar precautions against the dangers that come to a man when lying in his bed or when eating and drinking. This is their mistake."

The Invocator of the Ancestors, dressed in his solemn black robes, stood over the pigpen and counseled the pigs, saying, "Why should you object to dying? If I offered to feed you grain for three months, to keep vigil for ten days and fast for another three, then lay out the mats of white rushes and place your shoulders and rump the carved stand, surely you'd be willing to go along with it?" Someone who was planning things from the point of view of the pigs would say, "It would be better to eat bran and chaff and be left right there in the pen." Planning things from his own point of view, he is willing to go along with having the honors of cap and carriage while still alive and a fancy hearse to bear him to his stately funeral when he dies. Planning from the point of view of the pigs, he rejects these things. Planning from his own point of view, he chooses them. Why does he think [he's] so different from the pigs?

Once, when Duke Huan was hunting in the marshes, with Guan Zhong as his driver, he saw a ghost. The duke took hold of Guan Zhong's hand and said, "What did you see, Father Zhong?"

"I didn't see anything, my lord," answered the other.

After returning home, the duke began mumbling to himself until he took ill, remaining at home for several days. Huangzi Gao'ao, an official of Qi, said to the duke, "You are injuring yourself, my lord. How could a ghost be able to harm you? When accumulated energy[3] is dispersed outward in anger without being recovered, it becomes insufficient for your needs within. When it ascends without descending, it makes you ill-tempered. When it descends without ascending, it makes you forgetful. And if it neither ascends nor descends, but remains in the place of the heart at the center of the body, it makes you ill."

Duke Huan said, "But are there really such things as ghosts?"

He answered, "Indeed, there are. In the hearth there are the Lu, and in the stove, the Qi. Within the refuse heap inside the gate lives the Leiting. In the northeast the Pei'a and Guilong frolic, while the Yiyang dwells in the northwest. Then there are the Gangxiang of the water, the Xin of the hills, the Gui of the mountains, the Panghuang of the meadows, and the Weituo of the marshes."

---

3   "Energy" is *qi*. See Glossary.

The duke asked, "What does the Weituo look like?"

Huangzi answered, "The Weituo is as big as the hub of a carriage wheel and as long as its shaft, robed in purple and capped in red. This creature dislikes the rumblings of chariot wheels, and when it hears them it stands up with its hands on its head. Anyone who sees this creature generally goes on to become a hegemon of all the states."

Duke Huan burst out laughing and said, "That is what I saw!" Thereupon he put on his official clothes and took his seat at court, and before the end of the day, without his even realizing it, his illness was gone.

Ji Shengzi was training a fighting cock for the king. After ten days he was asked if the bird was ready. "Not yet," he said. "He's just become vain and confident in his own strength." Asked again ten days later, he said, "Not yet. He still responds to shadows and echoes." Asked again in another ten days he said, "Not yet. He still glares aggressively, his angry strength at full blast." Asked again ten days later, he finally said, "He is almost there. Now, even when another rooster crows, he does not flinch. He appears to all the world like a rooster made of wood, for his Virtuosity is whole and intact. The other roosters dare not face him: they just turn and run!"

Confucius was viewing the Lu waterfall, which plummets several hundred feet, whitening the waters for forty miles around, impassable to fishes and turtles. And yet he saw an old man swimming there in the torrent. Thinking the man had attempted suicide due to some suffering in his life, Confucius sent his disciples to run along the bank and try to pull him out. But the old man emerged several hundred paces downstream, walking along the bank singing, his hair streaming down his back. Confucius hurried after him and said, "I thought you were a ghost, but now I see you are a man! Do you have a course that allows you to tread upon the waters?"

"No, I have no course," said the old man. "I got my start in the given, developed via my own inborn nature, and reached completion through fate. I enter into the navels of the whirlpools and emerge with the surging eddies. I just follow the course of the water itself, without making any private one of my own. This is how I tread the waters."

Confucius said, "What do you mean by getting your start in the given, developing via your own inborn nature, and reaching completion through fate?"

"I was born on the land and thus I feel securely at home on the land. That's the given. I grew up with the water and thus I feel securely at home in the water. That's my own nature. And I am thus and so but without knowing how or why I am thus and so. That's fate."

Qing the Woodworker was carving a bell stand. When it was done, all who saw it were astonished, as if they had seen the doings of a ghost or spirit. When the Marquis of Lu saw it, he asked, "What technique do you have for this?"

Qing replied, "I am just an artisan—what technique could I have? However, there is one thing. When I am going to make a bell stand, I dare not let it deplete my vital energy. Rather, I fast to quiet my mind, and after three days, I no longer presume to care about praise or reward, rank or salary. After five days, I no longer presume to care about honor and disgrace, skill and clumsiness. After seven days, I become so still that I forget I have four limbs or a body. When this happens, for me it is as if the royal court has ceased to exist. My skill is concentrated and the outside world slides away. Then I enter into the mountain forests, viewing the inborn Heavenly nature of the trees. My body arrives at a certain spot, and already I see the completed bell stand there; only then do I apply my hand to it. Otherwise I leave the tree alone. So I am just matching the Heavenly to the Heavenly. This may be the reason the result suggests the work of spirits!"

Dongye Ji was introduced to Duke Zhuang to exhibit his driving skills. He advanced and retreated with the straightness of a taut cord and swerved left and right in arcs that could have been drawn with a compass. Duke Zhuang, taking the patterns of his motions to be unsurpassable, told him to make a hundred circuits along the same lines. Yan He encountered the carriages on the road and then entered the palace to see the duke, saying, "Ji's horses are going to collapse." The duke remained silent. After awhile, the horses did indeed collapse. The duke asked, "How did you know?" Yan He said, "His horses had come to the end of their strength but he kept making demands on them. That is why I said they would collapse."

Chui the Artisan's swooping freehand arcs could match the lines made with compasses and T-squares, for his fingers transformed along with the thing he was making, his mind never lingering to check or verify. Hence, his Numinous Platform[4] was unified and unshackled to any one place. The forgetting of the foot means the shoe fits comfortably. The forgetting of the waist means the belt fits comfortably. And when the understanding forgets right and wrong, the mind fits comfortably. When the encounter with each thing fits comfortably, the internal is not altered and the external is not made master. When everything fits, from beginning to end, even this fitting is forgotten, and that is the perfect fit.

There was a certain man named Sun Xiu who followed Master Bian Qingzi all the way to his gate and declared to him, "When I lived in the villages, never did anyone say I was an uncultivated man. When facing a challenge, never has anyone said I was a coward. And yet, when I cultivated the fields, I never got a good crop, and when I served a lord, the time was never right for advancement. So I have ended up being outcast from the villages and exiled from the towns. What crime have I committed against Heaven? Why have I met with this fate?"

---

4   Cf. Chapter 23, note 11, and the "Numinous Reservoir," 5:16, note 13.

Master Bian said, "Can it be that you've never heard how the Consummate Person conducts himself? He forgets his liver and gallbladder and drops his eyes and ears, drifting oblivious and 'uncommitted beyond the dust and grime, far-flung and unfettered in the great work of doing nothing in particular.'[5] This is called 'taking action but[6] not relying on it for any credit, helping things grow but not controlling them.' You, on the other hand, ornament your wisdom to astonish the stupid, cultivating your person to display yourself against the disreputable—so shiny and flashy, as if walking along wielding the sun and moon in your hands. You've managed to keep your body with all its nine openings intact, rather than being cut down midway by blindness, deafness, lameness, or deformity. You're luckier than most! What leisure do you have to resent how Heaven has treated you? Away with you!"

Sun Xiu departed, and Master Bian took his seat. After a while, he looked up to Heaven and sighed. A disciple asked, "Why do you sigh, master?"

Master Bian said, "Just now I instructed Sun Xiu by telling him of the Virtuosity of the Consummate Person. I am afraid he will be quite bewildered by it, leading him into great confusion."

His disciple said, "Not at all. Let's say Sun Xiu was in the right, and you, my master, were in the wrong. Well, the wrong certainly has no power to bewilder the right. But let's say Sun Xiu was in the wrong, and my master in the right. In that case, he was already confused when he came to you. In either case, what harm has been done?"

Master Bian said, "That's not how it is. Once a bird came to roost in the outskirts of Lu. The ruler of Lu was delighted by it, presenting to it a feast replete with all the finest meats and having the Ninefold Shao music performed for it. The bird soon started to appear worried and sad, looking around in a daze, not venturing to eat or drink. This is called trying to nourish a bird with what would nourish oneself. To nourish a bird as the bird itself would want to be nourished, you should let it perch in the deep forests and glide through the rivers and lakes, allowing it to eat whatever wiggly things it can find—for this creature such a life is as comfortable as walking along on level ground. Now Sun Xiu, an ignorant person of little learning, comes to me and I describe to him the Virtuosity of the Consummate Person. That is like taking a mouse for a ride in a carriage or trying to delight a quail with the music of drums and bells. How could he fail to be bewildered?"

---

5   Quoting 6:47–48.

6   *Daodejing* 10 and 51.

CHAPTER TWENTY
The Mountain Tree (Selection)

Zhuangzi was traveling in the mountains when he came upon a huge tree, lux-uriantly overgrown with branches and leaves. A woodcutter stopped beside it but in the end chose not to fell it. Asked the reason, he said, "There is nothing it can be used for." Zhuangzi said, "This tree is able to live out its natural life span because of its worthlessness."

When he left the mountains, he lodged for a night at the home of an old friend. His friend was delighted and ordered a servant to kill a goose for din-ner. The servant said, "There is one that can honk and one that cannot. Which should I kill?" The host said, "Kill the one that cannot honk."

The next day, Zhuangzi's disciple said to him, "The tree we saw yesterday could live out its natural life span because of its worthlessness, while our host's goose was killed for its worthlessness. What position would you take, Master?"

Zhuangzi said, "I would probably take a position somewhere between wor-thiness and worthlessness. But though that might look right, it turns out not to be—it still leads to entanglements. It would be another thing entirely to float and drift along, mounted on only the Course and its Virtuosity—untouched by both praise and blame, now a dragon, now a snake, changing with the times, unwilling to keep to any exclusive course of action. Now above, now below, with momentary harmony as your only measure—that is to float and drift within the ancestor of all things, which makes all things the things they are, but which no thing can make anything of. What could then entangle you? For the likes of Shennong and the Yellow Emperor, this was the only rule.

"But the inclinations of the ten thousand things and the traditional codes for human relationships put them in quite a different condition. Joined, they separate. Completed, they are destroyed. The scrupulous are beat down; the noble are criticized—whatever is accomplished is brought low. The talented among them scheme while the untalented just lie. What certainty could you get ahold of amid all this? It is all very sad, but note it well, my disciples! There is nothing for it but our homeland in the Course and its Virtuosity!"

[. . . .]

CHAPTER TWENTY-TWO
Knowinghood Journeyed North

Knowinghood[1] journeyed north beyond Darkwater, ascending the Hills of Hidden Jutting, where he met Nodoing Nosaying. Knowinghood said, "I want to ask you something. What should I think of and consider in order to know the Course? What should I adopt and serve in order to rest securely in the Course? What should I follow, what course should I take as my guide, in order to attain the Course?" He asked three questions, but Nodoing Nosaying did not answer. It wasn't that he was unwilling to answer. He did not know *how* to answer.

Having received no response, Knowinghood traveled back to the south of Clearwater, ascending the Hills of Doubt Silenced, where he met Wild-and-Twisty. He asked him the same questions. Wild-and-Twisty said, "Ah! This I know! Let me tell you!" But just as he was about to speak, he forgot what he was going to say.

Still having obtained no answer, Knowinghood returned to the Imperial Palace, where he asked the same questions of the Yellow Emperor.

"Only when you think of nothing and consider nothing," said the Yellow Emperor, "will you know the Course. Only when you adopt nothing and serve nothing will you rest securely in the Course. Only when you follow nothing and take no course as your guide will you attain the Course."

"Now you and I know this," said Knowinghood, "while the other two do not. Who is right?"

"Only Nodoing Nosaying is truly right," said the Yellow Emperor. "Wild-and-Twisty only seems to be right. As for you and me, we are nowhere near it. For 'he who knows does not speak, and he who speaks does not know. Hence, the sage practices the teaching of no words.'[2] The Course cannot be given, and Virtuosity cannot be received. But Humanity can be deliberately forged. Responsibility can do harm. And Ritual Propriety is just a mutual swindling. Hence, it is said, 'When the Course is lost, there is Virtuosity; when Virtuosity is lost, there is Humanity; when Humanity is lost, there is Ritual Propriety. Ritual Propriety is the fruitless flower of the Course and the beginning of disorder.'[3] And also, 'To practice the Course requires daily diminishment. Diminish again and yet again, until you reach nondoing, doing nothing and yet

---

[1] "Knowinghood" is *zhi* 知, here personified as the questing hero of a kind of adventure story and thus translated in this preposterous way, to echo the facetious tone of the original. See Glossary.

[2] Quoting *Daodejing* 56 and 2.

[3] *Daodejing* 38.

leaving nothing undone.'[4] Now you and I have already become *beings*—is it not difficult to return to the root? It is easy only for the Great Man. For life is the follower of death, and death is the beginning of life; who can discern any fixed order to them? The birth of man is just a convergence of energy. When it converges, he lives. When it scatters, he dies. Since life and death follow each other, what is there to worry about? It is in this way that all things are one. People take what they consider beautiful to be sacred and wonderful and take what they dislike to be odious and rotten. But the odious and rotten transforms into the sacred and wonderful, and the sacred and wonderful transforms into the odious and rotten. Thus do I say, 'Just open yourself into the single energy that is the world.' It is for the sake of this that the sage values oneness."

Knowinghood said, "I asked Nodoing Nosaying, and he gave me no response. Not that he wasn't willing to answer; he didn't even know how. I asked Wild-and-Twisty, and he didn't tell me either, although he was just about to. It wasn't that he decided not to answer; he forgot what he was going to say. Now I have asked you, and you know the answer. Why do you say you are far from it?"

The Yellow Emperor said, "The one is truly right, because he did not know. The other is a semblance of it, because he forgot. But you and I are nowhere near it, because we know it."

When Wild-and-Twisty heard about this conversation, he concluded that the Yellow Emperor was a man who truly knew the meaning of words.

Heaven and earth possess vast beauties, but they do not speak of them. The four seasons have their unconcealed regularities, but they do not discuss them. Each of the ten thousand things makes its own perfect sense[5] but does not explain it. The sage traces back from the beauties of heaven and earth and thereby reaches through to the sense made by each of the ten thousand things. Thus it is that "the Consummate Person does nothing; the Great Sage initiates nothing": that is to say, they merely cast their gaze over Heaven and earth. For the illumination of their spirits is refined to an utmost subtlety, allowing them to transform along with other things every which way. Things die, are born, go round, go square, and no one knows the root of it. But it is spread out everywhere, and through it the ten thousand things have maintained themselves since ancient times. Even something as vast as the six directions never gets beyond it; even something as small as a hair in autumn depends on it to take form as a physical body. Each thing in the world to the end of its days is forever rising and falling, never remaining as it was; the yin and the yang and the four seasons go through their cycles, each one finding its place in the sequence. Obscure, it is present, but only by being as if absent. Ever gliding away, it shows no fixed form and thereby manifests its mysterious power. All things are nour-

---

4   *Daodejing* 48.
5   'Perfect sense" is *li* 理. See Glossary.

ished by it but without ever knowing it. This is what is called the root and foundation, and it is with this that our gaze may reach the Heavenly.

Nie Que asked Piyi about the Course.[6]

Piyi said, "Straighten your body and unify your vision, and the Heavenly harmony will arrive. Gather in your understanding[7], unify your thoughts, and the spirit will come to reside in you. Virtuosity will then beautify you; and the Course will dwell in you. Just be oblivious to it all, like a newborn calf who seeks no reasons."

But before he had even finished speaking, Nie Que had fallen asleep. Piyi was delighted and strolled away singing: "Body like withered bones, mind like dead ashes, his real understanding is genuine, not maintaining itself by means of precedents and purposes. Dim and obscure, free of intentions, unconsultable—what sort of man is he?"

Shun asked Cheng, "Can the Course be attained and possessed?"

Cheng said, "Even your body is not your own possession; how could you attain the Course?"

Shun said, "If my body is not my own possession, whose is it?"

Cheng said, "It is just a form lent by heaven and earth. Life is not your own possession; it is just a harmony lent by heaven and earth. Your inborn nature and allotment of vitality are not your own possessions; they are just a compliance lent by heaven and earth. Your sons and grandsons are not your own possessions; they are just sheddings lent by heaven and earth. So in all our travels we can never really know where we are going, in all our dwellings we can never really know what is maintaining us, in all our eating we can never really know what we are tasting. This is all the doing of the bright and vigorous energy of heaven and earth—how could it be obtained and possessed?"

Confucius said to Lao Dan, "You have some leisure today. I venture to ask about the perfect Course."

Lao Dan said, "You must fast, rinse out your mind, cleanse your seminal spirit until it gleams like snow, and smash your understanding[8] to bits! Indeed, the Course is profound, difficult to describe! Nonetheless, I will tell you a few outlying generalities about it. The bright is born from the dark, and the determinable is born from the formless. The seminal kernel of vitality and the spirit are born from the Course. It is from this seminal kernel that the physical body is originally born. All things generate and give form to one another. Those with

---

[6]   Cf. p. 17 and p. 50. Piyi ("Clothed") is usually identified with his teacher Puyizi from the latter passage.

[7]   "Understanding" is *zhi*. See Glossary.

[8]   "Understanding" is *zhi*. See Glossary.

nine holes in them are born from a womb; those with eight are born from an egg. Before they come there is no trace of them, and after they depart they are bound by no limits, traversing no gate and dwelling in no chamber, positioned only in the full-flung vastness of the four directions. He who accords with this is strong in body, unobstructed in thinking, keen of hearing and seeing; he makes no efforts in the use of his mind, responding to things with no fixed method. Heaven cannot help but be high, earth cannot help but be broad, the sun and moon cannot but proceed on their ways, all things cannot but arise and flourish—is this not their Course?

"Learning does not necessarily make one knowledgeable,[9] and skill in debate does not necessarily make one wise. This is why the sage eliminates them. But what the sage holds onto is what is not increased when one tries to increase it and not diminished when one tries to diminish it. So deep and unfathomable—like the ocean! So lofty and towering—it ends and then begins again! It turns forth and measures out the ten thousand things without ever running dry. So can your "Course of the exemplary man" be outside of it? The ten thousand things depend on it to go their own ways without ever exhausting it—is it not their Course?

"This Middle Kingdom is populated with *human beings*, but such creatures are ultimately neither yin nor yang. For they dwell between heaven and earth only temporarily assuming the form of a human being, always just on the verge of returning to their source. From the point of view of its root, life is just a temporarily congealed thing. Although some are long lived and some die young, how much of a difference is there really? It's all a matter of no more than a single instant—what room is there for the rightness of Yao and the wrongness of Jie? Every fruition has its own coherence.[10] Although humans encounter difficulties in their interactions with one another, this is precisely how they are able to interlock. The sage meets them without rebelling, lets them pass without holding on to them. To respond to them by harmonizing with them is the work of Virtuosity, but to respond to them as a matter of pure happenstance is the work of the Course itself. This is what enables emperors to flourish and kings to arise.

"Man's life between heaven and earth is like a white stallion galloping past a crack in a wall: just a sudden whoosh and then it is all over. Pouring and surging forth this way and that, everything emerges; slipping and sinking away, everything is submerged again. One transformation and you are alive, another and you're dead. Living creatures lament it, and human beings bemoan it. But this is just the unfastening of the Heavenly bow sheath and the dropping away of the Heavenly scabbard, the twisting and turning in the chaos until your vital spirits are ready to scatter away and then your body—hence, the Great Return!

---

9   "Knowledgeable" is *zhi*. See Glossary.

10   "Coherence" is *li*. See Glossary.

"The formless takes on a form; the formed veers back to the formless: this is something everyone knows and need not be managed in any way when it is about to happen. It is something everyone has a theory about, but when it arrives there is no more theorizing, and when there is theorizing that means it has not yet arrived. When it is seen clearly, that just means it has not really been encountered, so debate about it is no match for silence. The Course cannot be learned, so hearing about it is no match for plugging up your ears. This is called the Great Attainment."

Dongguozi asked Zhuangzi, "Where is this Course you speak of?"
Zhuangzi said, "There is nowhere it is not."
"You must be more specific."
"It is in the ants and crickets."
"So low?"
"It is in the grasses and weeds."
"Even lower?"
"It is in the tiles and shards."
"So extreme?"
"It is in the piss and shit."
Dongguozi made no reply. Zhuangzi continued, "Truly, your question misses the substance of the matter. When a shopper asks a meat inspector to test how fat a hog is, the lower on the animal he checks, the more revealing the results. Just free yourself of foregone conclusions and don't run away from any particular thing. That's what the perfect Course does, and the same is true of great words. 'The Ubiquitous,' 'The All-Pervasive,' 'The Omnipresent'—these are three terms with the same meaning. They all point to the same thing. Let us try to wander together in the palace of not-even-anything, merging it together into one single assertion that is nowhere brought to a halt! Let's try doing nothing together, shall we? Flavorless and unmoving! Blurred yet unmuddied! Blended yet in-between! Having emptied my will, I have no destination, no idea where I am. Coming and going, I know not where I come to rest. I come and I go in it, never knowing where it all ends. Soaring through the vastness, the Great Understanding[11] enters into me, never understanding where it is brought to a halt.

"That which makes beings beings is not separated from beings by any border. So the borders that the beings themselves take on—these are merely borders from the side of the beings. The borders that do no bordering, the borderlessness that nonetheless borders—this is what fills and empties beings, what decays and kills them. That which fills and empties them is not filled or emptied, that which decays and empties them is not decayed or emptied, that which roots and branches them is neither rooted nor branched, that which congeals and scatters them is neither congealed nor scattered."

---

[11] "Understanding" is *zhi*. See Glossary.

Ke Hegan and Shennong were both students under Old Dragon Ji. Shennong had shut the door for an afternoon nap on his desk when Ke Hegan came bursting in and said, "The Old Dragon is dead!" Shennong pulled himself up from the desk with his staff, and then clanging the staff down to the ground he laughed and said, "The Heavenly One knew I was a vulgar, lazy fool, so he died and abandoned me. It is all over! The master died without even leaving some crazy words to set me off with!"

Yin Gang, having come to pay his respects, heard this and said, "All the exemplary men of the world seek to bind themselves closely to a man who has embodied the Course. Now, what this one had attained of the Course was not even one ten-thousandth of an autumn hair, but even he knew enough to take his crazy words to the grave with him. How much more so one who has truly embodied the Course! Looking for it one finds no form, and listening one hears no sound. When people try to describe it, they can only say it is a darkness, an obscurity. This is merely how the Course is described; it is not the Course itself."

This is why, when Great Clarity asked Endless, "Do you know the Course?" Endless said, "I do not know."

But when he asked the same question to Nondoing, he was told, "I know the Course."

"Is your knowledge of the Course specifiable?"

"It is."

"May I ask its specifications?"

"I know that the Course can be lofty or it can be base, it can be a constraint or it can be a scattering. These are the specifications by which I know the Course."

Great Clarity reported this to Beginningless, saying, "So between Endless's not knowing and Nondoing's knowing, which is right and which is wrong?"

Beginningless said, "Not knowing is profound; knowing is shallow. Not knowing is internal; knowing is external."

At this, Great Clarity was provoked to let out a sigh. "Not knowing is knowing! Knowing is not knowing! Who knows the knowing of nonknowing?"[12]

Beginningless said, "The Course cannot be heard; whatever is heard is not it. The Course cannot be seen; whatever is seen is not it. The Course cannot be spoken; whatever is spoken is not it. Know that what forms forms has no form. The Course corresponds to no name."

He continued, "If someone answers when asked about the Course, he does not know the Course. Though one may ask about the Course, this does not mean one has heard of the Course. The Course is unsusceptible to questions, and any questions about it have no answers. To ask after it by asking no questions is to be through with all questions. To answer by giving no answers is to be free from all [opinions] harbored within. And to confront the ending of all questions with

---

[12] "Know" throughout this passage is *zhi* 知. See Glossary.

nothing harbored within—such a one externally sees no time and space and internally is without knowledge of any primordial beginning, and thus has no need to 'pass beyond the Kundun Mountains' or to 'wander in the great void.'"

Radiance asked Nothingness, "Do you exist or do you not exist?" He got no answer and could see no countenance there, just a darkness, an emptiness. Ceaselessly gazing after him, listening for him, groping for him, he could find nothing to see, nothing to hear, nothing to take hold of. Radiance said, "Perfection! Who can reach such a state? I can reach the state of there being nothingness, but not of there being no nothingness! Reaching it, nothingness becomes being. How can such a state be arrived at?"

The Grand Marshal had in his employ an old man of eighty who was still forging harness buckles without the slightest error. The Grand Marshal asked him, "Are you just skillful, or do you have the Course?"

He said, "I have that which I hold to. Since the age of twenty I took a delight only in making harness buckles. From then on I neglected all other things, noticing nothing besides harness buckles."

Thus, what one can make real use of depends on what one has no use for; usefulness grows from having no use for certain things. How much more is this the case for that which makes use of all things! What being fails to find support in it?

Ran Qiu asked Confucius, "Can the state before there was heaven and earth be known?"

Confucius said, "Yes. The past is like the present."

Ran Qiu had no more questions and withdrew, but he returned the next day and said, "Yesterday I asked you if the state before there was heaven and earth could be known, and you said it could, that the past was like the present. At the time this was crystal clear, but now it makes no sense to me anymore. May I ask what this means?"

Confucius said, "Your clarity yesterday came from your spirit's initial reception. Your present confusion is because you are now seeking it with something other than your spirit, is it not? No past, no present, no beginning, no end: before you have descendents you have descendents. Do you get it?"

Ran Qiu could not answer. Confucius continued, "It is enough that you cannot answer! It is not life that produces death, and it is not death that brings an end to life. For do life and death depend on something else? Both are parts of the same body, which confers on them their unity. If there is something before heaven and earth, could it be any specifiable being? What makes beings beings is no being, for as soon as a being has appeared, it is no longer *before* all beings. It may seem as if there is something there, but the something this is can only be nothingness. The sage's selfless love for all people is rooted in this."

Yan Yuan asked Confucius, "I have heard you say, 'Dismissing none, welcoming none.' May I ask how to roam in such a way?"

Confucius said, "The men of olden times changed externally but not internally. Nowadays, people change internally but not externally. That which transforms along with things is the sole Unchanging. Securely at peace in things whether they change or not, securely at peace even in dispersing along with them, it finds its necessity in never exceeding them in the slightest. That clansman of Xiwei roamed in his park, the Yellow Emperor in his garden, that Mr. Youyu in his palace, and Emperors Tang and Wu merely in their own chambers.[13] These were initially exemplary men, but then they took Confucians and Mohists for their teachers and thus wore themselves down with right and wrong. And how much more is this so for the men of the present age! The sage dwells among things without harming them. Because he doesn't harm them, they cannot harm him either. Because there is no harm either way, he can both welcome and dismiss others.

"The mountain forests, the great open plains! Shall they make me joyful, shall they fill me with happiness? But even before my joy is done, sorrow has come to take its place. When joy and sorrow come I cannot stop them from coming, and when they go I cannot keep them from going. How sad it is! In being merely some specific being, every person in the world is nothing but a temporary lodging house! Indeed, they understand what they encounter but not what is never encountered. They understand what to do about that which something can be done about, but they don't understand what to do about that which nothing can be done about. It is impossible to escape from having something you do not understand and something that nothing can be done about! Is it not tragic to try to escape from what cannot be escaped? Perfect words eliminate all words. Perfect action eliminates all action. But merely to put what your understanding understands into some kind of order—that is just shallowness."

---

[13] All of these figures are legendary sage-emperors.

Selections from the

MISCELLANEOUS CHAPTERS

CHAPTER TWENTY-THREE
Gengsang Chu

Lao Dan[1] had a follower named Gengsang Chu. After having grasped more than most of Lao Dan's Course, he traveled north and settled in the Zigzag Mountains. He dismissed the brazenly knowing[2] among his assistants and distanced himself from the solicitously humane[3] among his concubines, living among the lumpen masses and employing only the most callous stablehands as his servants. After three years, Zigzag enjoyed an especially abundant harvest, and the people of Zigzag started saying things like, "When Gengsang Chu first came here, I thought him alarmingly odd. But now I think that, though his daily yield falls short, his yearly yield is above and beyond. Perhaps he is a sage! Why don't we hold festivals for him as our impersonator of the dead, or build him a shrine in which to make offerings to him?"

When Gengsang Chu heard about this, he turned toward the south, inconsolable. His disciples were puzzled. "What do you find so strange?" he asked. "When the energy of spring bursts forth, all the plants come to life. When the treasures of the earth get full access to the autumn, they all mature for harvest. And do you think spring and autumn can do this without availing themselves of something? It is the Course of Heaven that is already moving in them! I have heard that when the Consummate Person dwells corpselike in his little circular cell, the common people are set into a crazed abandon, knowing nothing of what they are or where they're going. But now these little folk of Zigzag are whispering among themselves about setting me up like a ritual vessel in the ranks of the worthy. Am I then a target-man, an ideal? This is how I know that I have failed to fully release myself into the words of Lao Dan."

A disciple said, "Not at all. A narrow ditch is too small for a large fish to turn around in, but for the eels and minnows it's a windfall.[4] A small hill provides no place for a large beast to hide, but for the little foxes it's a stroke of enormous good fortune. Since the times of Yao and Shun, all the world has been honoring the worthy and elevating the capable, putting whatever is good and advantageous first. It's no surprise then that the common folk of Zigzag are also this way. You should do as they ask, Master!"

---

1. Laozi, legendary author of the *Daodejing*.
2. "Knowing" is *zhi* 知. See Glossary.
3. "Humane" is *ren* 仁. See Glossary.
4. Reading *li* 利 for *zhi* 制.

"Come here, my little ones!" said Gengsang Chu. "A creature large enough to swallow a chariot, should it go forth from its mountains unescorted, can still fall prey to net or snare. A fish big enough to gulp down a ship, if it is thrown onto the shore, will be menaced even by the ants. This is why the birds and beasts never tire of the heights nor the fish and turtles of the depths. A man who wants to keep the life in his body intact must know how to hide himself, however far away he must go.

"And by the way, what is really worth praising about those two [Yao and Shun]? All their debates and distinctions are like a man drilling a hole in someone's wall and setting up a straw plug in its place. It's like selecting out which hairs to comb, or counting the grains of rice before you cook them—what benefit does all this meticulous scheming really bring to the world? Elevating the worthy only makes the people compete with one another. Putting the understanding in charge just makes the people loot one another. Such things can do nothing to improve people's lives. Once they become diligent about their own advantage, the sons will end up killing their fathers and the ministers their rulers, burrowing through walls to rob each other in broad daylight. Mark my words, the root of real chaos lies in people like Yao and Shun, and its branches reach down for a thousand generations. A thousand generations of this and I guarantee it will end up with human beings eating one another for dinner!"

Nanrong Chu straightened up on his mat with a jolt, saying, "What then can someone like me, advanced in age, do to live up to what you are saying?"

Gengsang Chu said, "Keep your body whole, hold fast to the life in you, don't let your thoughts get lost in busy calculations, and in three years you will have lived up to it."

Nanrong Chu said, "All bodies are equipped with similar eyes and ears, and yet the blind and deaf cannot use theirs to see and hear. All bodies are equipped with similar minds, and yet the mad cannot use theirs to get control of themselves. All human bodies are basically analogous—is it external things that make them operate so differently, so that some of us, no matter how we may wish to try, just can't do what we set out to do? Now you say to me, 'Keep your body whole, hold fast to the life in you, don't let your thoughts get lost in busy calculations.' I try to learn the Course, but it only reaches as far as my ears."

Gengsang Chu said, "There is no more I can say. A flitting bee cannot bring to term a moth larva on the leaves; the tiny chickens of Yue cannot hatch a swan egg. But the big hens of Lu can do it. The basic character of the fowl is present in both, but because of the different stature of their abilities, one is up to the task and the other is not. My abilities are meager, insufficient to transform you. Why don't you go south to see Laozi?"

Nanrong Chu shouldered his provisions, and after seven days and nights arrived at Laozi's place. Laozi said, "Did you come here from Gengsang Chu's place?"

Nanrong Chu said, "Yes."

"Why did you bring so many people with you?" Laozi asked. Nanrong Chu, greatly alarmed, turned to look behind him.

"Don't you understand what I mean?"

Nanrong Chu looked down in shame. Then he raised his head with a sigh. "Now I have forgotten my answer, and with it the question I came here to ask."

"Tell me what you mean," Laozi said.

Nanrong Chu spoke. "If I know nothing, people call me slow and stupid. But if I get involved in knowledge,[5] I bring anxiety to myself. If I'm not humane, I harm others, but if I am, I bring trouble to myself. If I am irresponsible, I hurt others, but if I'm responsible, I burden myself.[6] How can I escape this dilemma? These three points sum up my problem, about which I have come here, on Gengsang Chu's recommendation, to seek your counsel."

Laozi said, "A moment ago, with one look into the blink of your eyes, I got the whole picture about you. Now your words have confirmed my suspicions. You're all regulated and confined by your own schemes, like someone who has lost his parents and then brandishes a pole to seek them in the depths of the sea. You are yourself the goner! You want to return to your real condition and inborn nature but can find no way in. A pitiful sight!"

Nanrong Chu asked to be allowed to lodge there, trying to summon up what he liked about himself and get rid of what he disliked. After torturing himself like this for ten days, he went again to see Laozi, who said, "So you've been trying to purify yourself—well, it seems well-cooked now, that pent-up sorrow you're preparing! And there's still plenty of the hateful stuff frothing over in there, eh? But if there are external things that entangle you, it's useless to come to grips with them by tying up your hands in them. That just connects them with [what's entangling you] within. And if something inside you is entangling you, it's useless to get a grip on it by further tying yourself up in it. That just connects it with [what's entangling you] from outside.[7] If you are entangled

---

[5] "Knowledge" is *zhi*. See Glossary.

[6] On Humanity and Responsibility (*ren yi* 仁義), see Glossary.

[7] This is an extremely obscure sentence. Here, I follow Yu Yue's substitution of *jiao* 繳 for *fan* 繁, and follow Guo Xiang's general construal of the sense, but taking *qian* 揵 in its meaning of "to connect" rather than "to block off." "What entangles from outside" is usually interpreted to mean sensory objects of pleasure, as well as profit, fame, and power, while "what entangles from within" is taken to mean obsessive thoughts, biased desires, erroneous concepts, and illusory beliefs. Without the substitution, the meaning would be something like the following: "But it's no good trying to control external entanglements by making yourself more complicated—that just bolsters more of the same on the inside. It's no good trying to control internal entanglements by tying yourself up in them—that just bolsters more of the same from the outside." But the same passage could also be interpreted in the opposite sense, taking the alternate meaning of "seal off" for the character meaning "to shoulder up" (*qian* 揵), rendering something like the following: "When external things entangle you, instead of trying to get control of them one by one in all their complex diversity, just close your-

either internally or externally, you will not even be able to maintain hold of the Course and its Virtuosity, much less release your hold on the Course so that you can walk it!"

Nanrong Chu said, "When a sick villager is asked by another villager what ails him, he can describe his sickness. But someone who knows wherein he is sick is not really so sick. When I hear the Great Course, on the contrary, it is like a medicine that just makes the illness worse. I would be content merely to hear of the standard procedure for preserving the life process."

Laozi said, "The standard procedure for preserving life—well, can you embrace oneness? Can you keep it from slipping away? Can you know good and bad fortune without divining? Can you stop? Can you leave off? Can you ignore how it is with others and seek it in yourself? Can you be unconstrained and oblivious? Can you become an infant? An infant screams all day without getting hoarse—the utmost harmony! He grabs hold of things all day without tightly clenching his fist—for his Virtuosity comes from both himself and the objects. He stares all day without blinking—for he does not one-sidedly privilege the external. Walk without knowing where you are going; stop without knowing what you are doing; slither along with all things, joining in their undulations. This is the procedure for preserving the life process."

Nanrong Chu said, "So is this then the Virtuosity of the Consummate Person?"

"No. This is just what is called melting the ice and breaking through the freeze—but are you capable of it? As for the Consummate Person, he takes his food from the earth but his joy from the Heavenly, not disturbing or being disturbed by either people or things, by either benefit or harm. He joins in none of their extravagances, nor in their plans or projects. Unfettered, he arrives. Oblivious, he departs. This is the procedure for preserving the life process."

"This then is the utmost," Nanrong Chu said.

"Not yet," said Laozi. "A moment ago I asked you if you were capable of becoming an infant. An infant acts without knowing what she's doing and moves along without knowing where she's going, her body like the branch of a withered tree and her mind like dead ashes. In this state, neither good nor bad fortune can reach her. And if even good and bad fortune are nothing to you, how can anything human plague you?"

Empty space is vast and unshifting, and so the radiance of Heaven shines forth through it. When the radiance of Heaven shines forth, it reveals the humanness of the human, the thingishness of things. Hence, when the humanness is

---

self off to them all and don't let them in. When internal factors entangle you, instead of trying to get control of them one by one in all their tangled threads, just contain them all and don't let them out." In either case, though, the point is clear: the attempt to "do something" about your undesirable qualities, handling them with strategies of control, is futile. Laozi suggests an alternative to this in the following paragraphs.

cultivated, it comes to possess its own unending sustainability[8] even in this very moment. Sustainability means that when abandoned by the Human, one is instead aided by the Heavenly. Abandoned by the Human, one is called a citizen of the Heavenly. Aided by the Heavenly, one is called a Son of Heaven.

One who wants truly to learn should learn what cannot be learned. One who wants truly to take action should do what no deliberate action can do. One who wants truly to distinguish what is so by debate should distinguish what no debate can distinguish to be so. When understanding[9] stops at and rests on what it does not understand, it has reached its perfection. If there were anything that deviated from This, it would be destroyed in [the turning of] Heaven the Potter's Wheel.

Let your body be moved only by the totality of things.[10]

Let your mind spring to life from its rootedness in the unthinking parts of yourself.

Reach through to others through respect for what is most central within yourself.

If you are like this and evils still beset you, it is the doing of Heaven, not of man. Hence, it will not be sufficient to undermine your completeness. It will not be able to gain entrance to your Numinous Platform.[11] The Numinous Platform has that which maintains it, but its exact locus is unknowable: it is that which is sustained although there is nothing that can sustain it. If it operates in any way that is not also a revelation of this something that makes it complete and real, it always goes wrong. If its own endeavors end up getting stuck inside it, so that it is unable to get rid of them, then every change is really another loss.

If you do evil openly, it can be punished by humans. If you do it secretly, it can be punished by ghosts. It is only after you have brought both humans and ghosts into your own daylight that you can truly go forth into your solitude. For when you accord with what is within you, you walk in the nameless. When you accord with the external, on the other hand, you aspire only to the expectation of some sort of payment. When you walk in the nameless, even your everyday activities have their own radiance. But when you aspire to the expectation of payment, you become merely a merchant. Everyone sees you tottering on tiptoes, but still you think you're towering above them.

To go along with other beings all the way to the end is to accept them into

---

8   "Sustainability" is *heng* 恆 . See reference in Glossary entry for *chang* 常.

9   "Understanding" is *zhi*. See Glossary.

10   Alternately, something like the following: "Supply yourself with adequate material things to support your body." But *bei* 備 in the rest of this passage is used pointedly to refer to totality in a more robust sense, rather than a mere "supply of adequate provisions."

11   "Numinous Platform" is *lingtai* 靈臺. Cf. "Numinous Reservoir" (*lingfu* 靈府) at 5:16.

yourself. Temporarily putting up with other beings for whatever advantage you can wrest from them, on the other hand, means that even your own body is something you do not accept and shelter—how then can you accept and shelter others? If you cannot accept and shelter others, you will have no intimates, and for one without intimates, everyone—including oneself—is a complete stranger.

There is no weapon more fearsome than your own will, for which even an Excalibur is no match. There is no thief greater than the yin and yang, which cannot be escaped anywhere between heaven and earth. But it is not really the yin and yang that pillage us. It is our own minds.

The Course runs through and connects everything. Its divisions are also formations. Its formations are also destructions. What is hateful about divisions is just that each part is taken as the totality. What is hateful about such totalizing is just that some present existence is what is then taken as the totality. It is for such as this that people go chasing the external without turning back, finding only their own ghosts. For to go outside yourself and attain what you're after is called attaining your own death, and the gain that is left as a result of destroying yourself can only be a kind of ghost.

It is only their resemblance to the unmanifest and formless that gives stability to manifest forms. Beings emerge, but not from any root. They vanish, but not through any opening. What is really substantial is in no one location, and what really endures has no beginning or end. Since there is emergence but without any opening through which to vanish, there is a kind of substantiality to it. What is substantial but located in no position is the whole expanse of space. What has duration but no beginning or end is the whole expanse of time. Beings are born and die, emerge and vanish within them, but in all this emerging and vanishing they show no form. They are called the Heavenly Door. The Heavenly Door is Nonbeing, for all beings emerge from Nonbeing. Beings cannot constitute their being out of being; they must come forth from Nonbeing. But neither does there exist some entity called Nonbeing. It is "This" in which the sage hides himself.

The understanding of the ancients had really got all the way there. Where had it arrived? To the point where, for some, there had never existed so-called things. This is really getting there, as far as you can go. When no things are there, nothing more can be—added![12] Next there were those for whom there were things, but who saw life as a loss and death as a homecoming, hence finally putting an end to the fixed division of separate identities. Next there were those who said, "In the beginning there is Nonbeing. Afterward, Being is born. Thereafter, life ends all at once in death." They took Nonbeing as the head, life as the trunk, and death as the backside, saying, "Whoever knows that Being and Nonbeing, life and death, are held together in a single grasp, he will be my friend." Though these three types differ, they are part of a single royal

---

[12]   Cf. 2:25.

clan, like the Zhaos and the Jings, whose name derives from their official duties, and the Shen clan, whose name derives from their territory. It is only in this sense that they are not the same.

Being alive is like being a sediment of grime at the bottom of a cooking vessel, ceaselessly dissolving and scattering, which is what we speak of as the shifting rightness of its "this." When you try to talk about shifting rightness, you find it is always other than whatever you have said. Even if you happened to be right about it, it would be impossible to know. Both the stomach and the feet of the dismembered animal are arrayed during the midwinter sacrifice; they can be separated and yet cannot be separated.[13] In inspecting a house, you make the rounds through its boudoir and ancestral shrine, but you will also not neglect a gander at the outhouse. The definition of what is right adopts the shifting rightness of "this."

Let us try to talk about shifting rightness. Rightness is rooted in the life process, but we let it be guided by the understanding,[14] so our rights and wrongs end up charioting us around. For every name, we think, there turns out to be a substantial reality, so we take ourselves too as some kind of palpable material. We try to control others, using ourselves as the regulating standard. That is why death is the only reward of all our attempts at regulation. In such a state we consider whoever is useful to the world wise, and whoever is useless foolish, honoring success and disgraced by failure. And it is also this shifting rightness that makes the people of this age regard the likes of the cicada and fledgling dove as being in the right.[15] For the embrace of the same viewpoint comes simply from being in the same position.

When you step on a stranger's foot in the marketplace, you apologize profusely for your rude carelessness. If it's your brother's foot, you laugh it off. But if it's the foot of someone extremely intimate, like your parent or child, you don't even mention it. Hence I say: Perfect Ritual Propriety sometimes lies in ignoring that the other person is even another person. Perfect Responsibility sees no object to which one must properly respond. Perfect Wisdom makes no plans. Perfect Humanity is especially intimate with no one. Perfect Trust requires no collateral.

Retract the will's raging arousal. Untie the mind's entanglements. Undo the ties of Virtuosity. Pierce through the blockages to the Course. It is rank, wealth, prominence, prestige, fame, and advantage that arouse the will. It is appear-

---

[13]   The parts may be rearranged, but no matter how you slice it, all the parts are there. The right arrangement during the sacrifice is different from the right arrangement for the living animal—a shifting rightness. But in either case, there has been no real change: all the parts are still there. Cf. the Inner Chapters story of the monkey keeper (2:24) and the idea of "hiding the world in the world" (6:28).

[14]   "Understanding" is *zhi*. See Glossary.

[15]   Cf. 1:5–6.

ances, actions, sexual beauty, conceptual coherence,[16] emotional energies, and intentions that entangle the mind. It is dislikes, desires, joy, anger, sorrow, and happiness that tie down Virtuosity. It is avoiding, approaching, taking, giving, understanding, and ability that block the Course. When these twenty-four items do not disrupt you, the mind is no longer pulled off center. Centered, it finds stillness. Still, it finds clarity. Once clear, it becomes empty, and once empty, it is able to "do nothing, and yet leave nothing undone."[17]

The Course is the full array of Virtuosities. The life process is Virtuosity shining forth. The inborn nature is the concrete material of the life process. The motion of the inborn nature is a kind of activity, but when activity becomes deliberate and artificial, it can be called the loss [of that inborn nature].

[Similarly], the understanding consciousness is originally an interface with the world, but as "wisdom"[18] it comes to be a kind of scheming. What consciousness does not know is like what is in one's peripheral vision, seen out of the corner of the eye. For when all your actions are "what you cannot help doing, outside of your control," we call it "Virtuosity." Conversely, when all your actions "come from yourself alone," we call it "being completely in control." These two descriptions are directly opposed, but the facts they describe actually agree.

Yi was skillful at hitting a target, but not at preventing others from praising him. The sage is skilled at the Heavenly but not at the Human. It is only the Whole Man who is skillful at the Heavenly and also good at the Human. Only an insect can be an insect, and it is only by being an insect that it can succeed in being the Heavenly. The Whole Man hates the Heavenly, for he hates what other people [contrast to themselves] as the Heavenly. How much more would he hate [identifying himself] as "The Heavenly!" or "The Human!"

Yi could hit any sparrow that came his way—authoritative shooting indeed! But if he could have viewed all the world as the cage that encompasses them, not a single sparrow could have escaped. Tang caged Yi Yin by making him a cook, and Duke Mu of Tai caged Boli Xi with a five-colored sheepskin.[19] Thus we see that it is always what they like most that cages people.

A one-footed cripple may cast off his fancy clothes, for he already stands beyond honor and disgrace. An escaped prisoner may climb great heights with-

---

16   "Conceptual Coherence" is *li* 理. See Glossary.

17   Cf. *Daodejing* 48.

18   *Zhi* appears twice in this sentence, first as "the understanding consciousness" and then as "wisdom." See Glossary.

19   Yi was a legendary archer of great skill, mentioned also in Chapter 5 and Chapter 24. Yi Yin was fond of showing off his skill as a cook, and Emperor Tang enticed him to work for him by letting him do so. Boli Xi was fond of sheepskin garments and was bribed into service by the duke's gift.

out fear, for he has forgotten all about life and death. If a man gets used to being insulted, he becomes impervious to shame, and finally forgets all about human viewpoints. Forgetting the Human makes you a man of the Heavenly. Only when a man merges into the Heavenly Harmony can he be respected without being delighted or insulted without being angry. Anger comes forth from him without himself being angry, so his anger is an expression of his nonanger. Actions come forth from him without himself being in action, so his actions are an expression of his nonaction. To seek stillness by pacifying your vital energy or to seek spiritual power by following your mind—these are still just forms of deliberate activity. If you want to do both right, though, follow along with what is unavoidable in you. For it is something like the unavoidable that constitutes the Course of the sage.

CHAPTER TWENTY-FOUR
Xu Wugui (Selections)

[. . . .]

Zhuangzi said, "If an archer can be called skillful for hitting a target not designated in advance, then everyone in the world is a master archer like Yi. Would you agree?"

Huizi said, "Yes."

Zhuangzi continued, "If the world has no universally recognized standard of right, so each man affirms his own idea of rightness as right, then everyone in the world is a sage like Yao. Would you agree?"

Huizi said, "Yes."

Zhuangzi said, "Well then. There are the Confucians, the Mohists, the Yangists, the Bingists,[1] and yourself. Among these five positions, which is ultimately right? Or is it like the case of Lu Qu? His disciple said, 'I have mastered your Course. I can get the cauldron boiling in the winter and make ice in the summer.' Lu Qu said, 'That is just using the yang to evoke the yang, and the yin to evoke the yin. It is not what I call the Course. Let me demonstrate my Course for you!' Then he tuned two zithers, placing one in the foyer and one in his room. When he struck the *gong* tone on one, the *gong* on the other sounded; when he struck the *jue* tone on one, the *jue* on the other sounded—for they were tuned the same way. But then he changed the tuning of one string, matching none of the Five Tones. When he plucked this tone, all

---

[1] Traditionally identified as the followers of the logician Gongsun Long (see Chapter 2, note 13, and Chapter 17). Some scholars have also suggested that this could be a distorted reference to followers of Song Xing or the proto-Daoist/Legalist Tian Pian (see Chapter 33).

twenty-five strings of the zither resonated at once. It was just a sound like all the rest, and yet it functioned as the lord of all the tones. Is that how it is?"[2]

Huizi said, "But how about if whenever I debate the Confucians, Mohists, Yangists, or Bingists, they are so bowled over by my words and weighed down by my statements that none can refute me?"

Zhuangzi said, "[It would be like] a man of Qi who sends his son to Song but assigns cripples to be his bodyguards. Or like someone who seeks out a euphonious bell but then muffles its sound by wrapping it in cloth. Or like someone who searches for his lost son but doesn't look beyond his own house. This is forgetting the right type of thing [to be used for the job]. A man of Chu was angered by the doorman at his lodgings [and so wished to depart but was still so angry,] in the middle of the night, when no one else was around, that he picked a fight with the ferryman. He didn't get anywhere, but he did manage to make some enemies for himself!"[3]

Zhuangzi was attending a funeral when he happened to pass Huizi's grave. He looked at his followers and said, "There was a man of Ying who, when a bit of plaster no thicker than a fly's wing got smeared on his nose, had Carpenter Shi slice it off. Carpenter Shi swung his ax with a whoosh, slicing it off exactly as requested, removing every bit of the plaster without harming the nose, leaving the man of Ying standing there completely unperturbed. When Lord Yuan of Song heard about this, he called Carpenter Shi to court and said, 'Try it on me!' Carpenter Shi said, 'It is true that I could once slice like that. But my material is now long dead.' Since Huizi died, I too have had no material to work on. There is no longer anyone I can really talk to."

---

2   Huizi had developed a form of argumentation that used the alteration of perspective to undermine hard and fast distinctions, leading to the conclusion that "all things are one" (see Introduction and Chapter 33). Zhuangzi evidently adopts this method from Huizi but conceives its status and function very differently. For it is this method that seems to develop into Zhuangzi's "going by the rightness of the present 'this'" (*yinshi*) (2:16, 2:22–23), the "wild card." (See Glossary, and "Zhuangzi as Philosopher" at www.hackettpublishing.com) This method, shared by Huizi and Zhuangzi, is apparently what is here compared to the one tone that matches none but makes all the other strings resonate. Thus this passage perhaps shows us the difference between Huizi and Zhuangzi. Zhuangzi points out that this "wild card" is still one more card— "it is just a sound like all the rest" and that it still doesn't resolve anything about what is so, above and beyond all argument, in the way Huizi thinks. It just means he can win every argument. But this is still "to labor your spirit trying to make all things one" (2:23). For Zhuangzi, the "wild card" view has certain special characteristics, can resonate with every string, can win every argument—but it is not for that reason to be regarded as the establishment of an objective truth.

3   To think that winning a dispute is the way to establish the truth is using the wrong type of thing for the job. All that is actually accomplished is bad blood with the defeated, but the whole point was to establish agreement, a harmonious relation, between the disputants. Similarly, the man of Chu wanted to get away from his lodgings and cross the river because of his anger at something there, but it was his anger that kept him from getting across the river.

[. . . .]

Confucius went to Chu, where the king held a feast in his honor. Sun Shu'ao stood holding the pouring vessel while Shinan Yiliao received the wine and made the libation, saying, "Ah, you are just like the men of old! They would have words to say on such an occasion!"

Confucius said, "I have learned something of the wordless words, but I have never spoken of them. I will speak of them now. You, Shinan Yiliao, merely juggled some balls around, and the conflict between Chu and Song was thereby resolved. And you, Sun Shu'ao, merely fell asleep with a feathered fan in your hand, and the people of Ying halted their troops.[4] As for me, I would need a beak three feet long [for my speech truly to do justice to such deeds]! For those [actions] are what is called a course that provides no guiding course, while what I'm doing now could be called a disputation that says nothing. Indeed, when Virtuosity is absorbed completely into the unity of the Course, and words come to an end in what the understanding does not understand, they have both reached their perfection. No Virtuosity can comprehensively cover the unity of the Course, and what understanding cannot understand cannot be adduced in any disputation. To become famed [for Virtuosity, understanding, and disputation] like the Confucians and Mohists is thus always an inauspicious sign.

"So it is that the ocean refuses none of the rivers flowing into it; its vastness is unsurpassed. Likewise, the sage encompasses heaven and earth, his bounty reaching all in the world, but no one knows who he is. The Great Man is born without titles, dies without posthumous honors, gathers no wealth, and establishes no name for himself. Skillful barking does not make a dog good, and skillful talking does not make a man even a worthy, much less a great man. Indeed, even being great does not make him great, much less a Virtuoso! Nothing is more complete than heaven and earth, but do they become so by seeking to be so? One who understands the great completeness seeks nothing, loses nothing, abandons nothing, never letting mere beings alter who he is. He returns only to his own self, yet he finds it inexhaustible. He follows the ancients, yet he never becomes their mere copy. This is the integrity, the genuine completeness, of the Great Man."

[. . . .]

There are the subserviently compliant; there are the precariously perched; there are the compromised and put-upon.

The subserviently compliant are those who learn the words of one teacher and then, secretly pleased with themselves—so subservient! so compliant!— remain partial to their own theory, regarding it as quite sufficient, without re-

---

4 According to Luo Miandao, Shinan Yiliao juggled ninety-nine balls, keeping ninety-eight in the air at all times. Like Sun Shu'ao's ability to nap in a similar situation, this inner repose, unaffected by external things, ended up having the most powerful effect on external things, as the armies stopped their fighting, transfixed.

alizing there has never been anything to possess there or anywhere. Thus, they are called the subserviently compliant.

The precariously perched are like lice on a pig. Choosing a place among its wide-set bristles, they think they have found an enormous palace or vast pleasure park for themselves. In the slits of the hooves or creases of its buttocks, or in the cleavage between the teats or the folds behind the knees, they think they have found a secure home in an auspicious site, not realizing that as soon as the butcher claps his hands and spreads forth the kindling, setting it aflame, they will be fried together with the pig. They flourish due to their place and likewise perish due to their place. Such are the precariously perched.

The compromised and put-upon are people like the emperor Shun. The mutton has no hankering for the ants, but the ants hanker after the mutton, for it is rank with musk. Shun's musky behavior attracted the delight of the people. Thus, he changed his residence three times, and in each case a city sprang up around him. After he moved to the wastelands of Deng, it became a metropolis of a hundred thousand families. When Yao learned of Shun's worthiness, he raised him up from the barren lands, saying, "We are hoping his arrival will bring us prosperity." When Shun was taken from the barren lands, he was already long in years and was losing both his vision and his hearing, but he was never able to return home to rest. This is what I mean by being compromised and put-upon.

Hence, the Spirit Man always hates the arrival of a crowd. For where there is a crowd there is no togetherness, and where there is no togetherness a crowd is no gain. He keeps no one too close and no one too distant, embracing his own Virtuosity, warming himself with his own harmony, thereby getting along with the world. This is what I call a Genuine Human Being. They cast off wisdom[5] just like the ants, but they also took their cue from the fishes, so at the same time they cast off all deliberate intentions just like the mutton. They viewed the eye with the eye, listened to the ear with the ear, recovered the mind with the mind. Their levelness was like that of a taut cord. Their transformations were a mere following along. For the Genuine Human Beings of olden times waited for[6] them all with the Heavenly. They did not intrude into the Heavenly with the Human.

Such were the Genuine Human Beings of old! Getting it, they lived; losing it, they died. Getting it, they died; losing it, they lived. It is like medicine. There are crow's head, balloonflower, cockscomb, and China root. Taken at the right time, any of them can be what puts everything in order, but the case by case vicissitudes are beyond exact verbal description.

When Gou Jian was trapped on Mt. Kuaiji with his three thousand armored soldiers, it was only Zhong who knew how to save them from destruction, but it was also only Zhong who was unaware of the subsequent danger to his own

---

5   "Wisdom" is *zhi* 知 . See Glossary.

6   "Waited for" is *dai* 待 . See Glossary. Cf. 4:9.

life [at Gou Jian's hands].[7] So I say, the owl's eyes are suited to certain conditions, and the crane's neck has its proper proportion. To remove them would cause the creature suffering. Hence it is said that although both the wind and the sun diminish the river when they pass over its face, nonetheless, even if both were fixed upon it at once, the river would be undisturbed; it merely relies on its source and continues its way. For the water holds firmly to the earth, the shadow holds firmly to the body, and all beings hold firmly to one another.

So it is that the eye is endangered by keen vision, the ear by sharp hearing, the mind by its self-sacrificing devotion to external things. Every ability endangers its own reservoir. Once this danger has taken shape, it is too late to change it. Once disaster sprouts, it grows and flourishes. To return them [to their source] requires effort, and the results take time. But people think [these abilities] are their most precious treasures—pathetic, is it not? The ceaseless destruction of nations and the slaughter of the people comes from never thinking to question this.

The feet occupy just the span of earth upon which they stand, but it is all the untrod land that allows them to travel well. Man's knowledge is puny, but it is all that he does not know that allows him to know what is meant by the Heavenly. To know it as the Great Oneness, as the Great Dark, as the Great Eye, as the Great Potter's Wheel, as the Great Method, as the Great Dependable, as the Great Stability—that is the perfection [of knowing]. As the Great Oneness it runs through and connects all things; as the Great Dark it unbinds them; as the Great Eye it beholds them; as the Great Potter's Wheel it traces their outlines; as the Great Method it forms their bodies; as the Great Dependable it harbors them; as the Great Stability it supports them. In all of them the Heavenly is there to follow, for in all there is a darkness that illuminates, a pivoting to a new beginning, providing always an alternate standard.[8] To understand it seems like not understanding, to know it seems like not knowing, for it can be known only by not knowing. It cannot be inquired after in terms of either the bounded or the unbounded. But within all the scraping and slippage there is a solidity that is never replaced through all the ages, never lacking. So may we not say that it has been plainly and effectively presented? Shall we not inquire into this? What else is all our perplexity for? To dissolve our perplexity into the ever unperplexed, thus returning it to the unperplexed, this would still be the greatest unperplexity.

---

7   Gou Jian (d. 464 B.C.E.?) was king of the kingdom of Yue. Wen Zhong, originally from the state of Chu, was considered a master strategist and became one of Gou Jian's top military advisers in his campaign to reclaim his throne after Yue was annexed by the state of Wu. After they had successfully destroyed the state of Wu and Gou Jian was once again king of Yue, Wen Zhong stayed on at his court to enjoy the honors earned by his contributions, only to meet his death when Gou Jian later suspected him of plotting a revolt.

8   This line can be parsed differently, but it is equally obscure either way. The other parsing might render, in accordance with Guo Xiang's reading, "In all of them, the Heavenly is there. Following along with them, its illumination appears. Vanishing into it, you find its axis, but if you try to begin something with it, it becomes an 'other.'"

CHAPTER TWENTY-FIVE
Zeyang (Selections)

[. . . .]

The sage gets through to the intertwining of things, so that everything forms a single body around him, but without knowing it to be "right." For this is his inborn nature. Whether communing with his allotted fate[1] or shaken into activity, he takes the Heavenly as his only teacher. Others follow him and try to pin labels on him, troubling themselves with their own understanding.[2] In no time they are brought to a complete halt, wondering what to do next.

One who is born beautiful, even if handed a mirror, will not realize her beauty surpasses others' unless someone tells her so. But whether she knows or hears of it or not, the delight she gives is unceasing, and the affection it inspires equally so. For this is her inborn nature. Other people stick a name on the sage's love for mankind. If no one tells him, he will not know he loves mankind. But whether he knows or hears of it or not, his love is unceasing, and the comfort it brings to others equally so. For it is his inborn nature.

The old homeland, the old neighborhood—even gazing at it from afar is to be penetrated through with joy. Even if the grave sites are overgrown with weeds, and nine out of ten of your old friends are now lying beneath them, the joy still flows unhampered in you. How much more so if you could still see what you had once seen and hear what you had once heard there—it would be like standing on an eighty-foot platform suspended over the crowd. Now, the man of the Renxiang clan[3] found the center of the circle.[4] He brought himself to completion by following along with things, staying right there with them no matter how they ended or began, no matter what their impulse or season. It is the one who constantly changes together with all things who is always one and unchanging—when has he ever had to abandon them for even a moment? Indeed, if you deliberately make the Heavenly your teacher, the Heavenly will not teach you. You will instead end up merely sacrificing yourself to each thing you encounter—is it any surprise that they then end up belaboring you? To the sage there have never existed any such things as "the Heavenly" or "the Human"—to him there have never been any beginnings at all, never any beings of any kind. He just moves along with the world without replacing anything, going through every kind of experience without any clogging. What need has he to join things into a unity?

---

[1] "Fate" is *ming* 命. See Glossary.

[2] "Understanding" is *zhi* 知. See Glossary.

[3] According to Guo Xiang, an ancient sage-king.

[4] Cf. 2:17.

Tang made Deng Heng, his palace guard, into his tutor. He followed this teacher without being constrained by him, for he had mastered this ability to complete himself by following along with things. He put Deng in charge of his nominal duties, and it was Tang's name that became an inadvertent example to others. In this way he was able to manifest himself in two ways at once.[5]

It was through getting to the end of all calculating thought that Confucius became the teacher he was. The man of the Rongcheng clan[6] said, "Remove the days and there are no more years; without the internal, nothing is external."

[. . . .]

Qu Boyu has been going along for sixty years and has changed sixty times. There was nothing he didn't initially affirm as right that he didn't later repudiate as wrong, so he could never be sure whether what he presently called right was not fifty-nine times wrong. All beings have that from which they are born, but no one can see their root; they have that from which they emerge, but none can see through what door they enter. Everyone esteems what his knowing knows, but none knows how to know by relying on what his knowing does not know.[7] Is this not the greatest uncertainty of all? Enough! Enough! There is nowhere to escape it! This is called saying both "It is right!" and "Is it right?"

[. . . .]

Know Little asked Vast Unbiased Harmony, "What is meant by 'Community Words?[8]'"

Vast Unbiased Harmony replied, "'A community' [is a name that] means the joining together of the people [designated by] ten family surnames and a hundred personal names so that they collectively form a set of customs. The different is joined into the same; the same is dispersed into the different. Now, you can point to the hundred parts of a horse's body and never come up with a horse, and yet the horse is right there, tethered in front of you; it is precisely through establishing the hundred parts that we call it 'horse.' Hence, hills and mountains pile up the low to make the high. The Yangzi and the Yellow River join the small to make the large. And the Great Man joins and brings all things together to make the unbiased. For this reason, that which comes in to him from outside has a host to receive it without being exclusively clung to, and what comes from within him is able to rectify other things without being rejected.

---

[5] "Manifest in two ways at once" is *liang xian* 兩見. Cf. *liang xing* 兩行 (Walking Two Roads) at 2:24.

[6] According to the Gao You commentary to the *Huainanzi*, Rongcheng was the creator of the calendar in the time of the Yellow Emperor.

[7] *Zhi* appears six times in this sentence. See Glossary.

[8] A strange term, unattested elsewhere. Here, it seems to imply "words that cover the entire community of beings."

"Each of the four seasons has its own type of weather,[9] but Heaven is not partial to any of them. Thus does the year come into being. The five bureaus of government have their different duties, but the ruler is not partial to any of them. Thus is the state well governed. Cultural affairs and warfare require different skills, but the Great Man is partial to neither. Thus is his Virtuosity complete. All things have their differing guidelines,[10] but the Course is not partial to any of them. Thus, it has no name. Since it has no name, it engages in no particular activity, and engaging in no particular activity, there is nothing it does not do.

The seasons have their ends and beginnings; generations have their alternations and transformations. Disaster and prosperity, paired together, come flowing over, so that to thwart one thing is to suit something else. Each particular thing spontaneously follows a different direction; to put one thing right knocks something else out of whack. It can be likened to a great swamp, where all the different trees alike dwell. It can be seen also in contemplating a great mountain, taken as a foundation for trees and rocks alike. Such are what we call Community Words."

Know Little said, "This being the case, is it sufficient to call it the Course?"

Vast Unbiased Harmony said, "No. If we calculate the number of things, it does not stop at ten thousand, and yet we set a limit by calling them the 'Ten Thousand Things'—this is just to speak of them with a provisional name due to their great quantity. So 'Heaven and earth' just means the vastest among forms, 'yin and yang' just means the vastest among forces,[11] and the 'Course' just means what is most unbiased among all activities. To use [the word 'Course'] as a provisional name for the vastness involved is permissible; but once you have this word, you tend to take the Course as being comparable and contrastable to something. To dispute and distinguish on this basis is to compare the Course to a class outside itself, like we do with the species of dogs as opposed to horses. This misses it by a wide margin."

Know Little said, "In that case, within the four directions and the six realms, how does the arising of the ten thousand things come about?"

Vast Unbiased Harmony said, "Yin and yang shine on each other, injure one another, heal one another. The four seasons replace one another, give birth to one another, slaughter one another. Bridged between them there arise all sorts of desires and aversions, rejections and attractions. The joining of male and female, like paired halves, becomes a regular presence in their midst. Safety and danger replace each other, disaster and prosperity give birth to each other, leisure and hurry grind against each other, aggregation and dispersal complete each other. This is the realm of which names and objects can be

---

9   "Weather" is *qi* 氣. See Glossary.

10   "Guidelines" is *li* 理. See Glossary.

11   "Forces" is *qi*. See Glossary.

recorded, of which even the most subtle can be registered. The mutual ordering of beings as they follow in succession, the bridgelike circulation of beings as they move each other around, reverting when they reach exhaustion, beginning again when they come to an end—this is what belongs to the realm of beings, what words can exhaust, what understanding[12] can reach. It gets to the limit of the realm of beings and no further. She who sees the Course doesn't follow after them when they perish nor trace them back to whence they arise. This is where speculation comes to an end."

Know Little said, "Between Jizhen's theory that 'no one does it' and Jiezi's theory that 'something causes it,' which is true to the facts and which is a merely partial apprehension of how it all fits together?"[13]

Vast Unbiased Harmony said, "Chickens squawk, dogs bark—this is something people know. But even someone with the greatest understanding cannot describe in words whence they come to be this way, nor can she plumb by thought what they will do next. We can go on splitting and analyzing things further, until 'the subtlety reaches the point where there are no more divisions possible, the vastness reaches the point where it cannot be encompassed.'[14] But even so, the theories that 'something causes it' or 'nothing does it' don't yet get out of the realm of beings and thus in the end they fall into error. 'Something causes it' implies something substantial; 'nothing does it' implies a total void. The named and the substantial refer to the presence of beings, but 'namelessness' and 'void' merely point us to the spaces between these beings. One can speak and think about these, but the more one talks the farther off one gets.

"What has not yet been born cannot be kept from coming; what has already died cannot be stopped from going. Life and death are not distant, and yet the way they fit together[15] cannot be apprehended. These theories that 'something causes it' or 'nothing does it' are merely crutches for your doubt to lean on. I gaze at its root, and its antecedents go back without end; I seek its furthest developments, and their coming stretches on without stop. Having no end and no stop—these are negations within the scope of language and thus share only in the sense made[16] within the realm of mere beings. 'Something causes it' and 'nothing does it'—these are attempted descriptions of the root, but actually they end and begin where beings do. The Course cannot be considered existent, nor can it be considered nonexistent. The name 'Course' is what we avail ourselves of so as to walk it. 'Something causes it' and 'nothing does it' each occupy only one corner of the realm of beings. What do they have to do with the Great Method?

---

12 "Understanding" is *zhi*. See Glossary.

13 "How it fits together" is *li*. See Glossary.

14 According to the opening dialogue in Chapter 17, these were stock propositions among the debaters of the time.

15 "The way they fit together" is *li*. See Glossary.

16 "Sense made" is *li*.

"If words were completely adequate, one could speak all day and all of it would be the Course. If words were completely inadequate, one could talk all day and all of it would concern only particular beings. The ultimate reaches both of the Course and of beings cannot be conveyed by either words or silence. Only where there is neither words nor silence does discussion really come to its ultimate end."

CHAPTER TWENTY-SIX
External Things (Selections)

[. . . .]

Huizi said to Zhuangzi, "Your words are useless."

Zhuangzi said, "It is only when you know uselessness that you can understand anything about the useful. The earth is certainly vast and wide, but a man at any time uses only as much of it as his two feet can cover. But if you were to dig away all the earth around his feet, down to the Yellow Springs, would that little patch he stands on be of any use to him?"

Huizi said, "It would be useless."

Zhuangzi said, "Then the usefulness of the useless should be quite obvious."

Zhuangzi said: "If a man has the capacity to wander, can anything keep him from wandering? And if he has no capacity to wander, can anything set him to wandering? Neither a will that flows away with things nor practices that separate one from things, alas, are the doings of utmost understanding[1] and abundant Virtuosity, are they? [Those who truly achieve these] cannot be made to turn back even if an avalanche descends upon them, will pay no heed even though fire may engulf them. Though they may play the role of lord or servant to one another, this is only a matter of the times. In another age, neither would be lower than the other. Hence I say, the Consummate Person keeps to no single course of behavior.

"The scholarly types esteem antiquity and disparage the present, and when they compare people of today to the likes of the ancient emperor Xiwei, who could fail to appear as a mere fleeting wave? But it is only the Consummate Person who can wander through this world without going awry, following others without losing himself, not modeling himself on their teachings, able to accept their ideas without becoming one of them.

"For the eye to penetrate through, unblocked by its objects, is clear vision. For the ear to penetrate through, unblocked by its objects, is keen hearing. For the nose to penetrate through, unblocked by its objects, is acute smelling. For the tongue to penetrate through, unblocked by its objects, is the sweetness

---

[1]   "Understanding" is *zhi* 知. See Glossary.

of tasting. Likewise, for the mind to penetrate through, unblocked by its objects, is real understanding,[2] and for understanding to penetrate through, unblocked by its objects, is Virtuosity. The Course, like any course, must not be blocked. For where there is blockage it becomes choked, and if it is choked it becomes stagnant. This is where all the trouble starts.

"The consciousness[3] of living creatures depends on their breath. It is not Heaven's fault if it becomes depleted. Heaven blows through them day and night without cease, but human beings see to it that all their openings are blocked off. Only when you reopen yourself all the way back down to the placenta can your mind wander in the Heavenly. When there is insufficient space in a house, the womenfolk will surely fall to quarreling. If the mind has no Heavenly wandering, the six apertures of perception will interfere with one another. This is why being in a vast mountain forest benefits a man more than whatever might be granted by the gods.

"Virtuosity overflows into a good name, and a good name overflows into violence. Preconceived plans are put to the test in an emergency, and cleverness[4] comes forth from conflict.[5] Obstructions are born from holding exclusively to official purposes, for it is when a multitude of factors combine appropriately that affairs come to their true fruition. In the springtime, when the sunlight and rain come at their proper times, the grasses and trees rage forth into life, and it is just when the hoes and sickles begin to cut them down that more than half of them come to be most firmly rooted, never understanding exactly how they do it.

"Peace and quiet can fortify one against disease, massage can ease the ailments of age, tranquility can halt anxiety, but these are the works of the already beleaguered. Those who are truly at ease have no place for them and never bother to find out about such things. The Spirit Man does not bother to find out about the sage's methods for unsettling the world, nor the sage about the worthy man's, nor the worthy man about the exemplary man's. Nor does the exemplary man bother to learn the petty man's way of collaborating with the times.

"In Yanmen there was a man whose skill in handling the mourning for his deceased parent earned him a post as official tutor. Thereafter over half of his townsmen died from their excessive mourning practices.

"Yao gave the empire to Xu You, and Xu You fled. Tang gave it to Wu Guang, and Wu Guang was furious at him. When Ji Tuo heard of this, he led his disciples to kneel and pray to the Kuan River, and all the feudal lords sent their condolences for his suffering. After three years, Shen Tu'ai threw himself into the Yellow River [to earn even greater fame for suffering].

---

2 "Understanding" is *zhi* 知. See Glossary.

3 "Consciousness" is also *zhi* 知. See Glossary.

4 "Cleverness" is also *zhi*. See Glossary.

5 The last phrase is an exact quote of 4:3.

"A fish trap is there for the fish. When you have got hold of the fish, you forget the trap. A snare is there for the rabbits. When you have got hold of the rabbit, you forget the snare. Words are there for the intent. When you have got hold of the intent, you forget the words. Where can I find a man who has forgotten words, so I can have a few words with him?"

CHAPTER TWENTY-SEVEN
Words Lodged Elsewhere

Almost all of my words are presented as coming from the mouths of other people, and of those the better part are further presented as citations from weighty ancient authorities.[1] But all such words are actually spillover-goblet[2] words, giving forth [new meanings] constantly, harmonizing them all through their Heavenly Transitions.

The nine-tenths or so attributed to others discuss a topic by borrowing an outside viewpoint. A father does not serve as matchmaker for his own son, for the praises of the father are no equal to those from the mouth of another—and the blame too then goes not to me, but to someone else! [In any case], those who agree will be responsive, while those who do not will object. For people call right whatever agrees with them and call wrong whatever differs from them.

The seven-tenths or so that are presented as citations from weighty ancient authorities are meant to defuse garrulous faultfinding, eliciting agreement with the words of these "venerable elders" instead. [But in fact], some of those who come before us in years, if they have not gone through the warp and the woof of things, from the root to the tip, in a way befitting their age, do not have any real priority over us. A man [of advanced years] with nothing to give him priority over others has not fulfilled the course of a human being, and a human being devoid of the course of a human being should really just be a called a stale, obsolete oldster.

These spillover-goblet words give forth [new meanings] constantly, so that all are harmonized through their Heavenly Transitions. They extend on and on without break and thus can remain in force to the end of one's years. When nothing is said, everything is equal. But words and this original equality are then not equal to each other. Thus it is that I speak only nonspeech. When you speak nonspeech, you can talk all your life without ever having said a word, or never utter a sound without ever failing to say something. There is some place

---

[1] Literally, "nine-tenths are words-lodged-elsewhere," and (of those) "seven-tenths are repeated [or 'weighted'] words."

[2] A hinged vessel that tips and empties when it gets too full.

from which each saying is acceptable, and some place from which it is unacceptable. There is some place from which it is so, and some place from which it is not so. Whence so? From being affirmed as so. Whence not so? From being denied to be so. Whence acceptable? From someone accepting it. Whence unacceptable? From someone not accepting it. There is necessarily some perspective from which each thing is right and acceptable. Thus, all things are right; all things are acceptable.[3] So what words other than spillover-goblet words, harmonizing through their Heavenly Transitions, could remain in force for very long? All beings are seeds of one another, yielding back and forth their different forms, beginning and ending like a circle, so that no fixed groupings apply. This is called Heaven the Potter's Wheel.[4] It is Heaven the Potter's Wheel that we see in their Heavenly Transitions.

Zhuangzi said to Huizi, "Confucius went along for sixty years and transformed sixty times. What he first considered right he later considered wrong. He could never know whether what he presently considered right was not fifty-nine times wrong."

Huizi said, "Confucius certainly devoted himself to the service of knowledge."[5]

Zhuangzi said, "No, Confucius had let go of such things! Did he not say so himself? Confucius said, 'I received my innate powers from the Great Root, and I stay alive by returning always to its mysterious efficacy.' Each of his crowings became a measure, each of his words became a model, but this was only because, when the choice between profit and responsibility was set before him, he would make a show of some likes, dislikes, rights, and wrongs to subdue the mouths of others. If they had submitted in their hearts as well, they would not have dared to stand against him, and he could have settled what the world needed settled. Enough! Enough! Let's just say that I am no match for him!"

Zengzi was twice employed, and his heart changed each time. He said, "In my first post, though my salary was only three pecks of rice, it brought benefit to my parents as well, so my heart was glad. In my second post, though my salary was raised to three thousand bushels of rice, it was too late [to be of use to my parents], so my heart was sad." His disciples asked Confucius about it, saying, "Someone like Zengzi must be unentangled in any fault!" Confucius said, "No, he is already entangled. If he were unentangled, what sorrow would he have had? Both three pecks and three thousand bushels would have meant no more than a mosquito or a sparrow flying past him!"

Yancheng Ziyou said to Dongguo Ziqi, "After a year of your teachings, I was a wild man. After two years, I became tame. After three years, I opened up.

---

3   Cf. 2:20–21.

4   Cf. 2:24.

5   "Knowledge" is *zhi* 知. See Glossary.

After four years, I saw myself as a being among beings. After five years, some-thing came forth to meet me. After six years, its ghostly presence entered into me. After seven years, the Heavenly took shape in me. After eight years, I no longer knew either death or life. After nine years came the Vast Wonder.

"When life is subordinated to definite purposes, death can be used to exhort the masses by claiming that it comes to them from a particular source.[6] And yet their birth into the visible world has no such source. But is even that really so? Where does life go? Where does it not go? Heaven has its calendrical pro-portions, earth has its bearings for man, but where among them can I seek out [this source]? 'One never knows where one will end up, so how can there not be such a thing as fate?' But no one knows where he comes from either, so how can there be such a thing as fate? 'There is a response to my actions, so how can there not be such things as ghosts?' But nothing is found there doing the responding, so how can there be any such thing as ghosts?"

The penumbras asked the shadow, "Previously you looked down and now you look up. Previously you tied back your hair but now it is loose. Previously you sat and now you stand. Previously you walked and now you stop. Why?"

The shadow said, "Quibble, quibble! What a petty question! I exist without knowing how or why! To say I'm like a cicada shell or a snakeskin may seem to be right, but ultimately that's not how it is. In sunshine or by firelight I mate-rialize, but in the shade or the nighttime I vanish. Is it that there is an *other* there on whom I depend?[7] Then all of you are all the more dependent on something! When he arrives, I arrive with him. When he goes, I go too. When he is powerful and bright, I am powerful and bright. Since I am so powerful and bright, what questions could I have?"[8]

Yang Ziju had gone south to Pei and invited Lao Dan, who was traveling in Qin to the west, to meet him in the borderland between them. He went to Liang, where he joined up with Laozi. In the middle of their journey, Laozi looked up to Heaven and sighed, saying, "I used to think you were teachable, but now I know it will never work."

Yang Ziju made no reply. But when they arrived at their lodgings, he brought the master a towel and comb and a pan of water to wash his hands and mouth, removed his shoes outside the door and came forward on his knees, saying, "Earlier I wanted to ask you about this, but since you were busy with the journey, I dared not do so. Now that you have some leisure, please tell me where my fault lies."

---

[6] Either fate, as the Confucians claimed, or the punishment of ghosts, as the Mohists claimed.

[7] "Depend" is *dai* 待. See 1:8, 2:44, 2:45, 2:48, 4:9, 6:5, 6:29, 7:15, and Glossary.

[8] Cf. 2:48.

Laozi said, "With all your supercilious glaring and staring, who could bear to be with you? The purest are those who appear defiled; the greatest Virtuosos are those who appear defective."

Yang Ziju's face changed with a jolt. "I will respectfully do as commanded," he said.

On the road to this meeting, the innkeepers had welcomed him to their homes and seen him off, the husbands bringing his mat, the wives bringing his towel and comb, all the other lodgers yielding their seats to him and making way for him around the hearth. On the road back, he had to fight the other lodgers for his seat.

CHAPTER THIRTY-TWO
Lie Yukou (Selection)

[. . . .]

Zhuangzi was dying, and his disciples wanted to give him a lavish funeral. Zhuangzi said to them, "I will have heaven and earth as my coffin and crypt, the sun and moon for my paired jades, the stars and constellations for my round and oblong gems, all creatures for my tomb gifts and pallbearers. My funeral accoutrements are already fully prepared! What could possibly be added?"

"But we fear the crows and vultures will eat you, Master," said they.

Zhuangzi said, "Above ground I'll be eaten by crows and vultures, below ground by ants and crickets. Now you want to rob the one to feed the other. Why such favoritism?"

[. . . .]

CHAPTER THIRTY-THREE
The World under Heaven

There are many in the world who apply themselves to some method or technique, and they all believe that what they possess is unimprovable. But in the end where among them is what the ancients called "the art of the Course"? I say, there is nowhere it is not.

But then, you may ask, whence does the spirit [of sagely holiness] descend? Whence do the illuminations [of kingly wisdom] emerge?

I answer: That which produces a sage, that which completes a king—both have one and the same origin.

He who is never separated from his source is called a Man of the Heavenly.

He who is never separated from the seminal quintessence of vitality is called a Spirit Man.

He who is never separated from his genuineness is called a Consummate Person.

He who regards Heaven as his source, Virtuosity as his root, and the Course as his gate, alive to the portents of every transformation, is called a Sage.

He for whom Humanity is the stuff of beneficence, Responsibility the guideline,[1] Ritual the normal practice, and Music the source of harmony, everywhere exuding compassion and humanity, is called an Exemplary Man.

But to use laws to define proper roles, to regard stated duties as the standard of evaluation, comparisons as the test of performance, and verification as the only decisive factor, viewing these as four hard-and-fast categories—one, two, three, four!—this is no more than a way for the government officials to keep order among themselves. Still, if they are unvaryingly committed to their duties and prioritize the feeding and clothing of the people, regulating the periods of plowing and leaving fallow, storing up the surpluses, always keeping in mind the weak, orphaned, and widowed, then even here there is some guideline for nourishing the people.

In contrast, however, how complete the ancients were! They combined the spirit with the illuminations,[2] coupled heaven with earth, nourished the ten thousand things and brought the world into harmony, their bounty extending even to the ordinary folk. They understood the fundamental principles and could also link them to the derivative standards. Unobstructed above, below, and all around, they connected up all that surrounded them, operating everywhere, in both the large and the small, in both the subtler matters and the coarser ones.

Much of their wisdom, as embodied in principles and standards, can still be found among the scribes handling the old regulations and inherited traditions, and many of the gentlemen of Zou and Lu still have some understanding of that part of it preserved in the classics of the *Book of Songs, Book of Documents, Book of Rites,* and *Book of Music.* The *Book of Songs* guides their wills, the *Book of Documents* guides their handling of affairs, the *Book of Rites* guides their behavior, the *Book of Music* guides their harmonizings, the *Book of Changes* guides their yin and yang, and the *Spring and Autumn Annals* guides their apportioning of roles and duties.[3] Their principles are scattered

---

[1] "Guideline," here and throughout this chapter, is *li* 理. See Glossary.

[2] I.e., the holiness (or "spirit," *shen* 神) of the sage and the wisdom (or "illumination," *ming* 明) of a true king. Cf. *supra.*

[3] These are the traditional "six classics" associated with the Confucian tradition, which was centered in Zou (home of Mencius) and Lu (home of Confucius). It is noteworthy that the author of this chapter conspicuously omits an entry on the Confucians as one of the present-day schools that understands only one side of the Course. Instead, they are presented as the direct inheritors of what is left of its completeness.

throughout the world but firmly established in these central states, so that now and then the scholars of the various schools will commend them and take them as their guide.

But the world is presently in great chaos. People no longer understand real sagehood and worthiness. The courses they practice and the virtuosities they attain no longer form a unity. Many in the world congratulate themselves complacently for their insight into some single aspect of it. It is as if the ears, eyes, nose, and mouth each had its own understanding, without being able to interconnect. This is how the skills of the various schools each excel in some part of it, each of which is useful at a certain time. But they are partial and incomplete, nook and corner scholars only. They may try to judge the beauties of heaven and earth, analyze the guidelines for all things, and investigate the comprehensiveness of the ancients. But very few of them can fully encompass the beauty of heaven and earth or take the measure of the richness of [sagely] spirit and [kingly] illumination. For this reason the Course allowing one to be inwardly a sage and outwardly a king is obscured and unclear, blocked and unexpressed. Each man in the world now fashions his own technique out of whatever part of it happens to suit his own desires. How sad! The various schools go forth without returning, making it impossible for them ever to come together. These latter-day scholars are unfortunately unable to perceive the purity of heaven and earth, or the total system of the ancients. It is their "arts of the Course" that will end up tearing the world to pieces.

To remain free of extravagance though born in a decadent age, not wasteful in the use of any of the ten thousand things, making no display in the observance of one's delineated obligations, rigorously disciplining oneself as if with rope and cords, and taking upon oneself all the troubles of the world: these were some aspects of the ancient Art of the Course. Mo Di [Mozi] and Qin Guli got wind of them and were delighted. But they went too far in what they did and complied too closely in what they kept themselves from doing. They began an "anti-music" campaign, classifying it as a form of "frugality in expenditure." In life there was to be no singing and in death no ceremonial attire. Mozi wanted to extend love everywhere equally, bringing advantage to everyone, and also rejected warfare. His course was to eschew all anger. He was fond of learning and well-informed, but his emphasis on uniformity differed from the former kings, so he slandered the ancient rituals and music. Now, the Yellow Emperor had his Xianchi symphony, Yao his Dazhang, Shun his Dashao, Yu his Daxia, Tang his Dahuo, King Wen his Biyong, and King Wu and [his brother] the Duke of Zhou together created their martial music. In the ancient mourning rites, noble and base each had their respective procedures, superiors and inferiors divided by rank. The Son of Heaven was buried in seven nested coffins, the feudal lords five, the great officers three, the knights two. But now Master Mo would have no singing in life and no ceremonial attire in death, making a three-inch-thick coffin of paulownia wood with nothing enclosing it the enforced standard for everyone. I'm afraid that to instruct people thus shows no real love for them. And to put it into practice personally certainly shows no real love for oneself!

This does not mean Mozi's course was a complete failure. But people sing, and he condemns their singing; they cry, and he condemns their crying; they make merry with music, and he condemns their music—does he really have any fellow-feeling for them? To be labored in life and then neglected in death—this course is excessively dry, and being so difficult to put into practice, it just brings sorrow and worry to the people. I fear this can never be used as the Course of the Sage. The people of the world cannot endure such a thorough rejection of what is in their own hearts. Although Mozi himself may have been up to the task, what use is that for the rest of the world? Thus isolating himself from the world, he was far from true kingship.

But Mozi praised his course, saying, "In olden times when Yu diverted the great flood, he channeled the rivers to reach the four barbarian tribes and all the nine provinces, creating three hundred major waterways, along with three thousand large streams and numberless small ones. Yu took up the shovel and basket with his own two hands, joining and interconnecting the waterways of the world until the down was scraped off his hams and the hair off his shins, drenched in extreme rains, hair raked through by violent winds. Thus did he bring security to all the nations. Yu was a great sage, and yet he was willing to labor his body for the world like this!" Such words caused many of the later Mohists to clothe themselves in hides or coarse fabrics and to shoe their feet in grass or hemp sandals, never resting day or night. They thought self-torture was the ultimate achievement, saying, "Anyone who can't do the same is not following Yu's course and is not qualified to be called a Mohist." Xiangli Qin's students, Wu Hou's disciples, and the southern Mohists such as Ku Huo, Yi Chi, and Deng Lingzi all recited the same Mohist canons but disagreed and argued to the point of calling one another heretical Mohists. They criticized one another with disputations about "hardness" and "whiteness," "sameness" and "difference," answering back to one another with words as incompatible as the odd and the even. They considered their Great Pontiff a sage, willingly making him their lord and master, each hoping to succeed him—it still goes on down to the present day.

Mo Di and Qin Huali had good intentions, but they went about it in the wrong way, causing the later Mohists to insist on doing nothing but torture themselves, goading one another on with their bare hams and bald shins. This is indeed the best kind of disorder, but the worst kind of order. Nonetheless, Mozi was truly one of the most outstanding persons this world has seen, the likes of which cannot be found today. Even when worn out and completely depleted, he never gave up—a man of genius, perhaps?

Unbound by conventions, unadorned by possessions, undemanding of others, not hostile to the mob, purifying the mind with the aspiration that all in the world enjoy peace and security, not stopping until both oneself and others have enough to nourish themselves with: these were some aspects of the ancient Art of the Course. Song Xing and Yi Wen got wind of them and were delighted. They wore caps in the shape of Mt. Hua as their emblem and based their interactions with all creatures on a policy of tolerance and noninterference. They spoke of the mind's ability to accept all things, calling this the cultivation of the mind itself, which would enable people to get along with one another happily and bring concord to all within the four seas. They would politely suggest that everyone establish this as their guiding principle. They said there was no disgrace in being insulted, wanting thereby to liberate the people from contention. They prohibited military aggression and called for universal disarmament, hoping thereby to save the world from warfare. They took this teaching all around the empire, counseling rulers and instructing the commoners. Although the world did not accept them, they insistently clamored on without giving up. Hence, it was said that although everyone, above or below, was tired of seeing them, they still managed to force their way into view.

But they did too much for others and too little for themselves. They would say things like, "It is enough if you would be kind enough to give me even five measures of rice. For I am afraid that you, my master, will not have enough to eat your fill. As for your humble servant here, although I may go hungry, I will in any case never forgot about the welfare of the world, and day or night I will not rest in my efforts." Or: "Is it really so necessary that I survive? Would I try to put on such airs, as if I alone were the man who could save the world?" They would also say, "An exemplary man does not make strict demands on others, nor impose his personal will on things." They held that anything not beneficial to all the world was not worth knowing. Their external practice was to ban military aggression and encourage disarmament, and their internal practice was to thin out their own passions and desires. In all they did, large and small, coarse and fine, their practices reached just this far and no further.

All-embracing and nonpartisan, unstrained and unbiased, unhesitating but without any fixed direction, going forth to things without secondary considerations, ignoring all calculations, uninvolved in any clever[4] schemes, choicelessly moving along with things: these were aspects of the ancient Art of the Course. Peng Meng, Tian Pian, and Shen Dao got wind of them and were delighted. They began by equalizing all things, saying, "Heaven can cover things but cannot support them; earth can support things but cannot cover them; the Great Course can encompass things but cannot distinguish between them." They knew that each thing had something acceptable and something unacceptable about it, and so they declared, "To make a choice is to lose the all-

---

[4] "Clever" is *zhi*. See Glossary. The term is rendered as "cleverness" throughout this passage, but its other connotations should also be kept in mind.

pervading; when any one thing is taught, something else is blocked out. But the Course excludes nothing."

Thus Shen Dao abandoned cleverness, rid himself of any personal position, and instead followed along with whatever was unavoidable. Letting all things flow on was for him the guideline of the Course. He said, "It is not clever to be clever. It is only because a person aspires to cleverness that dangers beset him." Unashamed and self-reliant, accepting no responsibilities, he laughed at the world's esteem for the worthy. Unconstrained and unattached, undertaking no moral practices, he critiqued the world's high regard for sages. By pounding and hammering off all his sharp protuberances, rounding himself off, he was able to roll and swirl along with anything that came his way. Abandoning both right and wrong, he managed to avoid entanglement. Unguided by cleverness or calculation, ignoring the before and after, he simply towered alone in his place. Moving only when pushed, proceeding only when pulled, he was like a twirl in the breeze, like a spinning feather, like a grindstone rolling on—complete, rejecting nothing, making no mistakes whether moving or at rest, free from blame. For what reason? An inanimate[5] object has no worries about establishing itself and does not get entrapped by the application of its cleverness. Neither its movement nor its stillness can ever stray from the guidelines, and thus it remains forever free from praise [and blame]. Hence, he said, "Just become like an inanimate object. There is no need for worthies or sages. Indeed, a clump of earth never strays from the Course." The ambitious achievers would laugh at him, saying, "Shen Dao's course is no practice for the living, but it is a perfect guideline for the dead!" In the end he was regarded as merely an eccentric.

Tian Pian was the same way. He studied under Peng Meng and learned from him the eschewal of all positive teachings. It was Peng Meng's teacher who said, "The ancient men of the Course simply reached the point of considering nothing either right or wrong. Their ways were like a passing wind gusting by—how can they be described?" These men insisted on doing the opposite of what others do, presenting to men's eyes no achievements worth beholding, but still they had to "round themselves off." What they called the Course was not really the Course, so even what was right in their words could not but turn out wrong. Peng Meng, Tian Pian, and Shen Dao did not really know the Course. But they had all heard something of its general overall character.

Regarding the hidden root as the finest quintessence and its manifest reifications as the cruder part, regarding accumulation as an insufficiency, dwelling tranquilly alone in the company only of whatever forms of spirit and illumination may come: these were some aspects of the ancient Art of the Course. Guan Yin and Lao Dan got wind of them and were delighted. They founded their way on the constancy of Nonbeing and centered it in the supreme One-

---

[5] A being without *zhi*. See Glossary.

ness. Externally, they had the appearance of pliant weakness and self-deprecating humility. Internally, it was the empty void that leaves all things unharmed which was their firmest reality.

Guan Yin said, "When nothing dwells within yourself, the forms of all things manifest in you naturally. In motion be like water, in stillness like a mirror, in responding like an echo. Vague and ambiguous, as if not really there! Still and quiet, like something transparent and clear! To merge with it is to form a harmony, but to try to gain something from it is to lose it. Never precede others; instead, follow behind them."

Lao Dan said, "Know the male but hold to the female; be the ravine of the world. Know the unstained, but hold to the disgraced; be the valley of the world.[6] Everyone else chooses to be the first, but I choose to be last. This is called accepting the filth of the world. Everyone else chooses to be full, but I choose to be empty, for it is because I store up nothing that I have more than enough—like a range of rolling hills stretching on before me, more than enough!" His personal demeanor seemed unhurried and careful to waste nothing. Free of deliberate activity, he laughed at the skillful. Everyone else sought to get what they wanted, but he found his completeness in the indirect twists and turns, saying, "Somehow or other it will work out all right." The depths were his foundation, the cords of restraint his regulating thread, for he said, "The hard will be smashed; the sharp will be dulled." He was broad-minded and tolerant with all creatures, never slicing his way into the domain of others. This can be called reaching the zenith. Indeed! Guan Yin and Lao Dan, these were truly the vast and broad Genuine Human Beings of olden times!

Blank and barren, without form! Changing and transforming, never constant! Dead? Alive? Standing side by side with heaven and earth? Moving along with the spirits and illuminations? So confused—where is it all going? So oblivious—where has it all gone? Since all the ten thousand things are inextricably netted together around us, none is worthy of exclusive allegiance. These were some aspects of the ancient Art of the Course. Zhuang Zhou [Zhuangzi] got wind of them and was delighted. He used ridiculous and far-flung descriptions, absurd and preposterous sayings, senseless and shapeless phrases, indulging himself unrestrainedly as the moment demanded, uncommitted to any one position, never looking at things exclusively from any one corner. He considered the world sunken in the mire, incapable of conversing seriously with himself, so he used spillover-goblet words for unbroken extension of his meanings, citations of weighty authorities for verification, words put into the mouths of others for broad acceptance.[7] He came and went alone with the quintessential spirit of heaven and earth but still never arrogantly separated himself off from the creatures of the world, for he rejected none of their views of right and wrong

---

6   Cf. *Daodejing* 28.

7   Cf. Chapter 27, beginning.

and thus was able to get along with worldly conventions. Although his writings are a string of strange and rare gems, their intertwining twistings will do one no harm. Even though his words are uneven, their very strangeness and monstrosity is worthy of contemplation. For his overabundance was truly an unstoppable force. Above he wandered with the Creator of Things, below he befriended whoever could put life and death outside themselves, free of any end or beginning. He opened himself broadly to the vastness at the root of things, abandoning himself to it even unto the very depths. He may be said to have attuned himself to whatever he encountered, thereby arriving up beyond them to the source of things. Even so, he was able to respond to every transformation, and thus [his writings] have a liberating effect on all creatures. The guidelines within them are undepletable, giving forth new meanings without shedding the old ones. Vague! Ambiguous! We have not got to the end of them yet.

Hui Shi had many theories: his writings filled five carts. But his course was uneven and mottled, and his words wide of the mark. His thinking ranged through all sorts of things. He said:

"The largest unit has nothing outside it. I call it the Great Unity. The smallest unit has nothing within it. I call it the Small Unity."

"What has no thickness cannot be piled up, and yet it extends for a thousand miles. Heaven is as low as earth, and the mountain as level as the lake."

"Just as the sun slants as soon as it reaches high noon, all beings start dying as soon as they are born."

"Within a Great Sameness there can be further subdivisions of sameness and difference. These are called Small Sameness and Small Difference. But all things are ultimately the same and also ultimately different. This is called Great Sameness and Great Difference."

"The south is both bounded and boundless, so one can go to Yue today and arrive yesterday."[8]

"Linked hoops can be unhooked."

"I know the center of the world: it is north of the state of Yan [which is in the north] and south of the state of Yue [which is in the south]. Love all things without exception, for heaven and earth are one body."

Hui Shi used these statements to make a great display in the world, showing them off in debate, and all the debaters in the world shared his delight in them, [adding]:

"Eggs have feathers. A hen has three feet. The state of Ying possesses the whole empire. A dog can be deemed a sheep. A horse lays eggs. Frogs have tails. Fire is not hot. 'The mountain' comes out of the mouth. The wheel does not touch the ground. The eye does not see. Pointing never reaches. Reaching can never end. A turtle is longer than a snake. The T-square is not square; the

---

8   Cf. Chapter 2, note 8.

compass cannot make a circle. The chisel does not surround its handle. A flying bird's shadow never moves. A speeding arrow in flight is sometimes neither moving nor at rest. A puppy is not a dog. A yellow horse and a black cow make a total of three. White dogs are black. An orphaned colt has never had a mother. If you remove half of a foot-long stick each day, it will not be depleted even after ten thousand generations."

The debaters responded to Hui Shi with these propositions, which kept them busy to the end of their days. Huan Tuan and Gongsun Long were debaters of this type. Covering over what is in people's hearts with their embellishments and altering their ideas, able to defeat their mouths but not to convince their hearts—this is the trap in which all such debaters get stuck. Hui Shi day after day used his cleverness to debate with others, accomplishing nothing more than the creation of a spectacle along with the other debaters. This is all it amounted to. But Hui Shi thought his eloquence was the most valuable thing in the world, saying, "Are heaven and earth any more magnificent? I have this heroic power in me without even relying on a past tradition!"

In the south there was an odd man named Huang Liao who wanted to know why heaven above did not crash down and why the earth below did not collapse underfoot, and the reasons for the wind, rain, thunder, and lightning. Hui Shi did not hesitate to answer, responding without even thinking, giving a comprehensive explanation of it all. He talked without rest, loquacious, unstoppable, and still he thought it was not enough, so he supplemented it with even stranger ideas. Since it was really all about opposing the views of others, so that he might earn fame for defeating them, he was unable to get along with the mass of men. His Virtuosity was weak but he forced his way heavy-handedly through things, so his path was in the end a dark one. Viewing Hui Shi's skills against the Course of Heaven and Earth, they look like the busy labors of a mosquito or a fly. What use are they to other creatures? That [uselessness] would still have been perfectly acceptable, if only he pushed all the way to its conclusion his idea of Oneness, which is to say, if he had valued the Course a bit more. He was so close! Instead, Hui Shi found no peace in it even for himself, scattering himself unceasingly into all things, ultimately gaining nothing more than fame as a skilled debater. A pity! Hui Shi's talents were fruitlessly dissipated running after things and never returning to himself. He was like a man trying to silence an echo with shouts or to outrun his own shadow. How sad!

Selections from

TRADITIONAL COMMENTARIES ON THE INNER CHAPTERS

Selections from
Traditional Commentaries on the Inner Chapters

Guo Xiang: Though some are larger and some are smaller, every being without exception is released into the range of its own spontaneous attainments, so that each being relies on its own innate character, each deed exactly matching its own capabilities. Since each fits perfectly into precisely the position it occupies, all are equally far-reaching and unfettered. How could any one be superior to any other? **1:1**

Wang Fuzhi: For us forms lodged here between heaven and earth there is only this wandering, this play, and nothing besides. It makes no difference how large or small: each stops only where it finds itself. Going forth but without any plan, coming back but not to any dwelling place—this is what it means to be free of dependence: not leaning on things to establish some identity for oneself, not leaning on projects to establish some merit for oneself, not leaning on actualities to establish some name for oneself. Large and small alike come to rest in the middle of Heaven the Potter's Wheel and thus each wanders far and unfettered. "Unfettered" means echoing beyond the dissolving tones—forgetting what has passed. "Far" means pulled into the distance—not limited to the understanding of consciousness. Hence, the theories of things can be made equal, the ruling force of life nourished, the physical form forgotten but its Virtuosity fulfilled, the world entered but its harm kept at bay, things responded to in a manner worthy of a true sovereign so that the empire comes to order.[1] All are ways of attunement with the great source, forgetting both life and death. All can be wandered in—indeed, all are nothing but this wandering.

Cheng Xuanying: When the physical form alters, the dispositions change with it. Formerly, being a fish, he swam the depths of the Northern Ocean. Now that he has become a bird, he soars over the Southern Sea. Although being submerged and being aloft may differ in nature, he is equally far-reaching and unfettered in both. Similarly, whether alive or dead, congealed or dispersed, one fits comfortably into whatever it is one is encountering. Whatever thousands of changes and ten thousands of transformations I may go through, not one of them fails to be myself.[2] **1:2**

---

[1] Alluding to the titles of the seven Inner Chapters, in Wang's interpretations of them.

[2] For further comment on this passage, go to www.hackettpublishing.com

1:3   LIN XIYI: This doesn't mean such a book really exists, necessarily. Zhuangzi invents a story and then cites this book as his own verification. This is another example of his playful theatrics.

1:4   SHI DEQING: This is a way of showing truly surpassing vastness. "Heat hazes" means the insubstantial waftings of steam above a sunlit lake, and "swirls of dust" means the wandering dust seen in a sunbeam coming through a crack in the wall. *"The back and forth blowings of living beings" refers to the birds and animals and insects of the world breathing back and forth at one another, down to the most subtle and minute breathing. The blue on blue of the sky is not its true color. It is just the result of the eye's power failing to reach the sparse remote expanses of empty space. The idea is that although Peng is certainly large, if he were viewed from above the vast unfilled expanses of empty space, he would appear as nothing more than a single *"wild horse" [heat haze] or "mote of dust"—how tiny and insignificant! Even though he may raise a wind that causes the waters to ripple for three thousand miles around, in the end it is no more vast than the breaths and gasps blown out by living beings. What vastness is there to it? Thus, the text says, *"Looking down upon him, he is just like this and no more." This means that although the sage may be vast, he is still confined to the realm of limited forms, with his own particular body, while the empty space that is the Course is formless and beyond description. What mere "being" can there be to it? This is to show that the sage's wandering is due to the Course, not to his limited form.

LÜ HUIQING: Wild horses [heat hazes] and dust motes are all* blown forth by the breath of the process of creation. This "breath" is the vital energy that fills up the space between heaven and earth, leaving no gaps. Man here within it looks up at the sky from below, seeing its blue on blue. Is it the true color of the sky or just the endlessness itself that he sees? There is no way to know. And precisely because there is no way to know, he need never take his own position to be a lowly one. Thus, when Peng looks down from above, how would he know that his position is a lofty one?

QIAN MU: Although the dust motes, scurrying like *wild horses, are extremely minute, they too have that which they depend on in order to move about.

1:5   SHI DEQING: This passage sums up the implications of the transformations of Peng and Kun, and their journey southward, a subtle metaphor for the fact that the great sage must first foster his powers in the depths and nourish himself amply before he can accede to his great function. The idea is that if the Northern Ocean is not deep, it cannot nourish Kun, and unless he has a great wind to support him when he transforms into Peng, he cannot travel to the Southern Oblivion no matter how he tries. This shows that without the vastness and depth of the Great Course, the fetus of the great sage cannot be gestated, and moreover that even when his grand body does come to completion, he will not be able to accede to his great function unless he is able to transform himself. Further, even when he attains this great function, if he is unable to ride upon the powerful transports provided by the interacting trends of ways of the world, he will be unable to act and move and thus will have no way to accomplish his brilliant works. Thus a deep and ample fostering and nurturing of his powers, which waits for the proper moment before it acts, is necessary to complete the substance and function of the great sage. Zhuangzi depicts the thick accumulations by reference to the surface of the water and the height of the wind, but the real idea of describing the thick accumulation of water is to point back to Kun. Rather than speaking of nourishing this fish, the text takes an oblique turn by pointing instead to the bearing up of boats. This is how Zhuangzi's writing twists and turns, making it impossible for readers to pin it down. If he spoke directly of Kun here, it would be unbearably stiff and clumsy. His intent is to make fun of the world's superficiality, of mere mouth-and-ear learning.

WANG FUZHI: The laughter of the dove and the cicada shows how a small 1:6 consciousness falls short. But even the traveler who stores up her provisions can make plans of only three months in advance; and of those of vast duration, longevity goes no further than that of Pengzu. This shows that a vast consciousness and vast duration are also bounded and limited. Thus, this passage only means to point out that a small consciousness knows nothing and that short duration is pitiful. It does not mean to imply that someone who flies ninety thousand miles high or lives for hundreds and thousands of years has reached the vastness of the unbounded. For this reason, the one who goes on a day trip and returns with his belly still full can also laugh at the pointless labor of the one who saves up provisions for three months. Neither the small who laugh at the large nor the large who pity the small have yet found the true ease of far and unfettered wandering.

SHI DEQING: There was something he had not yet firmly planted—that is, 1:7 he was able to forget reputation but had not yet forgotten his fixed identification with his particular self.

WANG FUZHI: "Even" Song Rongzi laughs, which indicates that we don't need to wait for the Consummate Person to find this laughable. But if the man esteemed in a single village or country does not take the attitude of the cicada laughing at Peng, but instead forgets his own smallness and wanders within it, then he could certainly just as well laugh at what Song Rongzi had not yet firmly planted. Song Rongzi did not yet understand how to laugh at himself. The fact that even he could laugh at these men is itself laughable. In the same way, "even" Pengzu has a reputation for longevity. "Firmly planted" means to grow wherever it is planted, emerging from the earth and blossoming into the open space above. Song Rongzi held firmly to his own definite self but was not yet able to go forth to things to complete the great function in them. Where there is something firmly planted, there is for that reason something that is left unplanted.

1:8   GUO XIANG: "Heaven and earth" is just a blanket term used to indicate all beings. It is all individual beings that form the very substance of heaven and earth, and it is each being's *self-so* that aligns true to itself. "Self-so" means what is so of itself, without being done by anyone or for any purpose. Thus, Peng's ability to fly high and the sparrow's ability to stay low, the great tree's ability to last long and the mushroom's ability to perish quickly, all these are done spontaneously, all are self-so; they are beyond the ability of anyone's particular activity. Because these are self-so capabilities not done by anyone or for any purpose, they are aligned true [to themselves]. Thus, to "chariot upon what is true both to Heaven and to earth" means to follow along with the character of each thing. To ride "atop the back-and-forth of the six atmospheric breaths" means to wander in the paths of transformation and change. If you travel forth like this, where can you go that will bring you to a halt? If you can ride upon whatever you happen to encounter, what will you have to depend on? This is how the perfect Virtuoso, who vanishingly unifies self and other, wanders far and unfettered. If you are depending on some particular conditions, even if you have the grace and ease of a Liezi, you will still be unable to travel when there is no wind. Such people can only wander far and unfettered after they attain that which they depend on—and how much more so is this the case for Peng? It is only one who can vanish into things and follow along with the great process of transformation who can be truly free of dependence and thus constantly unobstructed. And is it only she who is thereby freed of obstruction? No! She also complies with all dependent things, allowing each to attain what it depends on. Since they do not lose what they depend on, they too are joined with the Great Openness. So although I cannot make the dependent and the independent the same as each other, the fact that each rests securely in its own character, its Heavenly Mechanism unfolding of itself, receiving it but not knowing how or why—this is something I cannot make different among them. And if even the independent is ultimately no different from the dependent, how much less could there be any difference between the larger and smaller among the dependent?

SUN KUANG: "Ungoaded by praise" is the same as "having no one name." "Not involved in anxious calculations about bringing good fortune to himself" is the same as "having no particular merit." "Not being dependent" is the same as "having no fixed identity."

TAO WANGLING: The Consummate Person has no one fixed identity, so everything is his self. To differentiate it into the back-and-forth of the vital energies is how his merits take shape. To scatter it to form individual things is how his names take shape. Is he big, small, long, short, coming, going? Call him a wandering! But "wandering" is really just a forced name given to what he continually receives from the endless.

FANG YIZHI: Guo Xiang says, "He also complies with all dependent things, allowing each to attain what it depends on." But this little word "also" is superfluous. This way of putting it still falls one level short of the matter. Did you know that even to say "the self-so is free of all dependence" is also saying too much? The sage merely speaks of doing what one should do to the utmost, according to one's situation. Where does dependence enter into it? Only the truly self-so say nothing about the self-so.

WANG FUZHI: If you "chariot upon what is true both to Heaven and to earth," there is nothing that is not true and right. Heaven is high and earth is low, but such highness has no worry about going over the top, such lowness has no worry about wallowing in the mire. Rather, they include and enhance all beings without any of them interfering with one another, so that each of them can serve as a vista in which to wander. As for "riding atop the back-and-forth of the six atmospheric breaths," it is these six states themselves that transform and distinguish themselves. It is not the charioteer who distinguishes and transforms them. When it is cold, wander in the cold. When it is hot, wander in the heat. Then you can ride and wander even on the great droughts and great floods. In the endless alternations of mire and dry ground, of order and chaos, be endless together with them. Then there is an endless supply of greatnesses and also an endless supply of smallnesses. The village or country can be wandered in; inner, outer, praise, blame—all can be wandered in. The graceful wind can be wandered in, but the howling storm and the raging thunder, the scorching sun and the drenching rain can also be wandered in. When no fixed identities are established, all things can find their function. When no particular merits are dwelt in, all ways can be traveled securely. When no one name is made manifest, all realities are safe from loss.

SHI DEQING: Here we see that Yao was capable of ceding the empire and thus was capable of forgetting merit and identity. But he was not yet able to forget the reputation, the good name, that comes from ceding the empire. In this he is no better than Song Rongzi laughing at the world. | *1:9*

SHI DEQING: This shows that Xu You was capable of forgetting reputation and name, but he was not yet able to forget the identity of his personal identity and selfhood. In this he is no better than the tailorbird living on a single branch or the beaver filling its belly, both of which represent taking what one needs to satisfy oneself alone. This is like Liezi riding on the wind, not yet capable of forgetting his body. But the Spirit-Man on Mt. Guye is the one who forgets everything without exception. | *1:10*

SHI DEQING: Following up on the previous passage about Song Rongzi, which depicts three types of people to illustrate the three types of forgetting— of identity, of merit, and of name—this passage shows how Yao, in ceding the empire, is able to forget merit but not the good name that comes from his act of ceding, while Xu You, in refusing to accept the empire, is capable of forgetting name and reputation in the interest of satisfying himself, which means he is not yet capable of forgetting his fixed identity. We must look to the | *1:11* following passage about the Spirit-Man of Mt. Guye to find the truly spiritual person who transforms and enlarges himself to the next level, the great sage who forgets everything, giving a concrete example to show what "wandering far and unfettered" really means.

1:12　GUO XIANG:　The virgin girl is one who does not allow the external to harm the internal.

XIANG XIU:　The virgin girl who has reached her time is empty, tranquil, gentle, and yielding, harmonizing without clamor. It is not she who seeks others, but others who seek her.

CHENG XUANYING:　The *Classic of Mountains and Seas* says, "Mt. Guye is located beyond the encircling sea. A holy man lives there who gathers together the impulses of all things and responds to them. When the times require someone to yield and ritually defer, he becomes a Yao or a Shun; when the times need someone to wield the sword and spear, he becomes a Tang or a Wu."[3]

1:13　SHI DEQING:　This passage explains the previous one about Yao's ceding the empire to Xu You and the latter's refusing it. The meaning is that although Xu You did not accept the empire from Yao, he was still unable to get Yao to forget about his kingdom, or for that matter to forget about the name he deserved for ceding it, because Xu You himself had not yet forgotten his own fixed identity. But now, as soon as Yao saw the Spirit-Man, he suddenly forgot all about his kingdom. This is enough to show how the Spirit-Man rules the world, the great functional effectiveness of nondeliberate action. The whole meaning of the entire book is contained in this one phrase—it is not merely a summary of this first chapter about far and unfettered wandering. Zhuangzi's writing seems at first glance to be absurd and random, recklessly self-indulgent, but in reality the design is matchlessly rigorous and tightly structured.

WANG FUZHI:　Every creature has that which suits it comfortably; when it finds that, there is little more that needs to be done. But those who see themselves internally as having one fixed identity believe there is a world existing outside themselves, and those for whom there is a "world" on the one hand relating to "oneself" on the other will use that self to try to rule the world. Then they will bother themselves trying to do something about it, take credit for it as their own accomplishment, preside over it as the source of their reputation— restricting Peng and Kun to the space between the elm and the sandalwood tree, driving the cicada and the dove into the oblivion of the vast ocean, using Pengzu's longevity to cast blame on the dead child. All of this is using ceremonial caps to suit the tattooed men of Yue, keeping all creatures from their far and unfettered wandering. But one who does not allow others to wander far

---

[3]　Yao and Shun were sage-emperors who gained their position without recourse to arms; Tang and Wu were sage-emperors who took the throne by force, displacing a corrupt dynasty.

and unfettered can never do so himself. Only he who forgets all about "the world" can possess the world. If you allow each creature to get what it needs, what wandering could fail to suit you, wherever you may go?

SHI DEQING: Tangled weeds are solid inside; they have a central "heart-mind" and thus they serve as obstructions[. . . .] In this passage, by creating the tale of the far-reaching and unfettered Spirit-Man to illustrate the great use of uselessness, Zhuangzi is also offering an image of himself, meaning that no one in the world understands him. Huizi was the closest friend of his life, and thus he concocts this little song of ridicule to show his meaning. It also means that even a sage cannot manifest his full function to his own generation unless there is someone in the world who recognizes him for what he is. Although the tale is comic, it was written with a painful heart. To get the sense of a text like this you must not interpret it literally, for there is a whole further dimension of flavor going on implicitly. As the saying goes, poetry always has at least one *more* meaning. Students of this text must not fail to notice that parables of this type are quite numerous throughout the remaining chapters. This passage discusses a failure to skillfully use a large thing, but it has not yet touched upon the use of uselessness, which is developed in the following passage about the large tree. *1:14*

WANG FUZHI: People see the hundred-pound gourd as large and the anti-chapping balm as small because they are entrapped in the uselessness of these things, and hence they can be neither far-reaching nor unfettered. If instead we go by the ways in which these things can be used, then each is far-reaching and each is unfettered. To "concentrate the spirit" means not to be startled by the large and not to be disdainful of the small. When things arrive, one resides right in the things themselves, treating them as they treat themselves. Heaven and earth are my chariot; the six atmospheric states are my mounts. What difference between the large and the small remains to entrap my mind as in the tangled weeds?

QU DAJUN: Zhuangzi's teaching is all about freedom and self-sufficient enjoyment. The transformations of Peng and Kun are a metaphor for the mind. The homeland of not-even-anything and the vast wilds of open nowhere are where the mind is to be lodged. Loafing and wandering, far-reaching and unfettered—these describe the utmost enjoyment of one's own enjoyment. Transforming the mind into Peng and Kun, transforming the body into the great Stink Tree—since he is already free of any fixed identity, what particular merit or name could there be? *1:15*

GUO XIANG: Every creature without exception considers itself right and the others wrong, praising itself and defaming others. It is in precisely this sense that, although each embraces a different definition of right and wrong, self and other are exactly equal. *2:1*

YUAN HONGDAO: Between heaven and earth there is nothing that is free of rights and wrongs. The world is a city of rights and wrong. The body and mind are a house of rights and wrongs. Wisdom, stupidity, worthiness, and worthlessness are the fruits of rights and wrongs. All of history is a deserted battlefield of rights and wrongs. The people of the world drown and float in rights and wrongs, wrongs and rights, clinging to their rotting remnants, like fat insects dangling from the ends of branches. They either follow along with whatever they happen to see or bark back like dogs at whatever they happen to hear. Thus, they hand their minds over to their own habits and their mouths to the crowd, angry when others are angry, praising when others praise—for these are the rights and wrongs of the ordinary man in the street. To support the ways of old and use them to make judgments on the present, to strive for sagacity and correct foolishness, to disdain the common and praise the elegant—these are the rights and wrongs of the man of culture. To hide away in remote valleys, running toward purity and avoiding defilement—these are the rights and wrongs of the hermit in the wilderness. To investigate names against realities, critique hollow honors, esteem regulation and responsibility, find fault with empty absurdities—these are the rights and wrongs of the Legalists.[4] To be rooted in ancient deeds of Humanity and Responsibility and narrate them forward, distinguish between the sage-king Yao and the tyrant Jie, model themselves on Zisi and Mencius, praise true kings and condemn dictators—these are the rights and wrongs of the Confucians. To dislike fullness and prefer retreat, to cut off wisdom and discard sagacity—these are the rights and wrongs of the Daoists. To pursue quiescence and the extinction of passions, take joy in compassion and renunciation, praise discipline and reject lust and rage—these are the rights and wrongs of the Buddhists. Through these different paths and diverse doors their contending courses are put forth, and even an ocean of ink could never exhaust their writings. Alas! Right and wrong run amok through the minds and dispositions of people, and they cling to these as Truth. All the theories and assessments made by the worthies and sages, Confucians and Mohists, are ultimately rooted in nothing more than this.

WANG FUZHI: There were many makers of theories[5] in those days, but the most prominent among them were the Confucians and Mohists, contending with each other over right and wrong, unwilling to admit defeat. Each understood only his own position, at the same time setting up the other as the opposite to which he is coupled. Thus did they exhaust themselves, not knowing how to turn back. Initially they were motivated by a desire to speak the Course—and indeed all of it was the Course. But in setting up their doctrines they agitated their own vital energies, and this agitated energy in turn came to pull their consciousness on and on, overflowing uncontrollably in all direc-

---

⁴ Late Warring States school of philosophy, emphasizing the strict enforcement of impersonal law and fulfillment of clearly defined duties, represented most completely in the works of Hanfeizi.

⁵ I.e., *lun* 論 (assessments), as in the title of the chapter.

tions. Then they felt compelled to have a theory about every thing, unconcerned about whether it accorded with the Course or not. Theories of things are what we use to *appropriate the things we come into contact with when our bodies open out to the world, the better to fit them all together.[6] But these can never really be made equal. If you try to use the Course to force equality on them, you will just be dragged down into their midst, one more contender forever crossing swords with all the others. Instead, just go along with their unleveled disarray and compliantly listen, allowing each *to come to its own spontaneous end.[7] Then you will know where they arise from and also whence they cease: they all depend on the mutual blowings of the vital energies of living human beings, artfully fashioned into various transformations. Then you will see that they are not worth arguing about. Just encompass them from your position in the center, where they have never-yet-begun-to-be; listen compliantly for them to return to their silence once the transforming wind has passed. All are then made equal. Then you can let "the broad daylight of Heaven" [2:16] be what illuminates them and "taking them all in your embrace" [2:33–34] be what hides them. Let "Walking Two Roads" [2:24] be the initiating impulse and "purity of fully formed maturation" [2:41] be what joins them. Discard what those others call illumination and instead adopt the Illumination of the Obvious [2:15], our Genuine Knowledge [6:5]. For in allowing them to arise as they will, you also allow them to come to an end as they will, so that you are neither the same as them nor different from them. Just making use of whatever comes along, keeping silent will then be all you need to do. But if you do happen to put forth words, they will limitlessly overflow, allowing you to fully live out your years—so it is equally acceptable to use any and all words just as you like. If you refrain from setting yourself up as the measure to be compared to the opposing counterpart, what theories of things, what assessments, are not made equal? This is how Zhuangzi is able to ride roughshod over all the other schools and go beyond them all.

LIU XIANXIN: This chapter begins by showing the spontaneous self-rightness of all things and goes on to show how self and other are both right. This is what is called *equalizing things. Later readers usually mistakenly think it instead to be about eliminating right and wrong. But the neither-nor attitude where both extremes are to be forgotten is really a Buddhist position. The main principle of Buddhism is Emptiness: nothing is wanted; all is to be abandoned. The main principle of Daoism is vastness: everything is wanted; all is to be included. The two are fundamentally different; how could they be forced into agreement?

---

[6] Based on Wang's reading of the sentence translated, "We give, we receive, we act, we construct."

[7] See Chapter 2, note 3.

2:2   WANG FUZHI: When Ziqi previously leaned against the table, he was dis-
puting about Confucianism and Mohism. Now he has disintegrated into it all,
forgetting what he was saying. Ziyou sees in him the mind that has lost its cou-
pling with an opposite and thus asks this question. For discourse arises from being coupled to an opposite. You see the other as different from yourself, like an
enemy in whose face you must not back down, so you are obliged to respond.
But having a counterpart comes from having a self: my own consciousness and
its opinions are set up as "this," and outside of "this" all becomes "that." "That"
can then be my double, my partner, the opposite to which I am coupled. A
theory may be as comprehensive as you like, but if we examine its origin and
realize that it is no more than one nook portioned off within the center of the
circle, then each creature is "I," for which reason nothing can be uniquely established as I. "Each creature is I"—the one who is capable of seeing it this
way can only be the Heavenly itself. Since every "I" is then the Heavenly, to
what opposite could I be coupled? Hence, when the me is lost, the counterpart is also lost, and vice versa. They vanish together, and then all the unequal
are made equal. Words are products of the understanding consciousness.
Where there are words there is a self, which takes up residence in the mind
like a glowing fire in the ashes. When there is a mind that is always on the verge
of speaking, it manifests in the physical form, like plants about to sprout in the
springtime. From such and such a form we know such and such a mind. The
"astonishment that forgets all about it" [1:13] is the same as the physical form
shown in Huzi's "Virtuosity that blocks everything out" [7:9].

YE BINGJING: "I lost me" corresponds to the "transformation of things" that
ends the chapter. Not viewing any things as existing, all transform to form a
single me. Not seeing any me as existing, the me is "lost" and identified with
all things.

2:3   FANG YIZHI: All things are "paired counterparts." Letting go of the paired,
will you then cling to the unpaired One? But the paired and the unpaired themselves form a pair. Letting go of this pair, where will you then stand? Will you
keep going on in this way, mistaking [a reflection] for your own head?[8] Or fall
into the indeterminate Emptiness of nonarticulated chaos? To see the one outside the two is to add an extra head on top of your own head. To cling to the two
and forget the one is to try to remain alive by cutting off your own head. Once
you have understood this, you will be able to hear all three of the pipings.

2:4   SHI DEQING: The long wind blowing through the hollows is merely a
metaphor for how the Great Course noncoercively creates all things and is scat-

---

8   A reference to a story in the *Śūraṅgama Sūtra*, a Buddhist scripture. A man sees his
own reflection, and noting that the man in the mirror has a head, while he, looking down at
his own body, has nothing comparable to be seen on his shoulders, goes mad and begins
searching for his own head.

tered into all people like the wind drumming forth the sounds of the hollows. Each person is endowed with a different physical form and thus their views are not the same, so their discourses are at odds with one another, just as the hollows, being large or small, deep or shallow, receive the wind in various degrees and thus give forth different tones, high and low, loud and soft, long or short. This is why even what the various theories have in common can never compel them to reach agreement. Thus, whenever the ancients sang something even faintly in the past, the harmonizers of the future make of it something loud and extensive. Each harmonizes with something formerly sung: different people follow different masters and traditions. The original singer is already dead, but the harmonizers follow up ceaselessly with further discussions; this is like the way *the grasses and trees continue to rustle even after the wind has stopped.⁹ But the one energy of Heaven's wind is rooted in spontaneity, utterly free of any calculating mind, and so it can also create words that are without any deliberate and fixed position—the words of the sage. Other people, however, perversely cling to their own views. Their words derive from the calculating mind, rather than the nondeliberate mind, and thus right and wrong appear. Hence, the text will go on to say, "Words are not wind," showing that the reason the theories of things are not equalized is because they speak entirely from the calculating mind and views of self, without realizing their error. This is the key to all the pronouncements people make. Once you understand this, you are able to see the equality of things.

GUO XIANG: Just this is the piping of Heaven. How could the piping of Heaven be some separate additional thing? It is just the hollows and the panpipes and the like, combined with all living beings, that collectively form the unity called Heaven. Since Nonbeing is what does not exist, it cannot produce Being. And whatever Being there is, before it has been produced, has no way to bring about its own production. So what is it that generates all becoming? All at once, each spontaneously self-generates. Self-generation does not mean being generated by me, the self. The self cannot generate things, and likewise things cannot generate the self. Thus, the self is "so of itself." What is so of itself is called what is so of Heaven. The Heaven-so is what is not deliberately created [by a self or by an other]. Hence, we use the word "Heaven" to indicate that they are self-so, spontaneously so. It does not refer to the blue sky above! And yet, some think the piping of Heaven forces creatures to follow and obey it. But Heaven cannot even possess itself—how could it possess creatures? Heaven is just a collective name for all things. Since no one specific thing is Heaven, who could be the master to be served by creatures? Each thing self-generates, without recourse to anything that goes beyond itself. This is the Course of Heaven.

2:5

---

⁹ Shi Deqing, like many commentators, interprets the line I have rendered "the tempered attunements, all the cunning contentions" as a reference to the swaying motion and fading sounds of the trees after the wind has stopped.

LÜ HUIQING: Before, when he was leaning against the table, he was in the phase of responding to all things. Leaning against the table now he is in the state of relinquishing all things. If one knows whence the self arises, then its loss or preservation never ceases to reside in oneself. Everyone has heard what bamboo panpipes sound like and knows that they are empty inside—a nothingness. That in the self that makes it the self is the same way. Is not the way the ten thousand openings howl and wail similar to the way we are when we belabor our minds and bodies with our concept of self? And is not the emptiness of these hollows similar to how we are when we have lost our "me," becoming like dried wood or dead ashes? He says, *"Have you not heard?" and *"have you not seen?" to tell Ziyou that, although he has seen and heard the starting and stopping of the piping of the earth, he has not yet perceived the arising and perishing of the mind. Using what has already been seen and heard to investigate what has not yet been seen and heard, the Piping of Heaven can be known.

WANG PANG: The wind cannot call forth sound where there are no hollows, just as the process of transformation cannot belabor us when we harbor no thing within us to belabor. If you can drop off the bonds of the body and let the biased inclinations of deluded thoughts vanish, the illuminating comprehension will penetrate everywhere, so that the "me" does not belong to the "I." You then enter the wondrous mystery, where Creation and Transformation can no longer constrain you.

LIU CHENWENG: Even when the counterpart is lost, the self may remain firmly in place. But once the self too is lost, whence can debates about things arise? Even if someone picks a fight with you, he finds no opponent facing him.

LU XIXING: The piping of Heaven makes no sound and yet is able to sound forth all the world's sounds. This is what is described later as "Seeming to have a genuine controller but peculiarly devoid of any manifest sign of it." [2:8–9] [. . . .] "Each hole selects out its own tone" means that there are all sorts of different sounds and each causes itself to emerge; they take it from themselves alone, not from Heaven. So who is rousing the hollows to their wail?

SHI DEQING: When the ten thousand tones emerge all at once in the piping of earth, the single incipient impulse of the wind calls forth a vast variety of notes and echoes, but there is no right or wrong among them. In the case of the piping of man, however twisted and curvy manmade bamboo panpipes may be, in the end they have no calculating mind of their own, so the text needn't say anything more about them. The piping of Heaven means that the words spoken by every human being originally derive from the inconceivable wonder of the Heavenly Impulse, but simply because of the extra addition of the concept of self, they make the calculating mind their master, and so see their words as different from the wind blowing through the trees in the piping of earth. For this reason right and wrong come into conflict with each other. If words emerge from someone in whom the calculating impulse has been forgotten, on the other hand, then there is no longer any conflict between acceptable and unacceptable—how then can there be any right and wrong there deriving from self and other?

TAO WANGLING: When the "I" possesses a "me," there is a paired counterpart. When the "I" has lost the "me," the paired counterpart is forgotten. It is from the pairing of counterparts that right and wrong emerge, and from the "me" that "this and that" take shape. The entire thrust of the chapter is revealed fully right here at the beginning.

XUAN YING: The howls arising in dependence on the wind are the piping of earth, while precisely the wind's allowing of the hollows to howl spontaneously of themselves is the piping of Heaven.

WANG FUZHI: Without the understanding consciousness, words cannot proliferate. Consciousness may be large or small, and its words will alter accordingly. The small is not independently small—it appears small only in contrast to the large. But likewise, the large cannot be large on its own—it appears large only when set against the small. So the idle and spacey is also cramped and circumspect; the bland and flavorless is also detailed and fragmented. The idle and spacey is used to criticize the small consciousness, ridiculing its narrowness. Conversely, the cramped and circumspect is used to interrogate the vast consciousness, exposing how much it leaves out. The bland and flavorless is used to catch what small speech fails to grasp. Conversely, the detailed and fragmented is used to accentuate the insubstantiality of big talk. Thus, words arise competitively on all sides, taking shape as theories. The unevenness of all existences is what the understanding consciousness selects from them for itself. But who or what is it from which consciousness itself emerges? The text goes on to interrogate this in detail. **2:6**

WANG FUZHI: This passage vividly describes the fermenting process by which the understanding consciousness comes to be, the ceaseless endings and beginnings of the transforming impulses that make up all endeavors to reach theoretical knowledge. [In sleep] the spirit converges on itself, but we don't know where consciousness has vanished to. [Upon awaking] the physical form opens outward, but we don't know where consciousness has come from. Sleeping and waking are both aspects of this one body, and the Consummate Person does not distinguish between them. But the makers of theories take the opportunity to operate when the waking consciousness appears and thus distinguish it from sleep. How could sleep be not-myself if waking is myself? Once the body opens outward, they *appropriate whatever they encounter and join them together into a system. Thus, they accept what they consider acceptable and reject what they consider rejectable, storing it away most securely and defending it with hearts full of fear. Once they start, they cannot be made to go back, exerting themselves to the utmost in debate, running down one path and **2:7** ignoring everything else, until their strength is exhausted and their consciousness is fettered, stopping only when enfeebled or dead. But in essence it never goes beyond the consciousness of a narrow crack through a wall, continuing thought after thought, pulled along from one word to the next, with no knowledge of where it all sprouts from. On the other hand, if you don't attempt to understand where they sprout from, you are lost in the eight moods listed here, obeying something as unfixed as music from empty holes and as rootless as mushrooms of billowing steam. For if there really is anything making them sprout, it should not be completely unknowable. But what makes them sprout? The text continues to inquire.

2:8   CHENG XUANYING: If the spontaneity of nature were not there, what could generate me? But if I were not there, what could receive the spontaneity of nature?

LIN YUNMING: Lacking the operation of the Heavenly Impulse, I would be unable to generate myself on my own power. Lacking something of me to access it, it would be incapable of generating me on its own power.

2:9   LIU XIANXIN: The spirit is present in all the hundred parts of the human body. For the spirit is originally an undifferentiated totality, belonging exclusively to no one part. Similarly, the Course in all things, like the wind in all the hollows, is exclusively partial to no one among them.

2:10   WANG FUZHI: Some say, since oneself and these others, the various mental states, are formed in mutual dependence, like the appearance of magnetic phenomena in the presence of both iron and a magnet, this means there is really no one element that makes them sprout. But this is perhaps not really so in this case, in that unless the self selects and appropriates them, these things cannot operate. However, even if we admit there is some doer, we are unable to discover who or what it is. If we claim there is nothing doing it, we find on the contrary that the emergence of incipient impulses always comes from a self, holding and defending always has some point of reference, disliking and being bound always derive from something stored up. So shall we say there is a genuine controller? *"It is believable after it begins operating,"[10] but prior to this it shows no sign. Some condition manifests, but it has no one fixed form, so this controller is not constant and thus is certainly not a genuine controller. Hence, we cannot establish a genuine controller as the doer who makes them sprout.

Or, since [consciousness] emerges only after the body opens outward, some suggest the body is the source of the sprouting. Now, the bones, orifices, and organs all have an effect on consciousness. Is it dispersed among them? Then a single person's body would contain many consciousnesses; the eye and

---

   10   Wang's reading of the phrase translated, "Its ability to flow and to stop makes its presence plausible."

ear would be unable to communicate; inner and outer would not correspond. If it's not dispersed among them, it must be lodged in one or the other as its controller, in which we should take special delight. So which among these organs, bones, and orifices is the controller, and which are the servants and concubines? Because of this difficulty, one might suspect that the genuine master is located *outside* of the physical body. But then these two would be devoid of the presence of the other, completely out of contact, unable to control or be controlled by each other. Such a one could not exert any control at all, much less be the genuine controller.

Seeking everywhere, no firm ground is found. Thus, since no one can ever know whence they sprout, in the end we must say there is no entity operating these sproutings. The transforming energies of Heaven rouse and provoke them, causing knowing consciousness and then words to appear. How could humans control it themselves? Heaven spontaneously takes a certain form, transformations spontaneously operate, the vital energy spontaneously proceeds, and whether we understand it or not has no effect on it. Is it not the height of foolishness to seek a determiner of right and wrong amid all this?

LÜ HUIQING: Joy, anger, and so forth indicate the differing moods and emo- tions coming forth. These are all examples of *"blowing forth the ten thousand differences, allowing each to come to its own end."[11] They are like music from hollows, mushrooms of billowing steam, alternating before us day and night, but without our knowing whence they sprout. This is the doing of the nondoing that is the piping of Heaven. Are not all the differences in size and incli- nation of the various capacities of living creatures similar to the different shapes of the hollows in the towering trees? Are not the various moods and emotions, the joy and anger and sorrow and pleasure, the openness and the crampedness, the nervous and the stunned, quite like the different sounds, the yeeeeeing and yuuuuing roused howling forth from them? Is not the unfindability of the place from which the sounds of hollows and the steam-mushrooms arise quite like *the quivering of the holes after the wind has passed, not revealing where it has vanished to? Seeing it this way, in what does my being "me" really reside? How is my body not like dried wood, my mind not like dead ashes? Indeed, Heaven's piping is so difficult to know, the genuine ruler so hard to see, that it is only by losing oneself, disintegrating to the point of making the mind merge into them, that they can be found. "It is through obtaining all this day and night that we come to exist" tells us simply to understand that no one knows whence they sprout and thus to make the state of our minds match and merge into that unknownness. Finding no manifest sign of it, seeing no definite form, we find no doer, nothing that moves them and makes it all so. Searching in vain for it everywhere among forms and bodies, we learn that it has never been present in any locus. But searching the body exhaustively for the agent that moves it

2:11

---

[11] See Chapter 2, note 3.

and makes it so in vain also shows us that a genuine ruler resides in it. Everyone has a genuine ruler within, but whether its real state is discovered or not neither aids nor harms it. It can be neither drawn closer nor pushed away, whether one is mindful of it or not.

LIU CHENWENG: Joy and pleasure are like music responding to the limitless openness of space, while the pent-up and constrained emotions are like cloudy mist congealing into mushrooms and plants. But both of these are spontaneously so of themselves.

LI ZHI: The wind is a vital energy without any palpable form. But to get stuck on it as a definite energy makes of it a mere thing rather than something spiritlike—how then could it bring such a tempered accord, such crafty contentions? It is in this way that we must also understand the piping of Heaven. For when the wind blows through things, the ten thousand differences certainly do come forth. But it just allows each to select out its own tone—even the wind itself does not know who is ultimately the blower! And this not knowing of who or what is precisely what is meant by the Heavenly.

2:12   CHENG XUANYING: A fully formed mind means any clinging to a one-sided biased viewpoint, limited to one range of emotions or stuck in one set of objects.

2:13   QIAN CHENGZHI: "Understanding the process of alternation" would mean for the mind to understand the alternations of day and night and then take it upon itself to select out something as the genuine ruler [controlling the alternations].

QIAN MU: Qian Chengzhi's explanation is correct. "Understanding the process of alternation" means the same thing as "understanding transformation." Understanding transformation means being free from the fully formed mind. *"The mind selecting out something of itself" means that a moment of cognition recognizes and appropriates a previous moment of cognition and erroneously clings to it as the genuine self [i.e., the genuine ruler]. So though a fool may not understand the whole process of transformation and hence is unable to let his consciousness transform freely, he is still able to select out and appropriate something to play the role of his own mind [as the genuine ruler]. It's just that in his case it becomes fully formed as one particular thing and is unable to transform.

2:14   GUO XIANG: What I call "this" and "right," the other sees as "that" and "wrong," and vice versa. Hence, it is said to be "unfixed." The unfixed instability comes from the one-sidedness of the sentiments of self and other.

2:15   GUO XIANG: What the Confucians and Mohists consider right is considering something right and considering something else wrong. Not considering anything right or wrong is what they consider wrong. So to affirm what they negate and negate what they affirm, we must illuminate the sense in which there is no right or wrong. The best way to do this is to use the Confucians and Mohists to illuminate each other, to see each in the light of the other. Then we see how what each affirms as right is also not right, and how what each considers wrong is also not wrong. The rights are not right and the wrongs are not wrong, so there is no right and no wrong.

LÜ HUIQING: The Course is everywhere, so all words are the Course. How could the Course be so obscured that some words are true and others are false? All things are the Course, so words are also the Course. How could words be so obscured that some are right and others wrong? Knowing that the Course is everywhere, where can you go and fail to find it present? Knowing all words are the Course, where could they be present and fail to be acceptable? But the apparent absence and unacceptability emerge when the Course is hidden in small accomplishments and successes, obscuring the great totality of which they are parts, and when words are hidden by the ostentatious blossoms of honor and reputation, obscuring the substantial root from which they grew.

WANG FUZHI: Every affirmation affirms something. Every course leads somewhere. All are moved by the vital energies of Heaven, so every affirmation can indeed be affirmed. Wherever the understanding consciousness may reach, all of it is within the Course. Some partial, some comprehensive, some left, some right, but every course can be seen as some part of the Course. Those who limit themselves to their understanding consciousness, making it into a fully formed mind, depending on whatever way their vital energy is roused, failing to understand how both alternatives are always at once acceptable and unacceptable, instead considering only one way right and one way wrong—these people take the small completions and successes of their understanding and opinions and make them into a theory. The Confucians and Mohists were the most prominent among them in Zhuangzi's time. They contended with each other in order to ornament their honor and renown, and the Course was thereby obscured, along with the kind of words that affirm both alternatives. But they call that which allows them to contend and debate about right and wrong with such certainty "illumination." Astutely they grasp and make use of it—but how could this be the genuine Illumination of the Obvious? The understanding consciousness resembles the Illumination of the Obvious, so the benighted mistake it for such. The Illumination of the Obvious is like the sun, and conscious understanding is like a lamp. The sun illuminates all without needing to be lit, but the lamp is sometimes lit and sometimes extinguished, and can only illuminate a single chamber, leaving in darkness whatever is far from the flame. But still they consider it illumination. Thus, the Confucians and Mohists all say they make use of illumination, holding fast to their little corner glow. Whatever they already understand they call right; whatever they don't yet understand they call wrong. How could the Course fail to be obscured?

2:16   WANG KAIYUN: This means going by the rightness alone, in order to transform the wrongness. What all the world affirms as right cannot be negated as wrong by the sage, but what all the world negates as wrong can be affirmed by him as right. The ignorant are hard to awaken, so one must first try to follow along with them. You must first affirm them all as right, and then you can eliminate all wrongness.

LIU XIANXIN: Going by the rightness of the present "this" means following along with each one, affirming it as right. What is eliminated is only the tendency for self and other to negate and criticize each other.

2:17   GUO XIANG: Right and wrong endlessly replace each other, over and over again, which is why they are here described as a circle. The center of the circle is empty. Now, by taking right and wrong as a circle, thereby locating the place in the center, we realize that there is no right and no wrong. For that very reason, we can respond to both right and wrong. Because right and wrong are endless, the responses to them are also endless.

MA QICHANG: Zhuangzi's teaching of "going by the rightness of the present 'this'" is nothing like Zimo's "clinging to the center."[12] Because it is without any fixed position, it is described as "Walking Two Roads." Because it is free of any opposition between the two poles, it is described as "opening them up into a oneness." Following along with the rightness and affirming it as right, my "self" is no longer brought into it. For it is from a sense of "rightness" that views of selfhood are born. Affirming that and negating this, a fixed position opposed to something else arises, and this is what is called "being coupled to an opposite." When "that" and "this" are no longer coupled as opposites, we are simply "going by the rightness of the present 'this.'" This is what makes the center of the circle so wondrous.

2:18   GUO XIANG: Each creature in the world affirms itself as "this" and negates all the others as "that." Hence, each this/right and each that/wrong Walks Two Roads inexhaustibly. Only those who cross into the emptiness to find the center, holding nothing in their hearts but a vast openness, can wander along riding upon them all.

ZHU XI: Laozi says, "It is because of its nonbeing that the wheel can function" [*Daodejing* 11]. "Nonbeing" here means the empty space at the hub of

---

12   Cf. *Mencius* 7A26:

Yangzi [Yang Zhu] chose self-interest: even if he could have benefited the world by plucking a single hair out of his body, he would not have done it. Mozi loved all equally; even if he had to scrape his body smooth from crown to heel to benefit the world, he would have done it. Zimo clung to the middle position between them. The middle position is almost right, but if you cling to the middle without the power to change with circumstance, it is no better than clinging to one of the extremes. What is hateful about clinging to one extreme is that it harms the Course. One thing is picked up and a hundred others are neglected.

the wheel. It is only because it is empty at the center that it can receive the spokes and turn endlessly. The same meaning is found here.

CAO SHOUKUN: A circle has no starting point; wherever you start to trace it from, whether curving to the left or to the right, it always returns to the original position. So the original position is not really the endpoint, and the starting point is not really the beginning. Whichever way you go, it is unobstructed, which means also that whichever way you go you have the center with you. Thus, it can follow along [with each point] and thus bring it to completion, responding to all without end.

GUO XIANG: To consider oneself right and the other wrong is the constant condition of both self and other. Thus the other's finger, compared to my finger as the standard, distinctly fails to be a finger. This is "using [this] finger to show that a finger is not a finger." Conversely, my finger, compared to the other's finger as the standard, spectacularly fails to be a finger as well. This is "using not-this-finger to show that a finger is not a finger." To illuminate the absence of right and wrong, nothing is more effective than understanding "this" and "that" in terms of each other, which shows that they are the same in their self-affirmation and other-disapproval. Since all are seen as wrong, nothing in the world is right. Since all are seen as right, nothing in the world is wrong. How can this be shown? If right were really right, it would have to be such that there could be no one in the world who could consider it wrong. If wrong were really wrong, no one in the world could consider it right. But in reality there is no standard of right and wrong; they are in complete chaos. When you understand this, even though each one believes only in his own narrow viewpoint, you see the consistency between them, their sameness. For it is the same wherever one looks, above and below. Thus, the Consummate Person knows that heaven and earth are one finger, and all things one horse. He finds everywhere only a vast overflowing tranquility, where every creature exactly occupies its own position, all the same in their self-attainment, free of right and wrong. 2:19

LIN XIYI: This means that there is no right and wrong in the world; right and wrong appear only as a result of "self" versus "other." But if even heaven and earth cannot be established, can there be any division between self and other?

SHI DEQING: To use my index finger to show that the other's middle finger is not my index finger is not as good as doing it from her perspective, that is, using her middle finger to show that my index finger is not her middle finger [. . . .] To use the other's black horse to show that my white horse is not his black horse is not as good as using his black horse to show that my white horse is not his black horse. By switching places like this to view the matter, there is no duality between fingers or between horses, and thus right and wrong naturally disappear.

FANG YIZHI: To cut down trees in the mountain is destruction, but to make a house from them is formation. To crush up herbs is to divide them, but to blend them together is the formation of a medicine. When you use an animal's tendons and horns to make a bow, the bow is formed but the tendons and horns are destroyed. Viewing the entire situation, there is neither formation nor destruction, so they are opened up and connected into a oneness. In the sense that the full realization of the Human is precisely the Heavenly, there is still the principle that there are some things that can and should be formed and others that can and should be destroyed. Can we then say that this principle falls into neither formation nor destruction? Cunning wisdom clings to the way the roundness destroys the squareness, not realizing that it is really precisely the roundness that makes use of the squareness. Not realizing that it is the roundness that makes use of the squareness, have you really connected them [into a oneness]? And if you do not further know that the square *is* itself the round, can you be said to have realized [what this "making use of" means]? Fan Zhongan said, "When the hands function at full force, the whole body is present in your two hands. What distinction is there then between the left hand and the right? And yet, the liver is never mixed up with the kidney, nor the lungs with the spleen: their order of interconnection remains perfectly clear." Try looking in Fuxi's diagrams [in the *Book of Changes*] for the way "Walking Two Roads" manifests throughout the entire body, so that they "connect to form a oneness." The fisherman, the woodcutter, the farmer, the shepherd: each rests firm in his own role. The cold freezes; the heat burns: each extends through the scope of its own utmost activity. Some start out gradually from a certain beginning, intensifying until they come to be precisely the opposite of what they started as, and yet each phase comes at its own proper time. In some the inside separates from the outside, until the inside and outside turn around and come together again, and yet each function still has its own determinate role. Is this not what "Equalizing Assessments of Things" means by saying that "heaven and earth are one finger"? Quite clearly these are not cases of something dying off completely and subsequently being born again. To call it merely a "finger" is really just said in jest.

QIAN MU: This means that to stand in my position to understand that he is not me is not as good as standing in his position to understand that I am not him.

2:20   SHI DEQING: Each thing has a certain genuine rightness to it. For example, in medicine there is ginseng and bird-beak powder. When ginseng is to be used, bird-beak powder is not right; when bird beak is to be used, ginseng is not right. This is what it means to say that each thing has a certain real rightness.

2:21   SHI DEQING: It is like carving up a great tree to make wooden vessels. To the trees it is fragmentation, but to the vessels it is completion, so its fragmentation is precisely a completion. Although the vessel is completed, the tree is destroyed. Thus, how could we cling to a single fixed view of what is completion and what is destruction?

LIN XIYI: Completion and destruction are the way things impinge on one 2:22 another. But without destruction there is no completion, and without completion there is no destruction. For example, when a mountain tree is cut down, it is destruction, but when it is then used to make a house, it is the completion of something. It is like the preparation of medicines: grinding and gnawing them is division, which allows them to mix and combine to form the right medicine. Archery bows can be made from animal horns and tendons: to the bow it is completion; to the horns and tendons it is destruction. If the Qin dynasty did not fall, the Han dynasty could not have risen; though it was completion to the Han, it was destruction to the Qin. From this point of view, there is from the beginning no pure completion, which means there is also no real destruction. Thus, they open into one another and connect to form a oneness.

HU YUANJUN: "Laboring his spirit trying to make all things one" is a refer- 2:23 ence to Huizi.

JIAO HONG: *"Not using" means not using his own viewpoint. "Entrusting 2:24 it to the everyday function of each being" means going by the viewpoints of others. "The everyday function" means the sustainable ordinary activities of other people[. . . .] For each thing when actively functioning opens up into others, and when not actively functioning becomes an obstruction[. . . .] In sum, it's all about "going by," following along with, these beings. If the meaning of this is unclear, consider the monkey keeper. He neither added to nor subtracted from the number of chestnuts on his own initiative, but rather "went by" the joy or anger of the monkeys to adjust the distribution. Was he not "going by" them? Thus, the sage externally goes by others, making use of all sorts of rights and wrongs to harmonize with them, but internally he embodies Heaven the Potter's Wheel, free of all rights and wrongs. He doesn't let the rights and wrongs that are the traces of his actions obstruct his mind's freedom from rights and wrongs. Thus, he is described as "Walking Two Roads."

QIAN CHENGZHI: The Course opens them up into one another to form a oneness. But only someone who is skilled at following along with them is able to make use of the twoness rather than the oneness. For the oneness is lodged in the twoness.

CAO SHOUKUN: "Walking Two Roads" means that whichever way it may turn, right or left, from the center of the circle, it always returns back to the same point.

GUO XIANG: This means to forget heaven and earth and let all things go. 2:25 Outside, they were unaware of space and time; inside, they were oblivious to their own existence. Hence they were open and unfettered, able to move along with all things, responding to each and all.

WANG FUZHI: To have boundaries between them means things are things and 2:26 the self is the self, period. Neither self nor its opposing counterpart can then ever disappear. You are then roused by the vital energies, lacerated by things and grinding against them in all their rights and wrongs. One is then no better off than Song Rongzi. When there are separate things, there will be dependence. One is then no better off than Liezi [1:8]. This is to be limited to the known, unable to reach the state of the Heavenly, where there have not yet begun to be any things. Since something is unreached, there is a waning, an incompleteness.

2:27   GUO XIANG: Possible sounds are innumerable. Hence, however many hands the blowers of flutes and the strummers of strings may deploy, most of the possible sounds are always left out. But the very reason they take hold of their flutes and pluck their strings is to make sound manifest in its fullness. When they present a certain sound, some sounds are left out. When they present no sound, all sounds are intact. So to have something fully formed which also creates a waning, *let Zhao play his zither. To have nothing fully formed and nothing waning, *let him not play his zither.

LIN XIYI: He has already described the principle of waning and fullness, but now the example of playing the zither explains it most precisely. If you take your zither and strum it, any given tune you play will naturally have a beginning and end. But this "beginning and end" are really only born after the strumming begins; if you do not strum, where is there any beginning or end? This is like a moment of human thought: if it does not arise, there is no sameness or difference between being and nonbeing, self and things.

SHI DEQING: Zhao Wen was skilled at playing the zither; this was the waxing full—the complete accomplishment, the perfection and success—of the family's vocation. But his son was not skilled at playing the zither; this was the waning of the family's reputation. The idea here is that if he had not initially had the ambition to earn a reputation for zither playing, his son would not have been able to ruin that reputation.

FANG YIZHI: Zhuangzi was originally just raising two questions, two parallel doubts. Whether the zither is played or not, sound retains its original intactness. What obstruction is there then between full formation and waning? Guo Xiang only got half of the point.

2:28   LIN XIYI: If any deed is considered rightly done in accordance with what its own abilities are, then whatever I happen to be capable of at this moment can also be called rightly done. But if we go by the fact that the deed of the present moment is also in some sense or other not yet rightly done, then nothing done by myself or anyone else in the world is rightly done. "Fully accomplished" here means "rightly done."

LI ZHI: Why do I say these three were not fully accomplished, even to the end of their days? Because Zhao Wen did not know how to slump on a desk, and Huizi did not know how to wave a baton.

HU YUANJUN: If you could really make things obvious to those for whom they are not obvious, and call this being fully accomplished, then everyone would be fully accomplished. But actually both myself and each other creature can only understand what is obvious to ourselves, which we can never really make obvious to others. If the fact that what is obvious to me is not obvious to others is called failure to be fully accomplished, then no one is fully accomplished.

LÜ HUIQING: The Course is everywhere, so all things are the Course, and 2:29 there are no things outside the Course. This is why the ancients took it that there were no things: they took each thing as the Course. When knowledge rests in this, it has reached its utmost. Next, there were those for whom there were things, but no boundaries between them. They couldn't yet see each thing as the Course, but they could use the Course to open up a connection between things. Next were those for whom there were boundaries, but still no rights or wrongs. They couldn't yet use the Course to open up a connection between things, but they were able to dismiss all things so as to come together with the Course.

ZHAO YIFU: It is from drifting chaos and doubt-wracked confusion that the illumination emerges. This alone is esteemed by the sage.

SHI DEQING: This passage concludes a point that has been building up from a long way back. The first level of the discussion runs from "human speech is not just a blowing of air" [2:14] to "if you want to affirm what they negate and negate what they affirm, nothing compares to the Illumination of the Obvious" [2:15]. The second level begins with "When this axis finds its place in the center" [2:17] and ends with the next "nothing compares to the Illumination of the Obvious" [2:19]. The term "The Course" is finally revealed as the living eye of the whole chapter in the next section, running from the discussion of fingers and horses, showing how the Course opens up through them to make them one, up until, "Such a person would not define rightness in any one particular way but would instead entrust it to the everyday function [of each being]" [2:23]. Next comes the story of the monkeys [2:24], which shows—by means of its allusion to "causing no loss [i.e., 'waning']"—how the waning of the Course was the full forming of the cherishing of one thing over another. This full forming [i.e., "completion," "success"] finally reveals the meaning of the term "fully formed" in the earlier references to *taking "what you have received [i.e., the body] as fully formed" [2:11] and following "whatever has so far taken shape, fully formed, in our minds, making that our teacher," [2:12]. The meaning is that preferential cherishings wax full when the received body is taken as something fully formed, and this brings the waning of the Course. This is what it means for there to be fullness and waning. *If one follows one's fully formed mind as teacher, on the other hand, there is originally no fullness or waning.[13] It is because one takes the body one receives as fully formed that there come to be debates and disputes, and right and wrong wax bright. Thus, the whole chapter revolves around [the contrast of] the two terms "the fully formed body" and "the fully formed mind" [2:11–12]. The obscuring of the Course in small completions and of words in the ostentatious blossoms of reputation all come from failure to awaken to the Great Course. So the text first hints at it by saying, "nothing compares to the Illumination of the Obvious," goes on to discuss "the Course as Axis," after which it repeats that "nothing compares to the Illumination of the Obvious." Here it finally gets to the bottom of the matter, concluding with the discussion of fullness and waning. The first benighted one to be referenced is Huizi, whose insistent debates on "hardness" and "whiteness" blighted his life to the end of his days. Hence the concluding passage points to the sage in the Radiance of Drift and Doubt [2:29]— that is, a person who does not consider himself to be in the right. The whole thing concludes with the one who "really gets all the way through them, who does not define any one thing as right, but rather entrusts himself to the everyday function [of each being]," and thus ends with, "This is what I call the Illumination of the Obvious." The passage starts all the way back at "Human speech is not just a blowing of air" and doesn't reach its completion until seven hundred or so characters later. The prose and meaning here are like a snake slithering through the grasses: you see only some shaking and swaying of the grass, but not the snake's body. Only those with eyes for this will be able to discern it. In the discussion of the fullness and waning of three masters, Zhao Wen's family profession had its fullness and waning, Master Kuang's physical body had its fullness and waning, and Huizi's course had its fullness and waning. This is meant to tie together the earlier comments on the Course being obscured by small completions and words by ostentatious reputation.

WANG FUZHI: What those others call illumination is not the Illumination of the Obvious. The understanding consciousness, whether idle and spacey or cramped and circumspect, contends over large and small within the so-called wisdom of a single nook and corner. The Radiance of Drift and Doubt, conversely, hands them all over to their own everyday functions, free of rights and wrongs, fullness and waning. It "takes all that [one's] understanding consciousness knows and unifies it into a singularity," [5:10] and this is the Genuine Knowledge [6:5]. Only then can it be called using the Illumination of the Obvious. For the Radiance of Drift and Doubt basks Heaven the Potter's Wheel in the Heavenly Illumination. Vague! Obscure! Such a mind can never be-

---

13   Note that Shi Deqing, like many interpreters, takes "the fully formed mind" to be something Zhuangzi is praising, identifying it with the Buddhist idea of original enlightenment. Others, including myself, take it to mean something like "biased, prejudiced mind" and thus is something being critiqued. But Shi's point about the importance of the trope of the "fully formed" in this chapter is undeniable.

come fully formed in the image of its own convictions. Dark and dim is its drift; floating and ubiquitous is its doubt. And thus its radiance shines everywhere. For when preferential attachments take shape, the Course wanes, and thus is it that the Course can never wax full. But the waning of the Course is really just the waning of these creatures themselves, with no effect on the reality of the Course, so at the same time we can say that it never wanes. Theories proliferate promiscuously, authoritative doctrines take shape one by one, and this brings on the waning of the Course. Hence no words anywhere in the world are really right. But they are all roused and moved within Heaven the Potter's Wheel, availing themselves of the incipient impulses of the vital energies to begin and end on their own, without affecting its reality. Thus, we can Walk Two Roads [2:24], and each everyday function can be lodged in temporarily. Hence, no words in the world can really be considered wrong. With neither right nor wrong, making use of whatever we may lodge in, either the successful formation of complete accomplishment or its total lack is acceptable, and every drift and every doubt is already radiant. Doubting both the Confucians and Mohists, so both are seen to be wrong, what theories of things, what assessments, fail to be equalized? "The wise do not speak; the good do not dispute" [*Daodejing* 81]. But to both speak and dispute, and yet remain free of both speech and dispute—that is what makes one a sage.

LIN XIYI: This passage grows out of the word "this" in the preceding statement: "He makes no definition of what is *this/right" [2:29]. Hence he says here, "I don't know if it belongs in the same category as 'this' or not." Such is the living pulse in Zhuangzi's every choice of words. Earlier he said, "Words are not just blowings of air"; here he turns around and hollers forth this phrase, "I now want to try to say something about 'this,'" which is another example of the living pulse that links the before and after of his prose. If the similar and the dissimilar put themselves in the others' shoes, looking at themselves from the perspective of the other, the similar and the dissimilar become similar. The meaning is basically that if I can see the other as myself and see myself as the other, then I can see how the other is the same as me. Hence, he says, "there is nothing to distinguish it from *the other." This is the meaning of "using a finger to show a finger" and "using a horse to show a horse." 2:30

WANG FUZHI: Here he wishes to disclose his main point but refutes it in advance to show that it is not to be taken as any one definite theory, lest it become something fully formed. This is another example of the Radiance of Drift and Doubt. "Let me try to say it" refers to the passage starting "There is a beginning." "This" refers to the Course. He says "this" rather than "the Course" because to use the term "the Course" for whatever course one has personally experienced creates a self and sets up a genuine Course in opposition to the courses of the Confucians and Mohists, thus establishing an opposing counterpart. So instead he points to whatever is illumined obviously right here before him—"this"—with neither counterpart nor name, an exemplar of drift 2:31

and doubt, but lodged in the everyday function, and calls it "this." Since "this" is present wherever one may go, there is nothing that is "that." All existences and nonexistences in the world are alike called "this," so "this" and "that" are no longer coupled as opposites. But since one is speaking, even if one's words perfectly accord with "this," it is still basically similar to the words of the Confucians and Mohists. Only silence would be dissimilar to them, similar only to the Course. No speech can ever be quite right. To speak as the text proceeds to do is still to say something. But this assertion, pushed to its ultimate, peculiarly arrives at the nonexistence of nonexistence, so although it says something, it also certainly says nothing. It cannot be compared to those who set up theories on the basis of minds fully formed through the blowing of the vital energy's impulses. Hence saying something is here saying nothing—a drift and doubt without any need to take a definite form. Thus even speaking here becomes acceptable.

2:32   CHENG XUANYING: Different creatures are born with differing forms and energies, some large and some small, some long-lived and some short-lived. But in terms of their being precisely what it is their nature to be, each is itself sufficient to the task. So if we take being sufficient to its own nature as the standard of bigness, nothing in the world is bigger than an autumn hair. If we take having no excess going beyond its nature as the standard of smallness, nothing in the world is smaller than Mt. Tai. If Mt. Tai is small, nothing in the world is large. If an autumn hair is large, nothing in the world is small. The same applies to a long life span and a short life span. For this reason, although heaven and earth are vast, the nature of each being just what it is, and hence affirming itself as right, is equal in both. Although things are diverse, they are equal in that each by nature affirms itself; the sense in which each being is exactly capable of being just what it is is the same for each. The previous section showed how there is no beginning and no end, no Being and no Nonbeing. This passage shows how there is no large and no small, no longevity and no early death.

LIN XIYI: The idea here is that once you have named some particular thing an autumn hair, if it becomes slightly bigger it can no longer be called that autumn hair. If Mt. Tai gets slightly smaller, it can no longer be called Mt. Tai. If you take Mt. Tai as big, you find that heaven and earth are even bigger, so Mt. Tai can also be called small. To use the name "dead child" is to set a quantitative limit on what counts as "dead child." Someone who lives a little longer then cannot be called "dead child." Although Pengzu is considered an exemplar of longevity, compared to heaven and earth, he too died young. If you examine these two lines carefully, you find that they are the same as "Can this be called success, being fully accomplished at something? In that case, even I am fully accomplished. Can this be called failure, the lack of full accomplishment of something? If so, neither I nor anything else can be considered fully accomplished" [2:28]. When you can see it this way, even things as large as heaven and earth are born together with you within the vastness of space, so heaven and earth are not really big. All things are born together with me between heaven and earth, so each plant, each tree, each bird, each worm is similar to me, of the same type as me. Hence he says, "Heaven and earth are born together with me, and the ten thousand things and I are one."

SHI DEQING: This last sentence is extremely difficult to understand. For the previous passage already brought the discussion back to the Great Course, and here the Great Course is used to unify right and wrong. The idea is that if we view limited forms from the perspective of limited forms, large and small, long-lived and short-lived are all definitely fixed and unchangeable. But if we instead view limited forms from the perspective of the Great Course, then although the tip of an autumn hair is small, its substance is none other than the entire vastness of all space, while Mt. Tai, as a limited form, is merely a pebble in the vastness of space. Thus, nothing is bigger than an autumn hair, and Mt. Tai is small. Although a dead child is short-lived, he remains the same as his source in the beginningless, while Pengzu is just one brief event in the span of beginninglessness. So none live longer than a dead child, and Pengzu died young. If we look at all things from the perspective of the Course in this way, then the small is not small, the large not large, the short-lived not short-lived, and the long-lived not long-lived. Thus heaven and earth have the same root and all things share a single body. What right or wrong could there be among them?

LÜ HUIQING: It is because people do not understand whence thoughts of   2:33
self and other and of right and wrong begin that they are unable to discard self and other or forget right and wrong. To understand the principle indicated here, you must observe the beginning of thoughts. Hence, he says, "There is a beginning." But the beginning originally has no place from which it comes to be, and this itself is precisely how things begin. Hence he goes on to say, "There is a not-yet-beginning," in order to eliminate any idea that there is something it all comes from. But even when this is eliminated, it is still not really gone; it continues to exist simply as the indeterminate "what it all comes from." So he continues on to say, "There is a not-yet-beginning-to-not-yet-begin-to-be-a-beginning," thus eliminating the idea that there is a "something" to be eliminated. Now there is neither anything it all comes from nor anything to be eliminated, so whatever arises in my mind comes as a sudden attainment, showing me that whatever exists now emerges in its entirety from nothing at all. Once I know this, survival or destruction are in my own hands. If I want it gone, I just do not give rise to it. Indeed, neither something from which it emerges nor a definite nothing can be found, which is why you must awaken to it in the space of a single turn of the head, when it suddenly comes together in all its clarity. Hence, he says, "Suddenly there is Nonbeing." It is impossible to tell which is Being and which is Nonbeing, which allows us to forget words and thus attain a state of mind that matches and merges into [that state of indeterminacy].

Nonetheless, what I have now said has also never gotten at any *thing*, so how could I tell the difference between saying something and saying nothing, between meaning and meaninglessness? This allows us to see that words have never said anything, have nothing they speak of. Indeed, once I know whence my mind arises, for me an autumn hair, Mt. Tai, a dead child, Pengzu, and all things between heaven and earth arise from this same place. Then how could large or small, long or short duration, have any constant substance? If there is me, there is heaven and earth—so heaven and earth are generated together with me. If there is no me, the ten thousand things are also gone—so I am one with all things.

QIAN MU: "Not going anywhere" means that both myself and others rest in our own allotments, for that is what is meant by "going by the rightness of the present 'this.'" It is also what is meant by coming to rest within [the center of] Heaven the Potter's Wheel.

2:34   CHENG XUANYING: Sheltering and protecting all types of creatures, his love is ubiquitous but free of any deliberate intent to be so. It is like the arrival of a verdant springtime, which is not deliberately practicing the virtue of Humanity.

2:35   GUO XIANG: These five are all examples of how deliberate activity harms the rightness of things. Unable to rest in their original natures, they seek something outside themselves. To seek outside for what cannot be gained by seeking is compared to a circle trying to imitate a square, or a fish emulating a bird. Although one may hope to emulate the flight of a pair of phoenixes and model oneself on the sun and the moon, as "this" gets closer, "that" gets more remote. The more you attain through your accurate imitation, the more you lose your own nature. The fetters of such one-sided esteem can be removed by the equalizing of all things.

2:36   CHENG XUANYING: It is like a mirror suspended high in a chamber, reflecting whatever comes before it. Where the awareness comes from is unknown to itself. We can call this a reflecting that is at the same time a forgetting, a forgetting that can also reflect things.

SHI DEQING: This gives the conclusion to the previous passage beginning with "The understanding of the ancients really got all the way there" [2:25].

2:37   JIAO HONG: The Shadowy Splendor means a knowledge that is nonetheless a nonknowledge.

WANG FUZHI: Hiding it in his embrace makes its splendor shadowy. To shade it does not mean to border and partition it off, relying on it as one's own private Virtuosity. Rather, all are included within one's own sheltering shade. This is called the Heavenly Reservoir. Since I am Heaven's reservoir, Heaven cannot make a piping of me, blowing forth from me a crowing. Its radiance cannot be used to show it to others. It is chaotic and uncategorizable—hence it is adrift. It can be either this or that, is neither this nor that, having nothing fully formed as its teacher—hence it is doubt. Embracing the drift and doubt in your own shade so as to include the illumination of Heaven is called the Shadowy Splendor. Knowing all, not-knowing all, [conscious of everything but without "understanding" it,] this is what is called "the understanding consciousness coming to rest in what it doesn't understand." With neither self nor counterpart, one cannot be trumpeted and drummed forth by the impulses of the vital energies.

ZHAO YIFU: When understanding rests in nonunderstanding, no name can be affixed to it; thus does *the Course arrive in you. When you can understand this, you become empty within. This is called the Heavenly Reservoir, which means that from which all things emerge. "Poured into without ever getting full, ladled out of without ever running out"—this refers to its endlessness. "Ever not-knowing its own source" means it is continuously renounced together with our knowledge of it. "Shadowy Splendor" means its illumination derives from its darkness.

JIAO HONG: When the Course is made explicit, when words demonstrate something, when Humanity is made constant, when rectitude is pure and courage is bold, their corners stick out, coming close to squareness. "Square" here means "bordered." Alas! The world knows that nonknowing is perfection but does not know that not to know and yet thereby to know is even greater. This is what is meant by demonstration without words, the Course that is not a course. Here, Being is precisely Nonbeing, form is precisely emptiness—is that not the unfillable that is ever poured into, the inexhaustible that is ever ladled out of: the Heavenly Reservoir? One never knows where it all comes from. The Shadowy Radiance is precisely this knowing without knowing.

WANG FUZHI: When the ten suns shone, there was no this and that, no large 2:38 and small, no right and wrong. The Radiance of Drift and Doubt does not derive its illumination from laboring the spirit trying to make things one. The sun in the heavens is the everyday function lodged in by Heaven. Virtuosity is Heaven's Reservoir, which can lodge also in ten suns. If Yao insists on comparing right and wrong with these three who are dwelling in the grasses and brambles, he is just another bit of grass and bramble himself.

SHI DEQING: He cannot be understood in terms of benefit and harm. 2:39

LÜ HUIQING: The Course cannot be known, which is why knowing knows 2:40 it not while nonknowing knows it. This shows just what kind of entity the Course is! Now, human beings take the places of comfort and ease known by their bodies as the right place to dwell, the flesh of livestock known by their mouths as the right thing to eat, and the beautiful shapes known by their eyes as the right sexual partners, just as eels and monkeys have their places of comfort, snakes and hawks have their delectables, and fish and birds and deer all have their own kinds of mates as counterparts. "This" and "that" each takes its own understanding as the standard of correct knowing. So how could whatever is known by humans or any other creature tell us anything about the real right dwelling place, right flavor, or right sexual beauty? Truly, it is because no right dwelling, flavor, or beauty can be known that we can know that what we know about these things is never "right."

ZHU BOXIU: Previous commentators have failed to explain what it is that all things have in common. In my opinion, what both humans and all creatures have in common is the inborn nature, while they differ in their biased dispositions. When the inborn nature degenerates into the dispositions, each creature affirms itself as right, "this" and "that" embrace their one-sided views, fingers and horses are used to criticize one another as wrong. Their assessments all differ, creating hatred and disparagement; their disputes go to extremes, giving rise to conflict and struggle. Finally, even liver and gallbladder regard each other as if they were the distant states of Chu and Yue, and fathers and sons treat each other like strangers on the street. In actuality, it all comes from one thing: the understanding consciousness, which senselessly produces these distinctions. So Wang Ni's three responses of "How could I know that?" were meant to provoke Nie Que to seek the nonknowing in himself and thus find the inborn nature, which is what is so of all creatures, vanishing into the principle of the Great Openness. This is close to it, but fearing the other still might not get it, he followed up by showing the different things suitable to humans, birds, and animals, the nonrightness of each dwelling, flavor, and form of sexual beauty. This being the case, how could what is called knowing truly be knowing, or what is called nonknowing truly be nonknowing?

2:41   GUO XIANG: "Pure" means unmixed. Taking part in the diversity of ten thousand harvests, present to all their changes—most people would call this being very mixed indeed. Hence, they slavishly labor their bodies and terrorize their minds, trying to get rid of one thing and going after some other thing. Only the great sage, because he is free of attachments, moves directly forward like an oblivious sprouting-forth, one with every transformation. One with every transformation, he roams always in the Singular. So although he may mix and participate in a hundred thousand different harvests, a thousand differences and ten thousand diversities, past and present form a single fully formed maturation, as a course is formed by walking it. All things are a single rightness, each is just "so," as things are made thus by calling them thus. Each thing is thus; each time is perfectly formed: this is what is here called purity.

LIN XIYI: "Each thing is just so, each thing is right," for each thing affirms whatever is so of it, each person has her own private opinion. So from heaven to earth and from ancient times to the present, they have piled up limitless affirmations, limitless "thises," limitless "rightnesses." Thus, it says, *"Heaping up [enfolding] affirmations." "Heaping up" here means they pile on top of one another, press one another down.

WANG FUZHI: All makers of theories pursue order—are they unaware that the world is fundamentally a chaotic drift? They all pursue illumination—don't they know that the world is fundamentally a murky mush? They seek order and illumination and call this Humanity and Responsibility, demonstrating them as right against wrong. But in essence right and wrong are nothing but benefit and harm. However, what this one calls benefit that one calls harm, and vice versa. There is no single constant standard of benefit and harm, but when the understanding consciousness makes a master of what has fully formed in the mind, it refuses to be constrained to its own domain, delighting in one thing and rejecting another, honoring what it delights in and looking down on what it rejects, thus leading to ceaseless conflicts. Now, a slave is looked down on by people, but every slave has something he excels at which makes him honored among his own class, so he too is always honorable. What space is there for words, either the bland and flavorless or the detailed and fragmented [2:6], in trying to make sense of Humanity and Responsibility, or right and wrong? How could there be any constancy to the distinctions made in debates about benefit and harm, right and wrong? Sometimes they change in a day, sometimes in a month, but within several decades they will certainly change, within a hundred years they will certainly change quite greatly, and in a thousand years the old will be replaced entirely.

ZHANG BINGLIN: The metaphor of dreaming and waking does not mean   2:42 that life is a dream and death is an awakening. The great awakening from the great dream means that one knows life to be a dream, and thus one does not seek long life, but equally one knows that both life and death are dreams, and so one does not seek the quiescence of death either.

LÜ HUIQING: The sage knows nothing of benefit or harm, so he neither   2:43 seeks nor avoids anything. He is ever satisfied, so he seeks no happiness. He knows everything is the Course, so he follows no specific course. His saying something is how he says nothing, and his saying nothing is how he says something. It is only his complete freedom from fixed intentions that allows him to be thus. Ju Quezi had heard that Confucius took it to be rude and careless talk, while he himself regarded it as depicting the practice of the Mysterious Course, but both of them were wrong. For the Course is conveyed by neither speech nor silence. A rooster is produced from an egg, but an egg is not a rooster. Roast fowl is obtained with a crossbow pellet, but a crossbow pellet is not a roast. Similarly, the Mysterious Course is obtained through what one learns, but what one learns is not the Mysterious Course.

WANG PANG: "Shoulder to shoulder with the sun and moon" means he makes a unity of day and night. "Scooping up time and space" means he equalizes far and near.

WANG FUZHI: We delight in life because of the consciousness that comes with life. But consciousness has no support as soon as life ends—not to speak of ten thousand years later. When conscious of the pleasure of drinking wine, we are unconscious of the sorrow of weeping. When conscious of the sorrow of weeping, we are unconscious of the joy of hunting. When one opens outward, the other converges inward, so the joy and the sorrow obscure each other. So how could we know anything about the ten thousand years that follow our own deaths? But then there is no reason to delight in life or hate death. It is not only the transforming sounds that are blown forth by the vital energy of Heaven; all the functions of our organs and bones, including the wondrous consciousness of our minds, are merely transformations of the impulses of the vital energy. When consciousness reaches this point, life and death are forgotten, and benefit and harm become insignificant. Once benefit and harm are forgotten, right and wrong vanish as well, and Humanity and Responsibility can no longer survive either. When Humanity and Responsibility perish, the success and failure of theories has no fixed measure. By means of the chaotic drift and murky mush you can pay heed to the unknowability of those ten thousand years. This is what is meant by "the understanding consciousness coming to rest in what it does not know" [2:36].

2:44 SHI DEQING: The living pulse of Zhuangzi's writing integrates it from top to bottom, like an underground spring. This chapter speaks laterally and vertically, up and down and back and forth, for over three thousand characters, finally arriving at this one word "other" to conclude it. What power it has! Looking back to the beginning of the discussion, with its subtle hints about a "genuine ruler," we find that he said there merely that "without an other there is no me," making this word "other" the ruling principle of the discussion. At the end here the phrase "wait for yet some other" is suddenly and boldly thrown forth. When you see to the bottom of the workings involved here, the transformations of this kind of prose are understood in all their inconceivable spiritual marvel.

2:45 GUO XIANG: The disputes about right and wrong are what are here called the transforming sounds. Since their dependence on one another is not sufficient to allow any one of them to straighten out any other, it is tantamount to no dependence at all.

SHI DEQING: The sudden appearance of something from nothing is called a "[magical] transformation." "Transforming voices" describes things like the echoes in a mountain valley. The idea is that if we contemplate sounds as if they were echoes in an empty valley, free of all biased emotional consciousness, what right and wrong would there be to them? This line ties together the earlier discussion of the piping of the earth, where the long wind through the hollows brought forth all the varying tones and harmonies: all were "transforming voices." If we contemplate the words of human beings as being like the sounds blown forth from the hollows, there will be no clinging to right and wrong. Right and wrong derive from words that emerge from a calculating mind, which thus competitively cling to the rights and wrongs of self against other. At the beginning of the discussion, he said, "human speech is not just a blowing of air" [2:14], introducing the question of right and wrong. Now, the chapter on equalizing things has reached its end, so it must bring us back to the piping of the earth. So here it says, *"The transforming sounds depend on it." This is the completion of the work of equalizing things. If words and sounds come forth like the piping of the earth, they emerge from the Heavenly innocence of becoming, completely free of any calculating intentions, and this is the genuine piping of Heaven. Looking back at the original description of the piping of the earth, it was a thunderous, earth-shaking passage—now it reaches its final conclusion in this very lightly touched-off little phrase, *"The transforming sounds depend on it." What a spirit was in that breast, what thinking, what endlessly changing literary power—that writing can reach such heights is truly beyond comprehension.

GUO XIANG: Forgetting what year it is, life and death are mysteriously uni-   2:46
fied. Forgetting what should or should not be, right and wrong are threaded onto a single string. The shaking loose of right and wrong, life and death, to form a oneness is the utmost guideline. The utmost guideline pervades unobstructedly without end, and thus one who entrusts herself to it is never able to be brought to halt.

LIN XIYI: When both the year and what should be are forgotten, you are jostled and shaken, drummed and agitated into dancing motion, in the realm where there are no things. This "jostled and shaken" means the same thing as "far and unfettered." Once you are cast far and unfettered into the realm where there are no things, you are lodged securely to the end of your days in the realm of no things.

FANG YIZHI: To be lodged securely in the boundlessness is to be lodged in the everyday functions of things. Each thing, each incipient impulse is dependent, and at the same time each is independent. This is the point Zhuangzi holds in the back of his throat, but he lets it overflow into his "spillover-goblet words," his "attributed words" [see Chapter 27], his dimness, and his drifting.

WANG FUZHI: When life and death are forgotten, this is forgetting what year it is. When right and wrong are forgotten, this is forgetting what should or should not be.

YAN FU: Whatever fits into neither this category nor that category, the in-   2:47
between, is called the "Neither-of-the-Two."[. . .] The penumbra's asking the shadow is the kind of "neither-of-the-two" that is somewhere in between the darkness of the shadow and the brightness of the light.

GUO XIANG: Some in the world say that the penumbra is dependent on the   2:48
shadow, the shadow is dependent on the physical form, and the physical form is dependent on the Creator. But I ask: As for this Creator, is he existent or is

he nonexistent? If he is nonexistent, how can he create beings? If he is existent, having a definite form himself, then he is not qualified to form all the various forms. Thus, only after you understand that the forms form themselves can you understand what is meant by creation. Hence, of all things involved in the realm of existence, even the penumbra, there has never been one that did not transform itself in its own solitary singularity, constantly positioned in the realm where all agency vanishes. Thus, creation is without any lord or master, and each being creates itself; for each being to create itself and not be conditioned by or dependent on anything else is what is meant by "true both to heaven and to earth" [1:8]. Thus, when self and other follow each other, and form and shadow simultaneously come to be, although they are obliquely joined, it is not ultimately a relation of dependence. One who understands this principle allows each of the ten thousand things to return to its source within its own self without depending on anything outside itself, externally without apology and internally without pride. Thus, all come into being as if enticed but don't know how or why they have come to be; all alike attain what they get without knowing how or why they do so. Now, if even in the case of the penumbra's following of the shadow we can still say they simultaneously come to be but without mutual dependence, then although the ten thousand things come together to collectively form the Heavenly, nonetheless each of them in perfect distinctness appears on its own in independent solitude. Thus, the penumbra is not controlled by the shadow, nor is the shadow caused by the physical form, nor is the physical form a transformation produced by Nonbeing. Transforming and not transforming, being so and not being so, following others or proceeding from one's own self, none are not self-so; how could the self discern how or why it is so? Thus, if we let them proceed without trying to help them along, root and branch, inner and outer, all will unobstructedly attain to being what they are and vanishingly leave no trace. If we seek out their nearby causal links and thereby forget that they are all ultimately self-so, positing a source for things outside of themselves, thus depriving them of the master lying within themselves, then preferences and esteem will be born. Even if we try to push this aside and make things equal, once this esteem has lodged in their breasts, how could any peaceful evenness ever be attained?

2:49   GUO XIANG: The distinction between dreaming and waking is no different from the differentiation, the debate, between life and death. The reason he could flutter about joyfully, following his whims just as he liked, was because these distinctions, and the temporary roles that go with them, are in each moment fixed, not at all because there is no distinction between them.

LÜ HUIQING: The penumbra belongs to the same type of being as the shadow but still doesn't understand that the shadow is independent of the body. Similarly, you and I and other humans are all the same type of being, but we don't know that each of us is independent of any other [. . .]. No thing knows any other thing, and so each returns to its own root. No being depends on any other, so each "is no longer coupled as an opposite" [2:17]. What then fails to be equalized?

JIAO HONG: Jiang Yu has said, "You know about the previous state of dreaming when awake, but when dreaming you know nothing about the previous state of wakefulness. In this sense, wakefulness is certainly more real than dreaming. But on the other hand, wakefulness is limited to the realm of thinking, while the foreknowledge of dreams goes beyond thinking. Hence, dreams are more wondrously efficacious than wakefulness. And yet, every utterance and motion undergone in a short morning's wakefulness will forever connect to further categories of reality, but whatever is seen and heard in even the longest dream will vanish without any continuity into the future." This describes how everything in the dream vanishes with a single instant of wakefulness. The difference between the two is as vast as this. How much more distinct are the great transformations of coming and going into existence, life and death! If you are not the right person for it, how can you avoid being transported about and submerged in the process of creation? Nonetheless, if you can awaken to the meaning of dreaming and waking, the coming and going into existence of life and death are really too insignificant to even discuss.

WANG XIANQIAN: Zhuang Zhou and the butterfly must have some distinction between their two identities, but in the dream and just after awakening, this distinction is unknown. You can say that it is Zhuang Zhou being the butterfly, or that it is the butterfly being Zhuang Zhou. Either is acceptable—and just this is their oneness, their transformation into each other

LI ZHI: To say that *"surely each has its own share" ["count as distinct"] means that we cannot say one has it and the other lacks it, that this one is awake and that one is dreaming, that Zhou is right and the butterfly is wrong.

SHI DAOSHENG: The transforming sounds, the things and their shadows, these are not dependent on one another. The butterfly is not dependent on Zhou, nor Zhou on the butterfly. The dream is not dependent on wakefulness, nor wakefulness on the dream. That is why Zhuangzi understands nothing of how it is that "I lose me," and all beings understand nothing of how it is that they transform themselves. In the penumbra's question to the shadow, the inquiry is traced all the way back to the Creator of Things, himself oblivious and unable to know how it's done, which gives us a rough sketch of the matter, as if in the splashed-ink style.

WANG FUZHI: When theories and assessments are the panpipes, it is the theorists who are the blowers. When humans are the panpipes, it is Heaven that is the blower. And when Heaven itself is the panpipes, it is the sudden arising of the incipient impulses that are the blowers. The vastness of the four seas, the duration of ten thousand years, the faintness of every insect's echo, the blast of all the sky's thunders—use of my ears alone is unable to hear it all, use of my mind alone is unable to know it all. Profound indeed is their failure, their limitation! But leaving them in silence, letting "them all bask in the broad daylight of Heaven" [2:16]—that gets to the heart of the matter. When I am silent there is that which allows me to be so, and when I bask them all in the broad daylight, illuminating them all, there is that which allows me to do so. In every case, what allows this is a certain following along, a "going by" [*yin* 因] something. If you dislike following along, because it beholdens you to the coercion of an other, and try to flee to empty space to escape this interference, you will not succeed. Even empty space is an interfering "other"—and where will you go to escape it? Profound indeed is this failure, this limitation! When those who don't comprehend this roam in the limited, believing it to be the limitless, those who do comprehend it laugh at them. But when those who do comprehend it roam in the limitless, they do so by finding that wherever they go, there is in fact a limit. Everywhere one goes between heaven and earth one encounters their vital energies; everywhere one goes among the ten thousand things one encounters their initiating impulses: others. To touch them is to contravene them; to contravene them is to touch them. Forced to give it a name, this is called "equality." I equal out the assessments of things, but at the same time the assessments of things equal me out. What can be done about this? When wisdom comes to its limit and the Course cannot be found, where else can we search for a secure way in which to hide ourselves? Zhuangzi says, "The sage hides it in his embrace" [2:33–34]. Is this not the most skillful choice of a technique?

Nonetheless, I must debate this, make an additional distinction. To hide things in your embrace is to run away from things, and to run away from things still leaves you in conflict with things. What does this mean? You hate being defeated by things, you hate having to follow the dictates of things, you hate having to compete with things, having no means by which to dominate them, and so you run away from them. And if you have hatred in your heart, you are already in conflict. To run from them in order to free yourself from defeat, from following dictates, from competing, thinking this will allow you to dominate them—this is all already conflict. If you are in conflict with them, the initiating impulse of your embrace of them will exceed the content of your theories. Within your impregnable silence there will still be the rumblings of violent thunderclouds. Then even the "wordless demonstration" is still a demonstration embroiled in rights and wrongs, and even "the Course that is not a course" is still a course built on the ostentatious blossoms of empty renown [2:36]. Almost all such people end up cast about like the wind and waves.

But the real reason the sage is said to hide it all in his embrace is that he is "there taking part in the diversity of ten thousand harvests, but in each he tastes one and the same purity of fully formed maturation" [2:41]. Thus, he can say what others have said without worrying about following their dictates, say what others have never said without meeting defeat, say what others cannot say or dare not say, thereby doing much more than merely dominating them. What does this mean? What has been said, what has not been said, what others cannot or dare not say—all are included in the ten thousand harvests brought to the oneness of full maturation. Speaking is OK, and not speaking is also OK—for both speaking and not speaking are included in this embrace. You can then approve of Yao and Shun without thereby disapproving of Tang and Wu, or approve of the naturalness of a deer's antlers among the branches without thereby disapproving of ritual and music. Humanity and Responsibility have no clearcut beginnings and ends, and loss and gain have no borderline between them. "Gazing all around, dawdling with satisfaction" [3:6] to fully realize this embrace—that is the only way one can be hidden securely in the embrace. Otherwise, it is nothing more than choosing a technique—and the sage has no use for techniques.

FANG YIZHI: Present equally in transcending the world and in coming forth into the world there is a "primary master within the master, a ruling host within the host."[14] Luckily we have happened upon this one word for it, "Du" [督; the ruling meridian running vertically through the center of our backs], which overcomes both action and nonaction by following along with varying conditions. This allows us sometimes to proclaim that the body is merely the four elements, so as to undermine any clinging to the physical body. But if you cling to this statement itself, you get yourself "rounded off on all sides" [like Shen Dao in Chapter 33]. Sometimes we proclaim that there is nothing beyond the physical body, to undermine any clinging to the idea of a mind separate from the body. But if you cling to this statement itself, you become a slithering, legless insect. The sage gathers together the entire world to form his own body and mind and joins in the celebration of ten thousand generations of "resting content in the time" and "finding his place in the flow" [3:8], depending "on Heaven's unwrought perforations" [3:5]. This is the greatest elixir of life there is—what can he do if everyone seems to ignore it? Here he gathers into a single flaming torch all those who are on the brink of death, all those who are stalwartly ready to die, all those who have already sliced their bones apart and returned them to their parents. Who can fail to enjoy the warmth at the mouth of this oven, to bask in the light of this lamp? Now I ask: Where is the primary host in charge of "putting life outside yourself" [6:35], and also of "the unborn and nonalive [that generate life]" [6:38], and yet also of "resting content" in life? To ignore the unseen power in one's back and its normal course, insistently making pronouncements, waving your knife around at random until surrounded by a pile of bones—this disease is the most difficult to treat. Zhuangzi smiles a chilly smile and says, "Here you are, unable to escape the contingen-

3:1

---

[14] "The master within the master" (or "host within the host") is a crucial phrase in the Caodong (JP: Sōtō) teaching of Chan (JP: Zen) Buddhism (See *Ruizhou Dongshan Liangjie chanshi yulu*, T47.525a). The word "master" (*zhu* 主) is the same as that translated as "primacy" in the title of this chapter.

cies of being alive. If you suddenly hear my words about nourishing those near to you and fully living out your years [3:3], maybe you can be half healed."

3:2   GUO XIANG: This person can lift great weights while that one can carry only light objects, in both cases without any strain to their spirit and energy; this is what is meant by the shaping limits of their physical strength. But a person motivated to do the lifting by love of fame or victory alone cannot satisfy his wish even if he exhausts all his power; this is what is meant by the lack of bounding limits characteristic of the mind bent on knowledge. Hence, what we call the mind bent on knowledge, the understanding consciousness, is born of losing one's proper match with what one is, and it can be extinguished by vanishing into one's own limits. To vanish into one's own limits means to go along with one's exact allotment, not adding even the weight of a hair to it. Thus, even if you are bearing ten thousand pounds on your back, as long as this accords with your own ability, you will be oblivious to any feeling of weight on the body, free of any consciousness of it. Even if you are responding to ten thousand situations, you will be, as if vanishing into them, unaware of any affairs requiring effort. This is what is *primary to the nourishment of life.[15]

LÜ HUIQING: The life process follows the body and thus ends where the body ends. But the mind bent on knowledge chases after object after object without limit.

SHI DEQING: Man's life is like a horse galloping past a crack in the wall— his time is limited. "The mind bent on knowledge" means deluded thoughts and cogitations, which come to us day and night without limit.

WANG FUZHI: The transformations of consciousness, on the basis of its joy, anger, sorrow, happiness, foresight, regrets, transformations, and stagnations, produce the "Eight Virtues" of left and right, roles and the behaviors they call for, divisions and distinctions, competition and struggle [2:33–34]. When you try to augment your vital energy in order to chase after these things, you only end up dissipating more and more of that energy outside of yourself, thereby doing more and more damage to the harmony inside yourself. But this contributes nothing to maintaining the patterned channels of the life process. Once these are endangered, one's "survival is just a waiting for the end" [2:11].

3:3   SHI DAOSHENG: This ruling force resides entirely in flowing along the central meridian as the normal course. Then you can do what you do in the realm of evil or in the realm of good without reaching the point of reputation or punishment. (Fang Yizhi comments: Daosheng added the phrase "in the realm of" before the words "good" and "evil," precisely revealing the kind of "tending toward" that occurs when you get sight of the middle meridian. He shows us the full force exerted by the lion as it fells either a rabbit or an elephant.)

---

15   See Chapter 3, note 1.

FANG YIZHI: The *Yinfujing*[16] says, "Heaven's unsurpassed selfishness, when put to use, is perfectly unbiased." Unbiased means precisely unselfish. Thus is all evil transformed into goodness. Two naked people—but it is not lasciviousness. Changing the order of imperial succession—but it is not covetousness. Excising passages and discoursing at length—but it is not showing off the talent of disputation. Yi Yin and the Duke of Zhou [take hold of the policies of the Shang and Zhou dynasties, respectively]—but it is not tyrannical maneuvering. When your intent is the realization of Humanity, nothing you do is evil. Once you have understood "the process of transformation and nourishing [of all things]" and the "Great Root" [described in the Confucian *Doctrine of the Mean*] and put forth your standards and guidelines accordingly, you naturally hit the mark of the Mean without effort, neither indulging nor eliminating your desires.

WANG FUZHI: The central meridian of energy along the front of the body is called the Ren [任], that along the spine is called the Du [督]. The Du meridian remains still, leaning neither left nor right, occupying the position of a channel of energy but without palpable physical form. To follow along the Du is to proceed along the empty channel with a clear, weightless, subtle energy, halting wherever one cannot further proceed. This flow is naturally smooth, for it always finds the center. By not claiming renown for goodness, you stay far from the punishment for evil, so your roaming never fails to be unfettered and far-reaching. You live out your years fully and then come to an end, making no choice about what you will then overflow into. Fully living out your years, your responses to things will bring no harm anywhere in the world. Resting at peace in the unknowability of the "ten thousand harvests [before and after your life]" [2:41], give yourself over to "the ending of the firewood" [3:8]. Then all the years you have life, you will be alive. Though dead, such a life continues on firm and unperishing.[17]

XIANG XIU: "Understanding consciousness, beholden to its specific purposes" means what operates exclusively set on its own area of control and investigation. "Promptings of the spirit" means letting the hand go where it wants, releasing the attention to move freely. It means whatever may be found without deliberate seeking.   3:4

GUO XIANG: This means keeping the eye from being subordinated to other, external things.   3.5

LÜ HUIQING: It is the "being," the presence, of things that obstructs, while the emptiness of the Course is open, allowing free passage. Before you have   3.6

---

[16] A short but influential Daoist text of unknown authorship, probably composed during the Tang dynasty (618–907).

[17] For further comment on this passage, go to www.hackettpublishing.com.

heard the Course, everything you see is a thing. Afterward, everything is the Course. "Encounter it with the spirit rather than scrutinizing it with the eyes" means to let your mind match it and merge with it rather than trying to know it with your understanding or cognize it with consciousness. When the understanding consciousness, beholden to its specific purposes, comes to a halt, the promptings of the spirit flow forth naturally. The passage from "depend on Heaven's unwrought perforations" to "knotted nodes" describes what it is like to "never see the entire ox"—or to be entirely free of seeing the ox. Freely passing through wherever you may go, since each thing is the Course, is also like this. "All I looked at was oxen"—in other words, to see it only as an ox, as a thing—and "the changing of the blade" are metaphors for harming the flow of life. "The blade as if just off the whetstone after nineteen years" is a metaphor for not harming the flow of life. Having a form but no real "being" there—is this not what is meant by saying that the joints have spaces within them? That there has never really existed any such thing as "life"—is this not what is meant by the blade having no thickness? "The play of the blade having more than enough room"—is this not like one who has embodied the Course playing amid all things?

YANG SHEN: The resonant thwing of the knife, each stroke ringing out the perfect note, this describes the measured tones and rhythm of the wielding of the blade, showing that between heaven and earth there is nothing that is not music [—and "music" means "joy"]. The merchant's hawking harmonizes with the temper of the Yellow Bell; the cook's knife matches the Dance of the Mulberry Grove, and thus it goes on, so that even the herding boy blowing at the leaves and the harem ladies scraping the washboards never fail to line up their tones perfectly in their own order. Where is there anywhere, when is there any moment, from which music—that is, joy—is lacking?

SHI DEQING: The cook stands for the sage, the ox for all the affairs of the world, from large matters like affairs of state to small matters like everyday behavior, all the things and events before one's eyes. The skill of carving up the ox is the wise method for ordering the world and the state, for handling life in general. The blade stands for the original nature, the host of the flow of life. To follow one's own nature in all one's actions is like the blade's cutting up the ox.

WANG FUZHI: Wherever great fame is at stake, wherever great punishment threatens, wherever great good and great evil are battling, there is great danger and great obstruction there. These are the "gnarled joints." But the dangers and obstructions are not really unavoidable: there is always some hollow within them. The problem is just that we inflate our own feelings, talents, and understanding consciousness into a "thickness" and then try to force our way in with them.

3.7   WANG FUZHI: When you try to subordinate the bounded [flow of life] to the unbounded [understanding consciousness bent on knowledge], you actually end up doing just the reverse: subordinating your consciousness to the flow of life. Doing good or evil, thereby creating a "thickness" [3:5], is nothing other than attempting to augment the flow of life. To devote yourself to the desires of the senses brings you close to punishment, and to devote yourself to the traces of knowledge and reputation brings you close to fame.[18]

GUO XIANG: The time passes away and never returns. The present moment   3:8 never pauses even slightly. Thus each breath in a man's life is a new attainment. The past breath is not the present breath: it is by taking our nourishment from each moment's breath that we enable our lives to continue on. The previous flame is not the present flame: it is by working each present piece of firewood that we enable the flame to transmit itself. The continuation of life and the transmitting of the flame are accomplished when the nourishment finds its proper limits. But the world does not know the real meaning of their ending and thus of their being reborn.

LIN XIYI: This is a metaphor for life and death. It is like fire burning firewood. If you gaze only upon the firewood that's been pointed out, you find that it will at some time be exhausted. But the fire in this world, from ancient times to the present, has been passed on constantly without being exhausted. We have never seen it come to an end.

LÜ HUIQING: Fire stands for the flow of life and firewood for the body. When this is understood, one knows that what makes life life has never had a beginning. How then can joy or sorrow seep in?

JIAO HONG: In my opinion, this means that when you count the firewood on your fingers, the firewood seems too much to handle—you run out of fingers to count on. When the fire is passed from one ember to another, you don't realize that it has at that moment ended. Indeed, the leaping metal can never escape the furnace and the floating bubble must return to the sea, which shows there is no life as opposed to death, that they are one. The text says earlier that life should be nurtured, but here life and death are considered to be one. Is this a contradiction? Rather, it means that those who understand that life and death are as one are the ones who are truly good at nurturing life.

ZHU BOXIU: The people of the world understand only how to nurture life; they do not understand how to nurture the host of life.

FANG YIZHI: Some say the firewood represents the body and the fire the soul. Some say the firewood represents phenomenal events and the fire the absolute Principle.[19] Some say that the fire is extinguished when separated from the

---

[18]   For further comment on this passage, go to www.hackettpublishing.com

[19]   "Principle" is *Li* 理 See Glossary.

firewood, and some that it is only the fire's light that is then extinguished while the immaterial reality of the fire is never extinguished. Some say the real fire fills all space but needs firewood in order to manifest as visible light. But please try wiping off your blade and cutting open the flame with it, thereby continuing the course of the fire. If you do not know how to cut open the flame, you naturally know nothing of how to "tend toward [the current of the central meridian] as [your] normal course" [3:3]. How then can you continue the course of the flame? So many mistakenly kill themselves off by living this kind of wasted life and dying this kind of a senseless death [. . . .] Zhuangzi gives us this one whispered phrase, "Its ending is unknown," and leaves it at that, thereby overturning both the narrow, annihilationist view that the spirit is destroyed at death and also the ignorant eternalist view of an immortal soul[. . . .] The sage takes nourishing the life of ten thousand generations as his ruling principle—that is, he uses the life of ten thousand generations to nourish the ruling host within him. Following along with Heaven and its unwrought perforations, tracing along the current to comprehend the normal course, the ending is unknown. Each thing then contentedly comes to its own end. Thus when he is happy, it is a happiness in which neither happiness nor sadness can get in at him. When he is sad, it is a sadness in which neither happiness nor sadness can get in at him. Happiness is then certainly happiness, but sadness is also a kind of happiness. In sharing the sorrow of the world, he becomes blue like Heaven when feeding on the blue, yellow like earth when feeding on the yellow, not worrying about the source of the fire but just making sure he uses good firewood. For you must clearly grasp that when it comes to the other side—the yonder beyond—there is nothing you can avoid and nothing you can do; all you can do is your deeds on this side. Do you understand that those who speak of the afterlife only offer one-sided manipulations of their own about the other side, thereby avoiding the normal course of the central current? Zhuangzi himself is in danger of it. I laugh and add: Zhuangzi too makes something of the other side in an attempt to nourish himself on this side, cooking up a pot of Buddha-flesh for his own nutriment. Will he not run across a rather "gnarled joint of bone" there [3:4–5]? Or, if not, find himself licking someone else's knife? One blow on the firewood under this pot and the whole house will be in need of the fire brigade. Manipulating the firewood like this, what can you transmit? Even if you smash the pot, you will be still be endangered. It would be better to just say, "Don't know," and leave it at that. Then you need have no worries about the destruction of "the master within the master."

WANG FUZHI: Those who *chase after the unbounded with the bounded fail to understand that the firewood comes to an end when the fire moves on. For the firewood can be counted to the end of the fingers, but the flame cannot be exhausted. What cannot be exhausted is the *ruling host of the flow of life. Is it not foolish to be lodged in the firewood, taking it to be the fire? When the human body is formed, the spirit comes to be attached to it. When the body breaks down and can no longer house the spirit, the spirit leaves it. But once the spirit leaves the body, it is no longer spirit. When lodged in the body, it is called spirit. When not lodged in a body, it is simply the Heavenly. But what difference is there in it whether lodged in a body or not? When you nourish this constant and unchanging host of the flow of life, which is transmitted without perishing, "tasting the single flavor of full maturation in ten thousand diverse harvests" [2:41], you come and go freely with the times whether the firewood is much or little, counting it out to its end. What is "unknown" about it is that it might wander in the void, or then again it might be lodged in another—a mouse liver or a bug's arm [6:41]. None of these are unacceptable. How could such a one be willing to obey the Lord's dangle and belabor himself over good and evil? What moves on is the host, while what comes to an end is the guest. Nourish the host, treat the guest as a guest, and then you can die without perishing. How could sorrow or joy then find their way into you?

QIAN MU: The fire represents the Great Course. Buddhist works sometimes use fire and firewood as a metaphor for the spirit and the body, respectively, but this is not Zhuangzi's original meaning.

GUO XIANG: Living in a human community, it is impossible to separate   4:1
yourself completely from other people. But because of the many transformations of the human world, different behaviors are appropriate to each time. Only those who are free of any fixed intentions of their own, not insisting on their own way, can follow wherever the changes may go without bearing their entanglements as a burden.

SHI DEQING: This chapter describes the sage's course for handling life in the world. The previous chapter on the *nourishing of the host of life concerned keeping the business of the world from harming the life in you, but what really nourishes life is an inner skill that can only be made your own and verified by involving yourself in the ways of the world. A person who is truly able to nourish the flow of his life will handle living in the world without boasting of his talents, seeking reputation, or forcing his way when there is no call for it. Naturally, in serving a ruler or carrying out orders, this will keep him from any suspicion of exaggerating his merits or showing off his virtues. But the real power of it comes from the practice of "Fasting of the Mind" [4:9] and "sitting and forgetting" [6:54]. By keeping the self empty throughout all your involvements with the world, you can remain free of trouble. What follows is an extremely thorough description of the difficulties encountered in navigating through the ways of the world and the emotions of human beings. But trouble is inevitable unless you know how to be "empty and await the operation of things" [like the vital energies; 4:10], minimizing your impulse to seek reputation and show off your skills. Thus, the chapter ends with a discussion of talentlessness as the final word. Only those who can remain untroubled in spite of their involvement in all the complexities of the world show us what is meant by "the master" who is truly skilled at "nourishing life" [3:1]. In reality, this chapter and the previous one are explications of each other.

4:2   GUO XIANG: The Course needs the right person to practice it. If the right man is lacking, a hundred physicians may treat the illness, but they will just sink the matter further into doubt rather than curing the disease.

4:3   GUO XIANG: It is the esteem for names and reputation that undermines Virtuosity. It is the struggle for preeminence in "goodness" that creates the overgrowth of cleverness. Even villains such as Jie and Robber Zhi care for nothing more than gaining a reputation and attaining "goodness" in some sense.

4:4   GUO XIANG: If he is able to delight in worthiness and despise foolishness, submitting to what is right when he hears it, then he is already an enlightened ruler. An enlightened ruler would not be lacking worthy ministers already, so your journey there would have no special value. But if he's not already like this, your journey will surely only lead to harm. Thus, when you go forth with a deliberate intention, wherever you go will be wrong. When you respond to things with no deliberate intention, on the contrary, the responses come naturally of themselves, and wherever you go will be right.

4:5   WANG FUZHI: The mind is one; what complicates it with disturbances is right and wrong. All the clashes of right and wrong in the world derive from the cleverness of the understanding consciousness. The understanding creates an idea of rightness, rightness forms its counterpart wrongness, and thus hundreds of divergences sprout. Goodness has its own right and wrong, while violent tyranny has another concept of right and wrong, which constantly struggle with each other, leading to unspeakable mutual disturbance. The cleverness of consciousness arises from the mind and yet also comes to disorder the mind, which is why the questions one must ask in getting to the bottom of the human mind are inexhaustible.

4.6   WANG FUZHI: Right and wrong are nothing but names, matters of reputation. "Right" is a glorifying of the reputation; "wrong" is a defamation of the reputation.

4.7   WANG FUZHI: Neither "punctilious and diligent" nor "humble and focused" can work. For to be humble but dignified is not real humility, and to be focused but punctilious is not real focus.

4.8   WANG FUZHI: He wanted to have the proposed punctiliousness, humility, focus, and diligence within himself as his own possessions, but these were still not he himself. Clashing with and imposing himself upon others, exploiting their feelings in order to blame them while leaning on his own unsullied Humanity and Responsibility—this is why his humility was not true humility, his focus not real focus.

CHENG XUANYING: Because the mind possesses understanding and aware-   4:9
ness, it can come to manipulate its objects. Vital energy, on the other hand, is free of emotions and reasonings, empty and pliant, going along with things. So if we eliminate the understanding and awareness and adopt the empty pliancy instead, eliminating ever more again and again, we will gradually ascend to the wondrous mystery.

FANG YIZHI: The *Wenzi*[20] says, "The highest students hear with the spirit. The middling students hear with the mind. The lowest students hear with the ear. But when you hear with the vital energies, you are in all places at once."

JIAO HONG: The character *shi* [使] used above to mean "what moves me   4:10
into activity" is the same as that used to mean "to move at the behest of, to serve" in the phrases "to be sent into your activities at the behest of other humans" and "to be sent into activity by Heaven" and should be understood as such. Yan Hui had a decisive awakening when he heard that emptiness is the fasting of the mind, and thus he declared that it is when he is unable to move and operate as desired that he has a concept of self, and conversely it is when he moves and operates exactly as desired that he has no concept of self [. . . .] When serving humans, one can have a concept of self, and thus it is easy to use deception. When serving Heaven, one can have no concept of self, and thus it is hard to use deception. For to comprehend things without using the faculty of understanding is like a man walking without steps or a bird flying without wings: it is the Heavenly that then moves them, Heaven which they serve. This is what is meant by [Yan Hui's] emptiness.

TAO WANGLING: When Yan Hui could not find what really moved him, he was sent into his activities *by the Human [in him]. When he found it, he was sent into activity by the Heavenly.

SHI DEQING: This is a metaphor for the emptying of the mind. When a   4.11
room is empty, all it needs is a single crack in the wall. Then it will certainly receive the sunshine, and brightness will be born throughout the empty room. This means that when the mind is empty, the light of Heaven will spontaneously appear there.

GUO XIANG: This means no being is worth more than any other being. As   4.12
long as the eyes and ears are not subordinated to the mind's understanding,

---

[20] Daoist text, dating from the early Han dynasty, purporting to be a series of dialogues between Laozi and his student Wenzi.

they naturally open to whatever they encounter. Hence, a person never becomes what the world calls wise and discerning because he decides he wants to be wise and discerning. A person never comes to have what is called vision because he deliberately decides to see. If wise discernment and vision could be deliberately created because someone wanted them, then whoever wanted to be worthy could become worthy and anyone who deliberately endeavored to be a sage would be able to. This is obviously impossible. But the world does not understand that knowing knows spontaneously, and hence they want to deliberately operate some "knowing" to know with. They don't see that seeing sees spontaneously, and thus they try to deliberately operate some "seeing" to see with. And again, they don't know that life lives itself spontaneously, and thus they try to deliberately operate a "life" to live with. Seeing an eye, they search for Li Zhu's keen vision; seeing an ear, they hunt for Master Kuang's keen hearing. This causes their minds and spirits to gallop restlessly within and their eyes and ears to lose themselves in external things. They are uncomfortable in their own bodies and yet also unable to vanish into things. Such a person can never find the appropriate union with the changes of the human world or respond to the varying requirements of each new time.

LIN XIYI: The seeing and hearing of the eyes and ears all penetrate inward to the mind, but if I have no mind within to receive it, then although I allow all that the eyes and ears see and hear to enter without obstruction, it actually *remains outside the mind and its understanding. What does it mean to be beyond the mind's understanding? Just that if the mind is unmoving, external things cannot get inside. Although you hear what you hear and see what you see, you remain unmindful, free of deliberate intentions, about what is seen and heard.

CHEN XIANGDAO: When listening stops at the ear, it is limited to what the ear can hear. When the mind stops at what verifies its preconceptions, it is limited to what it can combine with. But when you listen with the vital energy, since the latter is omnipresent, vast, openly flowing, it can use the body without being used by the body, allowing it to respond to the operation of all things without being dependent on things. For it is empty and unobstructed, responding but not storing [7:14]. The vital energy is kept whole and intact through the unification of the intentions into a singularity, emptiness is brought about by a vital energy that is whole and intact, and the Course is gathered in with the arrival of emptiness. This is the meaning of "the fasting of the mind."

WANG FUZHI: The essential thing for the fasting of the mind is simply to be empty, nothing more. Vital energy means the force of life, the harmonious energy of august Heaven. When it is mixed together with mind's understanding, the mind comes to order the vital energy about, entering into its midst and obstructing its harmony. This is how the emptiness is lost. But the mind is originally free of understanding. An infant, for example, is without any understanding, but we cannot say she has no mind. When the mind retains the vital energy within itself, it makes the life process flourish,[21] no longer joining in with the projects of the world, so the Heavenly radiance is constantly preserved, perfectly empty and perfectly unified. The understanding takes shape when the mind embraces right and wrong and struggles with others over names and reputation. But it is originally born under the guidance of our seeing and hearing. Now, our faculty of vision projects its illumination from within outward, and although the external thereby flows into us, it is insufficient to displace the inner sense of being in control. The ear's hearing, on the contrary, is in its entirety a process of inviting the external into oneself. Hence, as soon as the heard is stored in the originally empty mind and taken as a substantial reality, the mind, precisely because it is empty, delights in having something substantial to rely on and thus uses these voices and sounds to distinguish between the good and the not good, forming the rightness of the self and dividing it off from the wrongness of others. So the cavity of the ear is originally empty, but it becomes a reservoir for receiving the substantial. Thus, when you "take the mind as teacher" [2:12], you are really only taking the ear as teacher. What the ear hears is taken as your mind and made into the authoritative teacher, and the vital energy is made to serve it, thereby forcibly obstructing the energy's original harmony. Then if you happen to encounter the violent energy of a tyrant in the prime of his life with his autocratic ways, you will inevitably get involved in a struggle with him over name and reputation, and the mutual plaguing will be unstoppable. "To play in his cage but entrust yourself to the unavoidable" means simply to purify your vital energy so that it can wait on the presence of all things. The ear can be made to hear and yet still refrain from accepting what it hears. The mind can be made to match itself to the harmony of the vital energy [within] and keep from matching itself to what the ear [hears externally]. When both the crazy, reckless words of the tyrant and the resentful curses of the masses are both no more to me than "transforming voices" [2:45], unable to unsettle my vital energy, then I, along with the emptiness by which august Heaven transforms things, am just what the Course comes to gather in. Externally I have no opposing counterpart, inside no self, thereby I can understand the mind and energy of others and await their transformations. Whatever opportunities, entrapments, powers, and authorities may present themselves, nothing is deliberately put forth from me. This is the ultimate reach of the art of wandering in the world of human beings. It comes to its full realization in [Yan Hui's] "'myself' has never begun to exist"[4:10].

---

[21] Wang uses the same phrase for this that at 6:26 is translated "considering life good," *shan wu sheng* 善吾生.

4:13   WANG FUZHI: Thinking of the gravity of his commission from Chu and the casual treatment he will receive in Qi, giving rise to an internal fever—this is all the result of seeking it in others. When the understanding consciousness takes shape ahead of time within you, the eyes and ears are confused by the external, shaken and jolted until all its perplexity comes rebounding back over you—then all the human world is shackles and leg chains!

4:14   WANG FUZHI: This is the uncontrived stability that comes with "possessing it in oneself." Only when you neither delight in life nor abhor death is your emptiness truly empty, your unity truly unified. "The service rendered to one's own heart" means a service that is free of all service to anything at all. When your service is free of service, the mind is free of mind. When the mind is forgotten, the body can be forgotten. For what do the five sense organs and the hundred parts of the body know of delighting in life or abhorring death? It is the mind alone that delights or abhors. When the stimulations received from sights and sounds by the eyes and ears are allowed into the mind to unsettle its vital energy, the internal yin and yang and the external affairs of the human world intertwine to give rise to all sorts of troubles that the mind cannot resolve and the body cannot escape. But when the vital energy resides in emptiness, it knows neither life nor death and is constantly able to settle itself there without any special effort. Then all your actions will be free of doubts.

4:15   CHENG XUANYING: Wind raises waves in water as words raise joy and anger in the mind.

WANG PANG: Things cannot disturb you if you remain free of words, but words are required if you are to respond to the things around you. Responding, you are no longer still. Hence, he says, "words are like wind and waves." When you do not act, your traces are hidden, but when you do, your traces are revealed. When the traces are revealed externally, the truth is obscured within. Hence, he says, *"actions are a loss of the real." Indeed, when no longer still, you start to move, and when the true is lost, it is hard to be at ease. Hence, he says, *"Winds and waves can easily shake a man, and loss of the real can easily endanger him."

LI ZHI: Words are like winds and waves, and the person who has to transmit words is as if tossed about on the wind and waves, with no firm support to grab hold of. That is why the matter easily goes astray, easily leads to danger.

4.16   WANG FUZHI: How could wandering depend on a mind determined to wander? It is just a lodging in the unavoidable. Life can then be a wandering, and death too can be a wandering.

4.17   LÜ HUIQING: The problem with compromises is that they get inside you, and then you become the same as the others. The problem with harmony is that it shows, and then you become different from the others. So you are collapsed, crippled by the toppling destruction, or else you are haunted and plagued by the reputation and renown, because you are like the others without knowing how to support and maintain your own self, or else you are unlike the others without knowing how to accommodate and follow them. "Playing the baby with him" and so on, "mastered to the point of flawlessness," allows you to be lawless with him without endangering the nation or lawful with him without endangering yourself. It's all a matter of going by whatever is already in his nature, following along with it and penetrating it without obstruction, opening it up. That is the wondrous work of going by someone's capacity and transforming it by pinpointing it, just as Mencius led King Xuan of Qi to the Kingly Course by way of the king's love of war and wealth [*Mencius* 1B3–5].

GUO XIANG: The king has less talent than his ministers, and that is exactly why the ministers work for him. The keen-eyed see for him, the keen-eared listen for him, the wise plan for him, the brave battle for him. What need he himself do? He simply remains silent and invisible and all the talents of others find their proper use. Hence, the talentless is what talent ultimately reverts to. Thus, all the world bears him forward without resentment, and he can ride upon all things without harm.   4:18

CHENG XUANYING: Discombobulation of the body means something like forgetting of the body, while discombobulation of Virtuosity means something like forgetting Virtuosity. The story shows that Shu, being physically disabled, was the right kind of person to forget the body, but not being a sage, he was not yet able to forget Virtuosity. The wisdom of one who forgets Virtuosity reaches all things, but he returns his wisdom to foolishnesss. His brilliance rivals the heavenly bodies, but he returns his brilliance to dimness. Thus, he can accomplish the work without taking credit, take action without relying on his accomplishment, ceding the credit and reputation to the various talented ones, vanishing into things and leaving no traces. Such is the forgetting of Virtuosity.   4:19

LI ZHI: Who is the Spirit Man? Precisely Shu the Discombobulated is he. Once you know that Shu the Discombobulated is the sacred one, you understand that Yan Hui's going to Wei, Ye Gong's going to Qi, and Yan He's transmission of messages are all examples of people who embitter their own lives. Even the Sage can do nothing to help such people. So all the methods described here are really just schemes for those "useful" people; the Spirit Man does not keep hold of such things. That is why the chapter winds up with Jieyu's ridicule of Confucius.   4:20

SHI DEQING: This chapter explains the meaning of Laozi's statement: "It occupies the places most despised by the mass of men, and thus it is close to the Course" [*Daodejing* 8].   5.1

TAN YUANCHUN: He offers no instruction and gives no opinion, and yet they go to him empty and return filled: this is a necessary phase in any relation   5.2

between students and teachers that is truly profound. But if someone were to say, "I only want to empty out whatever is there, but will carefully avoid filling in wherever nothing is," I'm afraid even Mr. Wang could do nothing for him.

5:3   GUO XIANG: He alters together with every alteration, so life and death make no alteration in him.

5:4   LIN XIYI: *"To bestow their fates on things" means that the transformations of all things are given their destinies by me alone. This is like what Chan [Zen] Buddhists mean when they say, "When the mind is deluded, it is turned by the *Lotus Sutra*; when it is enlightened, the mind turns the *Lotus Sutra*."[22]

5:5   GUO XIANG: Although what they take to be beautiful differs, they are all the same in having something or other they consider beautiful. Each takes its own beauty alone to be real beauty, so all things are one and the same with respect to their beauty. Each takes what it considers right to be the real rightness, so all things are one and the same with respect to their rightness. If we consider them different on account of their difference, each thing in the world is different. But he who takes the vast, all-pervading view of things, regarding heaven and earth as his own sense organs and all things as the parts of his own body, knows that their being different in this sense is no reason to view them as ultimately different. Thus he considers them all the same on account of their sameness. But he also knows that this sameness too is not to be considered a real and ultimate fact. Hence, beauty and ugliness, right and wrong, if we consider them absent on account of the sense in which they are not ultimately real, are all nonexistent.

LI ZHI: The liver and gallbladder are neighbors, but the liver is the liver and the gallbladder is the gallbladder: how could they be considered the same? But if you view what all things have in common, ignoring what is lost from them, you hear without ears and see without eyes, hear by seeing and see by hearing. What would you know about the different functions of the eye and the ear? Instead, you let your mind roam in the harmony of all Virtuosities [5:6].

5.6   CHENG XUANYING: It is sights and sounds that suit the eyes and ears. But it is because of our ordinary biases that we distinguish between pleasing sights and sounds and obstructive ones, between what suits and what does not suit the eyes and ears, the acceptable and the unacceptable. Wang Tai merges all things together, combining life and death into a oneness, so how could he embrace any views of beauty and ugliness in the relations of sense organs and their objects?

GUO XIANG: Having forgotten all about what is or isn't suitable, he goes along with whatever is there. One who goes along with everything finds suc-

---

22   From the *Platform Sutra* of the Sixth Patriarch of Chan, Huineng.

cess in all things without exception. Nor have I heard of anyone who finds success in all things losing his harmony. Thus, he who releases his mind into the midst of the Course and its Virtuosities lets himself go but never fails to hit the mark, remains vast and open and yet comfortably fitted to every situation.

LIU CHENWENG: Not knowing what suits the eyes and ears means not looking or listening for anything outside oneself, just like a newborn infant. Our seeing goes no further than visual forms, our hearing no further than audible sounds, so it is said that the eyes and the ears have what suits them. Not to know what suits the eyes and ears is a way of indicating the mysterious merging with things characteristic of the Consummate Person: his ear can hold an oceanful of water, his eye can contain Mt. Sumeru. Only in this way can one apprehend the releasing of the mind to play in the harmony of all Virtuosities [5:6].

WANG FUZHI: When Heaven first takes on form, it congeals into soil which 5:7 then gestates into the human body and its organs. In each case it takes on an appearance by following its own course and brings its form to completion in accordance with that appearance, so that all of these are one whole. When we "entrust ourselves to the everyday function [of each being]" [2:23], the soil is also one of my functions, not removed from me. When it becomes useless, the foot may reach its end before I do. Here too one must simply entrust oneself to the situation at hand. When such entrusting gathers in the foot, the foot has toes on it; when such entrusting gathers in the body as a whole, the body has life in it. Once the foot obtains them, its toes may either be kept intact or destroyed; once the body obtains it, its life may be either preserved or lost. It is their Course to be so; it is the Heavenly that they cannot be otherwise. But the preservation or destruction of these "neither add to nor subtract from [the] genuineness" [2:10] of the foot or the body, for once these things are lost, they become nothing more than cast-off earth. The great undivided oneness is complete in the most vast, but even a clump of soil "minute and insignificant" [5:22] has its place within it—how much more so a foot? The source of the transformations of things, the expanding and contracting of all existents, are the dust and dirt and dregs and leavings within it, all unified in the totality of transformation. When your mind wanders in this, how can it fail to find a harmony wherever it may go?

QU DAJUN: The mind is found through the understanding consciousness; 5.8 outside of the understanding consciousness there is nothing to be called the mind. The *constant mind is found through the mind; outside the mind there is nothing to be called the constant mind. The understanding consciousness is the mind, and the mind is the constant mind. Ultimately, the only difference between the sage and the fool lies in their degree of understanding. When you understand, all things are the mind. When you do not understand, all of the mind is just a thing. Zhuangzi's equalizing of things is an equalization of them all into our own minds: once there are no things outside the understanding consciousness and the mind, all things are equalized.

5:9   YANG WENHUI: From the point of view of [what the Buddhists call] conventional truth, "when one family becomes humane, humaneness arises throughout the nation. When one family practices yielding, the practice of yielding arises throughout the nation" [as the Confucian *Great Learning* says]. From the point of view of ultimate truth, though, when one person discovers the truth and returns to the source, everything filling space throughout the ten directions instantly returns to the source at once, vanishing into it without a trace.

5:10   GUO XIANG: Since his consciousness moves along together with each transformation, he vanishes into whatever he may encounter. This is the singularity of all that is in his awareness. Since his mind follows smoothly along with both life and death, it springs to life as whatever moment comes along. This is what is meant by the mind getting through unslaughtered.

LIN XIYI: "He regards even his own eyes and ears as mere semblances" means the same thing as "free of all preconceptions about which particular objects might suit the eyes and ears." His eye resembles an eye, but it is not restricted only to seeing. His ear looks like an ear, but it is not restricted only to hearing.

5:11   LÜ HUIQING: To study the Course is to study what cannot be studied. To walk the Course is to walk what cannot be walked. This is why one-footed Wang Tai is used as a metaphor for how it is done. Those who followed Confucius knew how to follow him in the ways he could walk, but not how to follow him in the ways he could not-walk. So even if every single man in Lu were his follower, he'd still be sharing it all with Wang Tai[. . . .] Confucius and Wang Tai are really simply the outside and inside of the same being.

WANG FUZHI: Chang Ji's doubt is that Wang Tai's attainment of a mind for the constant, allowing him to forget life and his own body, only freed him from his own fetters, having no way to reach other creatures. He did not understand that those who "do it for their own sake alone" do not in fact "use their understanding to *attain the mind." To really do it for one's own sake is actually a process of *losing* the self. It is rather he who has a self as opposed to a counterpart that creatures keep apart from themselves. For then benefit and harm, right and wrong are not equalized, so that the two never come into real contact. Then none can obtain their own straightest and fullest state. Taking all that his understanding knows as one and the same in its great source, the complex issues of the mind and understanding are stilled. Each being enjoys its own enjoyment, so when one comes face to face with this mirror which retains no forms, both forget all about any gain and loss to be got from the other. Then each can obtain its own straightest and fullest state. The pine and cypress do not seek winter lushness, but in the winter they spontaneously flourish. Shun did not meddle with the world, but the world spontaneously gathered around him. When you are able to forget gain and loss in yourself, the sense of being either the same as or different from other beings also vanishes. When you are able to forget even life and death, all things can be transformed, as a brave warrior does not notice the nine ranks of soldiers attacking him. Hence, it is the most singular entity, without counterpart, that restores their allotted life to all the transforming creatures. All beings naturally follow the person who doesn't bother himself over mere beings.

GUO XIANG: Because the world is constantly at war over benefit and harm, everyone in the world is Archer Yi, and anyone who does not cast off her body, forget her understanding, and undulate along with all things is lurking near Archer Yi's bull's-eye. Both Zhang Yi, who constantly ventured out into the world, and Shan Bao, who cloistered himself away,[23] could not avoid being hit. So whether you are hit or not is purely a matter of inexplicable fate. But the limited and constrained, in all their different encounters, do not realize this is all just inexplicable fate, so they think they have escaped being hit through their own skill and become conceited in their delight over themselves. Those who are hit, on the other hand, resent the absurdity of their situation and become broken-willed and self-hateful. All of these conditions come from failing to comprehend fate. Now, my birth is not born from me, and so in my hundred years of life, whether I sit or stand or walk or stop, move or stay still, whatever I go after and whatever I avoid, my emotions and my nature, my wisdom and my abilities, whatever I have or do not have, whatever I do and whatever I encounter, all is not really done by me. It is just how it all spontaneously fits together.[24] To pointlessly worry and lament amid all this is the error of going against the self-so. 5:12

LU XIXING: Toeless Shushan knew he still had something worth more than a foot, which he sought to keep intact. With that intact, he could look on the loss of his foot as the casting off of useless soil. But Confucius thought instead that he was trying to make up for the ugliness of his previous behavior, not understanding that this sort of man never gives the slightest thought to good or evil, beauty or ugliness. This is something that is very difficult for those fettered by their own ideologies to understand [. . . .] Indeed, the Consummate Person has no fixed identity, the sage has no one name, just as the hands and feet are originally free of fetters and cuffs. One becomes fettered and cuffed through the restrictions of one's own ideas about the differences between one being and another. To unlock your fetters and cuffs, you must reverse these concepts of difference and return them to unity, seeing life and death as a single string, acceptable and unacceptable as a single thread. 5:13

---

23 See Chapter 19 of the *Zhuangzi* (p. 79–80) for the story of Zhang Yi and Shan Bao.

24 "How it fits together" is *li* 理. See Glossary.

FANG YIZHI: But do you know what it means to cuff and fetter people with this talk of being released from cuffs and fetters? It is only when Heaven punishes man and man also punishes Heaven that the single thread and solitary string of the Course of the Mean becomes clear. This is the skillful use of one's cuffs and fetters, and this is certainly the ultimate ambition of "the casualty [of Heaven, as Confucius describes himself at 6:47–48]." The ordinary people of the world do not understand this and thus replace Zhuangzi's eyes with a pair of black beans.

5:14   LI ZHI: *"No longer seeing the similarity in her" means she no longer resembled the way she used to be. But the piglets loved their mother not for her body but for *the use they made of her body. As long as their mother continued to produce milk after she was dead, her body could still be used by them, so they had no reason to abandon her. Thus, when one who loves the use he can make of his bravery dies in battle, he is not buried with camouflage feathers; one who loves the use he can make of his foot has no love for shoes after the foot has been cut off. Because they are loved for the use that can be made of their intactness, the women in the emperor's harem do not pare their nails or pierce their ears, and the newly married are sent on no new missions because the anticipated use to which they can be put is loved. Now, if the intactness of the body can be so loved for the use that is made of it, how much more so will intact Virtuosity be loved?

5:15   GUO XIANG: The way things spontaneously fit together[25] is assuredly correct and can never be escaped. Hence, a person's birth is never a mistake, and whatever occurs in that life is never there randomly. However vast heaven and earth may be, however multitudinous the ten thousand things, what I have encountered has happened to come to be just this that it is and no more. This cannot be overturned even if heaven and earth, all the gods and spirits, the state and the family, and all the sages and worthies exhausted all their strength and wisdom trying to change it. So whatever you may miss could not have been met with, and whatever you may have met with could not have been missed. What you do not do you could not have done, and what you do you could not have not done. Just give them all over to their spontaneous rightness in being exactly what they are.

5:16   GUO XIANG: [Springtime means] what all living beings depend on.

CHENG XUANYING: Let your goodwill shine on all the living, your kindness nourishing every animal and plant, treating all beings with benevolence and generosity—such deeds are equal to the works of the verdant springtime.

LUO MIANDAO: "Day and night without cease" means that although life and death, poverty and wealth, may alternately appear before me, I have no open-

---

25   "The way things fit together" is *Li* 理. See Glossary.

ing into which they can enter, for I view them all as one. I merge them all together, *making springtime with all beings. It is as if one were to pass through all the four seasons of the year seeing them all as aspects of springtime, thus perceiving no separate summer, autumn, or winter. In this way, as I come into contact with beings, the life-giving season ceaselessly emerges from my own mind. The phrase "life-giving season" follows on the word "spring." This means the season is not born from the energies of yin and yang, but from my own mind.

JIAO HONG: Although death and life, surviving and perishing, and so forth transform like this, we cannot discover a doer who makes them so, and thus we name it "fate." If we could understand who or what created these things, how could we ever be free of sighs and sorrows? But as it is, they transform and depart day and night, alternating and moving along without cease, and yet even the wisest person can never discover their origin. This is what Zhuangzi means by, "There is a not-yet-beginning-to-be-a-beginning" [2:31]. Knowing this, how could I let it dislodge the great harmony of my Numinous Reservoir?

LIU CHENWENG: "Connecting with it" means never to refuse it—going 5:17 along with it and receiving whatever one may get from it, like something passing through one's hands, happy to survey whatever situation one finds oneself in without preserving it in one's mind, but thereby naturally preserving the life-giving force of the mind instead. The clouds and rain comes forth, the various types of beings flow out into their forms, and all of it is beyond description. This is indeed the perfection of Virtuosity.

WANG FUZHI: What steals our joy from us and entraps our innate powers is none other than our attempt to determine life, death, existing, perishing, and the rest of these sixteen states before they have actually been visited upon us. Then you are obliged to delight in or resist the world in advance, which only traps the sorrow within you. If this continues you end up putting on appearances to have an effect on the masses, trying to invite good fortune and avoid trouble. The Numinous Reservoir is then thrown into chaos while externally you maintain appearances—this kind of innate power robbed of its Virtuosity is what uses up the Heavenly in you. Only after considering this do we know how the harmony of the Numinous Reservoir, generating the life-giving season in one's own mind, yields an innate capacity that opens into all transformations and yet remains ever intact. How could creatures fail to admire it?

GUO XIANG: What affairs must obtain to come to a successful completion, 5:18 and what beings must obtain to be in harmony—that is what is meant by "Virtuosity."

CHENG XUANYING: His brightness equals that of the sun and moon, but he 5:19 returns it to dimness. His achievements match those of the very process of Creation, but he returns them to all other beings. This is Virtuosity taking no definite form. Hence [as *Daodejing* 55 says], "he who harbors Great Virtuosity can be compared to an infant," whom all the world joyfully supports and promotes without satiety. This is what it means to say that "none can do without him."

5:20   SHI DEQING: They forget that which they love but cannot seem to forget that which they do not really love—this is truly forgetful!

5:21   GUO XIANG: Having already received it all spontaneously, the coherence[26] of each thing is already quite sufficient. So even though you may try to avoid trouble with your deep thinking, or to understand restraints to escape disasters, in fact no thing is any way but the way it should be. Each is a coming together of heaven and earth, the convergence of the perfect coherence. Sometimes, naturally, some thinking and planning must be done, but it is not actually myself who is doing the thinking and planning. Sometimes, naturally, no thinking or planning is done, but it is not me failing to do the thinking and planning either. Some avoid harm only after thinking about how to do so, while others avoid harm without having thought about it at all. Some come to harm in spite of thinking about how to avoid it, while others come to harm without having thought about it at all. But none of this is done by the self. What then is there to do but let it all come when it spontaneously comes?

LÜ HUIQING: Because of his true forgetting of the forgettable, the sage roams "in that from which nothing ever escapes, where all things are maintained" [6:29]. For such a person, understanding is a bastard son, not a part of the original trunk of the family tree. Obligations and agreements are glue, used to tie together what has been dismantled. Virtuosity is a taking up and continuation, used to line up discrete existences. Skill is salesmanship, not what creates the valued item that is for sale.

LIN XIYI: Earlier, in the phrases "connecting up with This, your own mind becomes the site of the life-giving time" [5:17], "innate powers whole and intact," it is "Virtuosity that takes no definite external form" [5:17], [and] "takes all that his consciousness knows and unifies it into a singularity" [5:10] the taking up of something, Virtuosity, and understanding were all positive terms. Now they've all become negatively valued. Thus does his brush drum and dance over the page, giving no heed to what came before and what comes after—and this is why the *Zhuangzi* is considered a heretical text.

YAN FU: "Having no plans" is "connecting up with This," so that "your own mind becomes the site of the life-giving time" [5:17]. "Being unsplit" is discerning "what alone is unborrowed" [5:4]. "Being without loss" is "Seeing what is one and the same to all things" [5:7]. "Not being a commodity" is "not trying to add anything to the process of life" [5:23].

5:22   FANG YIZHI: Lacking the characteristic inclinations of a human being, right and wrong cannot get at him—saying this, Zhuangzi made a "skill" of his abil-

---

26   "Coherence" is *Li* 理. See Glossary.

ity to nurture himself with it. This in turn is what allowed the likes of Gaozi[27] to make a commodity of what he had glued together. Wang Gouzi said, "The sage is free of the characteristic human inclinations, the feelings." Wagong Yi said, "Is the sage then inanimate like a pillar?" Wang said, "Although the counting tallies have no human inclinations or feelings of their own, there is someone who operates them." Yi then asked, "Who is it then that operates the sage?" Wang made no reply. I say: What salesmenship!

WANG FUZHI: Whoever beautifies his external appearance is trying to show what his innate Virtuosity has attained, laboring his understanding to attain a skill, tying others down with restraints and trying to secure them with this glue. The sage is free of both gain and loss; unharmed by others, he has no schemes to use their gatherings or separations to sell them something—he is only wandering in it all. What fills him internally is Heaven—this is what moves his physical form [5:14], what is worth more than a foot [5:13], what is *free of falsehood ["the unborrowed"; 5:4] and never ceasing [5:16]. Since he is far-reaching and unfettered in all his wanderings, his interaction with each being is a new springtime—that is nothing more than the Heavenly in him. For Heaven is free of falsehood, so rain, dew, frost, and snow are all the truth. Heaven never ceases, so the four seasons continue in their sequence without break. Humans depend on it of their own accord, but Heaven does not trouble itself to do any of this deliberately.

SHI DEQING: Huizi's idea is that without emotions and desires, it is impossible to really fulfill one's role as a person, and thus he asks this question to suggest that without the characteristic inclinations, one fails to be a person. Zhuangzi answers with the real crux of the matter, saying in effect, "What I call being free of the characteristic human inclinations does not mean to absolutely destroy all the emotions that arise in your relations to rulers and parents, the emotions existing between sons and fathers or between men and women. It's just that the people of the world indulge their emotions and desires in their quest to augment the process of life, which however has the countereffect of harming the process of life. Thus, I only hope to cut off their inclination toward greedy desire, not to cut off all human relationships." 5:23

GUO XIANG: This is to say that whatever you may do—laboring your vitality, treating your spirit as a stranger, slumping over your desk now moaning and now nodding off—this is all what is commonly called the characteristic human inclinations, the way people really are. But when he says Heaven has picked this out, he indicates that these inclinations are not brought about by these inclinations themselves—how much less can they then be the real source of anything else! Thus, all things and all physical forms, in whatever they do or say, 5:24

---

27 Gaozi claimed that original human nature is definitively neutral, neither good nor evil. See *Mencius* 6A.

what they approach or what they avoid, all of it comes about without the interference of the characteristic human inclinations—so what useful function is there for these inclinations in dealing with such things?

LÜ HUIQING: Huizi did not understand how to be still precisely while in motion, so he slumped over his desk in pursuit of stillness. Not knowing this is precisely not knowing that "what moves his physical form" [5:14] is "chosen by Heaven," so [he] used it instead to crow on about hardness and whiteness.

CHEN JINGYUAN: The sage wanders beyond it all, forgetting both the body and Virtuosity. Though his Virtuosity is always functioning, he does not boast of it, and so the "glue," "bastard son," and so on have no way to sprout forth in him. He does not scheme over benefit and harm, so he has no use for understanding. He does not sever his emotions from his nature, so he has no use for glue. He loses nothing of any being, so he has no use for the attainments of Virtuosity. He presents no merchandise, so he has no use for salesmanship. These four are all sustained and nurtured spontaneously by the Heavenly in him, like the dung beetle rolling his balls of excrement, or the spider spinning his web—they know how to do these things without any conscious scheming. The dragonlike and tigerlike clouds, the pine and cypress canopy overhanging the forest—these are the glued-togethernesses that admit of no severing. Beasts and birds amid the woods and bamboos, the fish and turtles in the rivers and lakes—these are the attainments of Virtuosity that admit of no loss. Each creature benefiting itself, managing its own life—this is the salesmanship free of any merchandise to sell. All of these are nourishment provided by Heaven, so it is here called the Heavenly Sustenance. Having the physical form but not the characteristic inclinations, he "looks like a rooster fashioned from wood" [cf. Chapter 19, p. 81]. Every face, although it spans a mere foot across, each quite different, has the Course there within it. Each body, although it be only six feet long, with all hollows and orifices identical [to those of other bodies'], has the Heavenly operating within it. None of this is accomplished by the characteristic inclinations, the emotions. What emotional inclinations does Heaven have in allowing your body to be as it is? It is "just a temporarily congealed thing" [cf. Chapter 23, p. 101]. Now, you have a body just like everyone else, and yet you use it to crow forth forced distinctions between hardness and whiteness, making a racket in the face of the crowd and considering yourself a wise and worthy man, like the molten metal trying to jump out of the furnace [6:42]—is it not strange?

FANG YIZHI: Some ask why this chapter ends by bringing in Huizi again. Laughing I reply: Zhuangzi has just brought up a whole string of freakish lepers and cripples and made them emanate light and shake the earth [like a Buddha], at the same time wiping away all those "of pure countenance and rich fullness of the back" [*Mencius* 7A21] or "comfortable and at ease" [like Confucius; *Analects* 7.4]. He brings Huizi in at the end because of the way Huizi had bragged of the beauty of his disputations about 'hardness' and 'whiteness.' Zhuangzi simply wants us to see Huizi reflected in light of the lineup of cripples. At that time Huizi must have turned a contrary face at him and said: "And you, do you not 'recite'? Do you not 'nod off'? Why do you misuse your spirit, unable to 'fully realize your physical form' [*Mencius* 7A38], concerned only with fashioning these entangling vines about 'glue,' 'bastard sons,' 'continuing what is received,' and 'salesmanship'—crowing on about softness and blackness!"

WANG FUZHI: The Course confers all appearances, so all appearances, whether ugly or beautiful, are the Course. Heaven bestows all physical forms, so all forms, whether intact or damaged, are the Heavenly.

GUO XIANG: However vast heaven and earth may be, however multitudi-   6:1
nous the ten thousand things, the source and teacher of all of them is intentionlessness.

SHI DAOSHENG: It is that which knows the Heavenly and knows the Human that is the Teacher of both Heaven and Man. But how could either Heaven or Man know both Heaven and Man? It is only what is neither Heaven nor Man, but can be either Heaven or Man, that attains this knowledge—and such a one is the Source and Teacher of more than just Heaven and Man.

FANG YIZHI: The knowledge that is free of all knowing, or the knowledge consisting of conscious choosing and recognition? Like the ruler's relation to his prime minister? The scholar's relation to his official post? There is from the beginning neither a union nor a separation between Heaven and Man. It is a mistake to cling to either a unity or a duality between them. The Great Source as Teacher administers medicine [e.g., speaking of unity or duality] in accordance with the disease at hand; the understanding of the symptoms is what is truly divine about it. For understanding of symptoms is more divine than knowledge of causal precedents [. . . .] But without knowledge of causal precedents, [you may ask,] how can anything be "nurtured"? Don't use what you understand to disorder what you don't understand, and don't use what you don't understand to disorder what you should understand. Then you will have mastery over the "hammering and smelting" [6:52] of the furnace of creation.

CHENG XUANYING: "What is done by Heaven" means the alternating   6:2
brightness and darkness of the sun, moon, and stars, the life giving and life taking of the four seasons, the unfolding and re-enfolding of the wind and clouds, the cold and warm of the thunder and rain. *"What is done by Man" means grasping with the hand and walking with the feet, seeing with the eyes and hearing with the ears, knowing with the mind—in short, whatever humans endeavor to do, whether skillfully or clumsily.

SHI DEQING: The Heavenly means the natural, Heaven-so Great Course, which is what stands as source to all beings. "What is done by it" means that all things in heaven and earth are transformations of the entirety of the Great Course. Thus they are called "what the Heavenly does." For what is naturally so is done without doing, and yet it indirectly brings all things to completion. It is not due to any intention. "What is to be done by the Human" means that human beings are no more than one among the ten thousand things; it is just that they are the most miraculous, sensitive, and efficacious [*ling* 靈] among them, for they receive the entirety of the Great Course as their Human Nature, which controls their bodies. This is what is called the Genuine Controller [2:9–10]. Thus, when this Genuine Controller controls the seeing, hearing, awareness, and knowledge of human beings, every slight experience in their everyday lives is nothing but the wondrous function of the Great Course. Hence we know that the Human is itself the Heavenly. To know how the Human and Heavenly Virtuosities merge into one is the ultimate knowledge.

6:3   GUO XIANG: "Heaven" is just a way of saying "what is so of itself, the self-so." For doing cannot be done by someone "doing" doing. Doing is spontaneously doing; it is self-so. Knowing does not know by someone "doing" knowing. Knowing is spontaneously knowing; it is self-so. As self-so knowing, knowing is not a result of knowing, is unknown, is itself a kind of nonknowing. Being always in this sense a nonknowing, what we call knowing emerges from nonknowing. As self-so doing, doing is not the result of doing, is undone, is itself a kind of nondoing. Being always in this sense a nondoing, what we call doing comes from nondoing. Since doing comes from nondoing, nondoing is always the master. Since knowing comes from nonknowing, nonknowing is always the source. Hence, the Genuine Human Being discards knowledge and thereby knows, does nothing and thereby does. Self-so, she comes to life; sitting and forgetting, she finds herself. It is only for this reason that she is described as eliminating knowledge and discarding doing.

6:4   GUO XIANG: The human body spans just these seven feet of length, and yet the Five Constants[28] are necessarily an intrinsic part of it from the moment it is born. This tiny body requires all of heaven and earth to support it. Thus, all the things that exist between heaven and earth can never lack one another for even a single day. If even one being were missing, there would be no way for anything to be born. If even one principle failed to come to bear, there would be no

---

28   Sometimes interpreted in early texts as the Five Elemental Processes (the mineral, the vegetable, fire, water, and soil), sometime as the Five Standards (paternal responsibility, maternal love, elder-brotherly friendliness, younger-brotherly respect, and sonly filiality), sometimes as the five primary Confucian virtues (Humanity, Responsibility, Ritual, Wisdom, and Trustworthiness), and sometimes as the Five Relationships (ruler and subject, father and son, elder and younger brother, husband and wife, and friend and friend).

way to live out one's natural years to the end. But our knowing does not know all that this body possesses, and doing is not the agent that brings about every principle that exists. What knowing knows is little compared to the abundance of what is really present in the body. What doing accomplishes is little compared to the abundance of operating principles[. . . .] Now, some have a tireless love of knowledge, for the sake of which they trouble all the parts of their bodies. What they love is no more than a single branch, but thereby they damage the entire trunk and root. This is what is meant by using what you understand to harm what you do not understand. The richest kind of understanding, on the contrary, means to understand that human doing has its own limited range and thus to comply with one's own range of activity without forcing anything beyond it; it means to understand that what understanding understands also has its limits and thus to make use of it without being unmoored by it. Hence, when the understanding consciousness does not worry itself about the "unbounded" [3:2] that lies beyond it, knowing and nonknowing obscurely come together within one's own single body, so that both are complete and intact. This is what it means to use what you understand to nurture what you don't understand.

CHENG XUANYING: *"What is done by the Human" refers to the fact that the four limbs and hundred parts of his body each has its own function. *"What knowing knows" means, for example, the eye knowing colors. For the eye, colors are the known. *"What knowing doesn't know" means, for example, that the eye can know colors but not sounds. For the eye, sounds are the unknown. But even so, the eye sees on behalf of the hands and feet, and the feet walk on behalf of the eyes and ears. Although they have no intention to do anything for one another, they succeed in assisting one another. Thus, all the organs and parts of the body alternately serve one another, each having its own special jurisdiction. The mind's clarity and dimness too have their own limits. What knowing knows nourishes what knowing does not know when it operates to its utmost within its own limited realm without any forced attempts to know anything beyond it.

LÜ HUIQING: To know what the Heavenly does is to know that the Heavenly is that from which the self was born. This involves no doing at all, and the Human has no part in it. It is what the understanding consciousness cannot understand. What consciousness can understand is just the doings of the Human, so that what it understands can be used to nurture what it doesn't understand. This means to use the understanding consciousness to nourish life, rather than using life to follow the dictates of the understanding consciousness [3:2].

LI ZHI: It is difficult to talk about the Course of *Nonknowing. For once you start considering the attainment of what nourishes you as a kind of knowledge, you will think of losing it as a problem. 6:5

TAO WANGLING: It is the Course that serves as the source of all beings, and it is what is not yet fully formed in the mind that serves as the teacher of the mind. It is not only that life and death, coming and going, are its mere reflections, nor merely that Humanity, Responsibility, Ritual, and Music are only its names and appearances: even the word *"Awareness"²⁹ is something that falls on the side of the derivatives, a mere grandchild of it.

WANG FUZHI: To make what is as yet unborn come to life, to make what has come to life die, this is the doing of the Heavenly, which is beyond understanding. Within the span of being alive, however, there are some things which can be understood. Thus we may use our understanding consciousness to understand that everything that happens to us in life must be responded to as an unavoidable fact, and thereby to keep from laboring our vitality in the endless likes and dislikes that are born from delighting in life and abhorring death. Thus, our harmony remains undamaged, and we can allow death, the incomprehensible, to go however the Heavenly has it go. Then our understanding consciousness, not dissipated away, is kept where it is and accumulates richly. But even being alive cannot really be understood, for things like the Course giving us an appearance and Heaven giving us a physical form [5:24], the crowings of the piping of Heaven [2:5], and the transformation of the Heavenly in things [2:49] are definitely beyond our understanding. But on the other hand, even in death we can understand that though the firewood in the fingers is all used up, the fire is transmitted elsewhere [3:8]. One can thus merge life and death, the Heavenly and the Human, unifying the understanding of both in a single consciousness, so that though we are born it is never really birth, though we die it is never really death. This is the Genuine Knowledge of the Genuine Human Being. How could the Genuine Human Being appear concretely as a real person? How could Genuine Knowledge really involve knowing some particular thing? The Human is all the Heavenly, and all understanding is impervious to understanding. Thus it is that we can experience the vague indistinction, entrusting our knowledge to the "slippery mush" [2:41].³⁰

6:6   LÜ HUIQING: The Genuine Human Being embodies the pure and unadorned and is thus free of selfhood. So although he may make a mistake, he knows he could not have avoided making that mistake and thus has no regrets. Though he may be in the right, he knows he could not have avoided being right at that time, so he has no self-satisfaction. For such a person, the highness is his own doing, so who else is there to frighten there? The water and fire are also his own doing, so who else is there to be drowned or to feel hot? The understanding consciousness is certainly not the Course, but the Genuine Human Being's understanding can, in its very demise, ascend through the distant vistas of the Course in this manner.

---

²⁹   "Awareness" is *zhi* 知 . See Glossary. In the *Zhuangzi* passage, the term is translated as "Understanding." Here it is used by Tao in the Buddhist sense of pure, nonobjectified awareness.

³⁰   For further comment on this passage of the *Zhuangzi*, go to www.hackettpublishing.com.

WANG PANG: Both the Human and the Heavenly are the Course, and whoever fully realizes the Course will understand what both of these are able to do. But this understanding is done by nonunderstanding. Understanding the Heavenly with nonunderstanding, you comprehend the subtle guidelines of nondoing. Understanding the Human with nonunderstanding, you fully realize the ultimate reaches of deliberate doing. This is what Laozi means by "observing the subtleties by means of desirelessness and observing the outcomes by means of desire" [*Daodejing* 1]. [. . .] Genuine Knowledge is a nonknowing, allowing one to maintain the smooth compliance with which to handle all one's inadequacies; to hold to the nonaspiring femininity that [attains the perfection that] seems to be lacking something; to be free from schemes to bring anything to oneself and allow the *distinguished men of the world to come to one of their own accord. Thus, it says, they "did not revolt against their inadequacies," and so on.

ZHU BOXIU: If such a person makes an error in his responses and reception of things, it just happens to go that way—what regret could there be? If he gets it right, it's also just a case of its happening to go that way—what self-satisfaction could there be? It is like a tile blown from a roof or a drifting empty boat—it has no deliberate intention to impinge upon other beings, so no being resents it.

LI XIANGZHOU: He does not revolt against his inadequacies because he "does not know" of any inadequacies to revolt against. He does not aspire to completeness because he "does not know" there is any completeness to be aspired to. He does not *plan to become a distinguished man because he "does not know" there are such things as distinguished men to plan to become.

WANG FUZHI: This is the great function of Genuine Knowledge. Not revolting against inadequacies or aspiring for completeness, they forgot about appropriating and renouncing. Not planning their affairs, they forgot success and failure. Wrong without regret, right without self-satisfaction, they forgot honor and disgrace.

SHI DAOSHENG: The successive descriptions of the Genuine Human Beings of old that follow—these are manifestations of the very power of Creation embodied in the tip of Zhuangzi's brush, in the manner of a lion toying with a ball. It is precisely the same thing that "makes the spirits and the Lord-on-High divine, [and] generates heaven and earth" [6:32], washing away the habitual energies of human words and names, and the usual course of the human mind. When people of the world try to force their explanatory commentaries onto it, they are no different from the hunting dog Han Lu chasing after a clump of earth [i.e., wasting their efforts]. 6:7

WANG FUZHI: The mind follows the rise and fall of the breath. When the breath returns to the heels, the mind too does not float off.

GUO SONGTAO: Only when the breath is preserved even when there is no breathing is it really taken in deeply. Still and silent, neither coming nor going, neither in nor out, it cannot be bound by either depression or anger, nor affected by preferences and desires. None of the nine orifices or great organs can influence it. The breath pours in and withdraws down to the heels, which nourishes it deeply, subtly, vastly, lodging it in the endless.

6:8   WANG FUZHI: This describes their increased attempt to extend outward as they increasingly beat themselves back internally.

6:9   WANG FUZHI: They come forth immediately in response to every stimulus. Thus, [the Heavenly Impulse in them] is shallow.

6:10   SHI DEQING: The mass of men find life burdensome. Thus they regard it as a curse to have received it and take no pleasure in it. The Genuine Human Being sees his life as a vehicle bearing the Course, and thus he takes joy in receiving a physical form. Although he lives in the world of men, his mind never contravenes the Course. Because he forgets and is forgotten by the world, he returns to the source with every moment of experience.

MA QICHANG: "Receiving it, they delighted in it"—whether a mouse's liver or an insect's arm [6:41]; wherever they went was acceptable. "Forgetting all about it, they gave it back"—content in the time and finding their place in the following along, joy and anger could not get at them [3:8].

6:11   SHI DEQING: The Human is itself the Heavenly, for it does not depend on any deliberate making or doing. Thus he doesn't use the Human to assist the Heavenly, and this is called truly being a human, a Genuine Human Being.

6:12   GUO XIANG: Those who embody the Course and merge with all transformations identify with the gentleness of the warmth and also with the harshness of the cold, but without any deliberate intention. Thus they have the appearance of warmth and of harshness, their times of killing and of giving life, which are here given the borrowed names of "joy" and "anger."

6:13   SHI DEQING: They have no deliberate intentions concerning their joy and anger, just following along with the effects things create in them, sometimes joyful, sometimes angry, but never maintaining any one fixed state within themselves. Thus they are described as intermingling with the four seasons. They respond fittingly to things, but others don't know they are thus actually free of joy and anger, so it is said that "none can tell exactly what their ultimate end might be."

6:14   GUO XIANG: He is merely destroying in accordance with the people's desire to have it destroyed, so he does not lose their hearts. For when the bright sun ascends in the sky, its illumination shines in all directions. It does not shine on the people out of love for them. Hence the sage warms the world like the spontaneous harmony of the spring sun, and so those who receive his bounty have no need to thank him. He chills the world like the spontaneous descent of autumn frost, and so those who wither and fall do not resent him.

GUO XIANG: They fit together with things but form no party with them.   *6:15*

GUO XIANG: They wander ever in solitude but hold to no single predeter-   *6:16*
mined course.

GUO XIANG: They release all into the vastness, to the point where it takes   *6:17*
on a substantiality of its own.

GUO XIANG: They do not harm themselves with things.   *6:18*

GUO XIANG: They are drawn toward no one thing in particular.   *6:19*

GUO XIANG: Without conscious recognition, without understanding, the   *6:20*
Heavenly Impulse spontaneously emerges, so they are as if oblivious.

CHEN XIANGDAO: Doing what was called for but nonpartisan, they could not be classified as intimate or distant. Deficient but accepting nothing, they could not be classified as noble or base.[31] *Firmly contoured but not rigid, their actions were not completely rounded off, but they did not hold to them stubbornly. Empty but not insubstantial, their patterned appearance was impalpable but imperishable. Cheerfully seeming to enjoy themselves, they unobstructedly took their own pleasure. Impelled along by what they could not help doing, they responded only when forced to. Letting everything gather within but still manifesting outward, they stored their vitality within and yet expressed their spirit to the world. Giving it all away but with their Virtuosity resting securely in place, their bounty functioned externally without harming them internally. Whether leprous, haughty, or unbreached, the perfect activity is free of all deliberate doing. Oblivious, the perfect speech is free of all definite words.

SHI DEQING: Punishments are properly administered by never allowing the   *6:21*
slightest selfish bias to remain. This means that no selfish bias remained in his heart, and he took this as his true body.

LI ZHI: This describes how the Genuine Human Beings of old appeared externally, their outward semblance. "With punishments as their own body" and so on are all the ways they were taken to be "working hard to get there" [6:21].

GUO XIANG: "The Human" means to take the other as definitively other and   *6:22*
the self as definitively self.

MA QICHANG: "Oneness" means the single overriding ultimate reality of the All. "Non-oneness" means the individual ultimate reality of each particular thing.

---

[31]   Cf. *Daodejing* 56.

6:23   WANG FUZHI: If you possess Genuine Knowledge but reject the unevenness of things on the basis of what you know and like, setting up a solitary, empty, quiescent source in contrast to things, then you thereby posit the Heavenly and the Human, opposed counterparts that can never be one. You want to use the Heavenly to overcome the Human and set about waging war on the Human. But for the Heavenly to win out over the Human in this way is perhaps no real victory. For the Heavenly is Heavenly, to be sure, but the Human is also the Heavenly. To "labor your spirit trying to make all things one" [2:23] is to see the Heavenly but not the Human, thus obscuring that which takes the transformations of all things as its own fate [5:4], mixing them all into one thrust, the Genuineness of which cannot be increased or decreased [2:10]. The Genuine Human Being can resemble spring or autumn, can impose punishments or practice the yielding enjoined by ritual propriety, can be wise or virtuous, can destroy a country, can extend his bounty to ten thousand generations, and in all this he is just "vague and evasive" when he responds [5:13–14], coming swooping in and going swooping out [6:10], neither delighting nor rejecting, unifying them all through the Heavenly in him. Having one day of life, he lodges in that one day's everyday function, making opposed counterparts of neither the Heavenly and the Human nor of life and death, but rather unifying them all in the one source, so that each is "the first ray of dawn." [6:35]. This is why he is called one for whom nothing at all is false—the Genuine [Human Being].[32]

6:24   LI ZHI: It is what gives me life and thus it is called the true father; it is what makes me die, and thus it is the true ruler.

WANG FUZHI: What gives them life and takes it away is fate. Some are fated to long life, some to early death, some to give, some to receive. Day and night, the Heavenly and the Human, are then coupled as opposites, rather than experienced as the independent and uncoupled Genuineness. What neither lives nor dies is free of contrasting oppositions and thus towers above without counterpart. The presence of the "genuine ruler" [2:10] means freedom from any ruler. I am then fate itself; I am the ruler. When you find this, you are unending through all generations—how could life alone be worth loving?

LÜ HUIQING: What is liked is the good and beautiful, and what is disliked is the bad and ugly, but when you see the oneness of things rather than their differences, both equally emerge from this oneness. Thus, the liked and the disliked are one. Their oneness is like the transparency of water, and their nononeness is like the waves and ripples, which are also nothing but water. Once you know this, you need not be at rest to be at rest.

WANG PANG: It is because the Genuine Human Beings have no deliberate intentions that their liking and disliking are one. It is because they embrace

---

[32]   For further comment on this passage of the *Zhuangzi*, go to www. hacketpublishing.com.

both sides that the non-oneness is the same as the oneness. Unifying them by means of their freedom from deliberate intentions, they can follow along with whatever is spontaneously so, which makes them followers of the Heavenly. Embracing both sides so as to make them the same, it is at times as if they were agents who make it so, so they are also followers of the Human. Honor and disgrace are part of the naturally changing conditions of the world. Although the sage responds to them, his mind is in reality free of them. If he were to discard the conditions and emotions of the world and consider it right only to decisively forget all things, how could he be a follower of the Human? This is just what Zhuangzi critiques, but ironically it is just what the foolish Confucians of the present age criticize him for.

LU XIXING: It is here that he finally reveals the reason for not delighting in life or abhoring death. "Liking" is the same as "delighting," and "not-liking" is the same as "abhoring." The reason he neither delights nor abhors is that he knows their oneness. This oneness is none other than the Heavenly. Knowing their oneness, he does not use the Human to assist the Heavenly, nor does he use his mind to push away the Course. This is what it means to say that there must be a Genuine Human Being before there can be Genuine Knowledge— for what he knows is nothing more than this.

LI ZHI: Death and life are no more than night and day[. . . .] Night and day   6:25
are both Heaven, sky—since they are both Heaven, could they fail to be one? But since we have already called them night and day, how can they be called one? Thus, their oneness is one, their not-oneness is also one. They are neither one nor not-one.

GUO XIANG: Both life and death are just Fate. The case would be different if   6:26
there were no goodness to it at all. But since there is some goodness to it, it is not the goodness of life alone. So if I regard my life as good, my death is also good.

GUO XIANG: There is no greater example of the power belonging to power-   6:27
lessness than the fact of transformation itself. For it can take up all of heaven and earth and bring them to the new, shouldering mountains and hills to discard the old. Never ceasing for an instant, we find ourselves constantly thrown suddenly into newness. There is no moment when all things between heaven and earth are not moving along. The world is ever new but believes itself to be old. Our boat is replaced each day, but we see it still as the former one. The mountain is exchanged each day, but we see it as the previous one. The moment is lost in each gesture between us, disappearing into oblivion. Hence, the previous me is not the present me. "Me" goes away together with the present moment. How then could the past be held onto? And yet, the people of the world are unaware of this, senselessly declaring that whatever they may presently have encountered can be tied down and kept there. Deluded, are they not?

GUO XIANG: The human body is itself merely one thing encountered   6:28
among the ten thousand transformations. It is not qualified to be privileged as

the sole good. Whatever may be encountered in this endlessness is just as good as the human state; why should being human alone be worth delighting in, and every other state devoid of joy? What was initially nonhuman transforms into a human being. In so doing, what it formerly was has been lost. But you are overjoyed in spite of your loss of the old because you took joy in the new encounter. Change and transformation are endless. What will you fail to encounter? If you delight in the fact of encountering itself, your delight will have no end.

6:29   LÜ HUIQING: The Great Clump certainly has no feelings about me. If there is something good about my life nonetheless, the goodness of my death is assured—what delight or dislike should I have about them?

ZHU BOXIU: Hiding the boat or the *mountain are images for how impossible it is for humans living within Creation-Transformation to ever escape its changes and alterations. Any being in the world that can be hidden away somewhere can also escape to somewhere and thus it cannot be preserved. Only what is not hidden away in anything cannot escape to anywhere, so that all is preserved. The place from which nothing can escape, so that all is maintained, is what Zhuangzi earlier called "the homeland of not-even-anything, the vast wilds of open nowhere" [1:15]. The Course for hiding the world in the world is to find this place and let yourself wander within it, going along with whatever might inadvertently be encountered, vast and open, with a comprehensive vision that sees what it is that survives no matter where you may go. Though you may emerge from the incipient seeds of life only to return to them, in all the transformations of life and growth let yourself see only their daily newness. To where could anything escape? The people of the present world, clinging to their biased views, time and again take things to be their personal possessions, thinking the boat and *mountain are immovable while the ravine and swamp are good hiding places, that material objects have some unchanging part. They do not realize that the invisible pivot is secretly turning, the sundial shadow creeps over the inches without cease—all things, the earth itself, your own body, all are changing without realizing it. So is there any way to rise above all this escaping and changing? Yes: to hide away nothing, to hold onto nothing, letting your mind wander with the Heavenly. Since what you seek is not findable even in the present moment, what could it mean to say that anything has escaped or changed?

FANG YIZHI: Do you understand that your body "escapes" into the elements of earth, water, fire, and wind? Do you understand that the blue Heaven "escapes" into "bricks, tiles, piss, and shit" [as in Chapter 22, p. 89]? Do you understand that the Great Ultimate "escapes" into a horse's hair and a tortoise's shell? This is how it is that nothing ever escapes, so they all are maintained. But how do you distinguish between the "good life, good death, good long life, good early death" on the one hand and "each transformation and all transformations" on the other hand? When a stone stele is put under water, it remains dry, but when taken out of the water, it is wet. Never mind its wetness when it's taken out—who has perceived its underwater dryness?

WANG FUZHI: If in life you are free of blowing and spitting, making it equal to death, then in death you will be free of loss, making it equal to life. Hence to nurture the flow of life is really a matter of nourishing not life itself but rather that within it that can never die. In the push and pull of the great transformation, heaven revolves above and earth wanders below. Every instant the *mountain in the swamp and the boat in the ravine are leaving their original position, but man is unaware of it. Thus, through all the days of my life, my deaths are many indeed. Today's birth is yesterday's death. To hold onto the past or guess about the future is always a form of "thinking oneself secure there," but before even a blink of the eye, the past has vanished without remainder. But when you meld yourself into that which "never stops for a moment," both life and death are your hiding place. Following along with the ten thousand transformations, never stopping for a moment, I am myself what the totality of transformations depend on, maintaining each thing—what can then escape? But though you may "understand" this, it can really only be wandered in; it cannot be held onto. If you hold onto it, your oneness will be a one, but your non-oneness will not be a one. This is why Liezi's wind walking still had to depend on something and hence "escaped him" after fifteen days had passed [1:8].

GUO XIANG: It has the *real disposition of no disposition, hence it is without activity. It has the reliability of impermanence, hence it is without definite form. 6:30

CHENG XUANYING: It has realness in the same way as a mirror reflecting the facts; it has reliability in the same way as an echo manifesting in accordance with whatever stimulus confronts it. Silent, still, empty, flavorless, it is without activity. Looking for it, we do not see anything. Hence it is without definite form.

LÜ HUIQING: It is by getting hold of it that the eyes and ears see and hear, the hands and feet move and operate, so how could it be lacking a kind of realness? By getting hold of it, the summer and winter come and go, all things live and flourish—so how could it be lacking a kind of reliability? But we can find no doer that does these things. This is what is meant by saying it has no definite form.

JIAO HONG: The Great Source and Teacher is the Course. It is only here that he finally says explicitly that it is formless and actionless. But the claim that it has realness and reliability is made from the point of view of [what *Daodejing* 1 calls] "observing its manifestations." "Realness" is the motion coming from stillness, and "reliability" is the ways this motion nonetheless always remains matched with and merged into [the stillness].

6:31 GUO XIANG: This is to say that Nonbeing does not depend on Being for its Nonbeing.

6:32 GUO XIANG: How could Nonbeing generate anything or make anything divine? It precisely does not make the ghosts and Lord-on-High divine, and hence they can make themselves divine. This is the apotheosis accomplished by not apotheosizing. It precisely does not generate heaven and earth, and thus they can generate themselves. This is the generation accomplished by non-generating. Indeed, [for something other than themselves] to make them divine would ultimately never be able to make them truly divine; rather, it is precisely not making them divine that allows them to become divine. How then could merit be worth holding onto, or deeds be worth depending on?

6:33 GUO XIANG: This means that the Course is everywhere. Hence, it is in the high place without being high, in the deep place without being deep, in the long enduring without being of long duration, in the old without being old. There is nothing it is not being, but it is not being whatever it is; it is everywhere present but only as an absence. For what reaches everywhere both high and low can be called neither lofty nor base. What is present both within and without cannot be named either inner or outer. What moves along together with every change cannot be called of long duration. What is constantly nonexistent from beginning to end cannot be said to be old.

6:34 WANG FUZHI: Heaven and earth, the sun and stars, the mountains and rivers, gods and men, all are just particular everyday functions to which it entrusts itself, which it lodges in [2:22–23], each forming its own root and foundation—for there is nothing further to serve as their foundation. It is as if there were a genuine ruler [2:10] there—but how could there be even the least sign of him?

6:35 GUO XIANG: Once life is forgotten, death is no longer despised, and in that case one finds peace in whatever one may encounter—as if breaking free, one is unblocked, created anew in response to each encountered impetus. This is what it means to break through like the first rays of dawn.

6:36 GUO XIANG: To find peace in whatever you are currently encountering, forgetting what may have been received before or what might be received afterward—this is seeing the Singularity.

6:37 CHENG XUANYING: Going along with the daily newness of universal creation, he follows every transformation and change but is not swept away by the changing realm of things. Thus, there is to him no difference between the past and the present.

QIAN MU: "Seeing the Singularity" means being free of space. "No past and present" means being free of time.

6:38 GUO XIANG: If other things are entangled in turmoil while you alone remain untangled, all will fail. But if instead you go along with each entanglement, all will be indirectly brought to completion.

LÜ HUIQING: "Seeing the Singularity" means the same thing as "this and that [no longer] being coupled as opposites" [2:17]. "Free of past and present" means the same thing as "taking part in the diversity of ten thousand harvests, but in each [tasting] one and the same purity of fully formed maturation" [2:41]. "Unborn and undying" means death is me doing the killing, so I never die, and birth is me giving life, so I am never alive. "Welcoming, sending off, completing, destroying," it is I myself who is thus putting things into turmoil, so this "I" is never endangered. Hence, it is called the Tranquility of Turmoil.

LU XIXING: The world is a process of welcoming, sending off, completing, destroying, giving, receiving, doing, constructing. The people of this world cast their minds roaming within all of this, so no sooner has their mind sent something away then another state of mind arises welcoming it. One moment they fear destruction; the next moment they are seeking to create something, arising and perishing constantly, flickering back and forth. Detesting this condition, they try to push it away and eliminate it, not realizing that the state of mind that seeks to get rid of arising and perishing is itself just another instance of the same—how can it get one to the realm of neither birth nor death? Instead, welcome everything, dismiss everything, complete everything, destroy everything! Go along with the spontaneous arrival of each of the states without allowing any additional attitude of mind to interfere. This is called the Tranquility of Turmoil. "Tranquil Turmoil! It is what reaches completion only through turmoil" is a way of describing the great state of stability attained even within the chaotic disturbances of the world.

SHI DAOSHENG: This idea of "coming to completion through turmoil" is truly wondrous. With this alone you can interconnect and comprehend all the points made in the Inner Chapters. The idea of "putting the world outside yourself" connects to the story of Yao's yielding the throne to Xu You in Chapter 1 [1:9–11]. "Putting all things outside yourself" and "Putting life outside yourself" connect to "I have lost me" in Chapter 2 [2:2]. "The breaking through of the dawn" and "seeing the Singularity" connect to "the extinguishing of the firewood and the transmittal of the fire" in Chapter 3 [3:8]. "Free of past and present and then entering into the unborn and undying" connects with "the use of the useless" in Chapter 4 [4:20]. "What kills life does not die, what generates life is not born" connects to "Neither the Heavenly nor the Human win out over the other" in Chapter 6 [6:23]. "Sending off all things, welcoming all things, destroying all things, completing all things" connects to "something empty and serpentine in its twistings, admitting of no understanding of who or what" in Chapter 7 [7:10]. Truly it is qualified to be called the Great Source as Teacher.

WANG FUZHI: In sum, it is all a matter of putting life outside yourself. Since every life has a time when it will change and end, life has always the inherent capacity for changing and ending, which means it is always being put in turmoil. Thus it can never stand beyond it all to form a singular and independent body of its own. To understand death and life is to understand that the loss or retention of both the body and the spirit is a matter of the mighty power's shouldering them and stealing them off, while the unborn and undying throughout the ages never escapes to anywhere, so the survival or perishing of the body is not worth worrying or rejoicing over. Hence, when things come in all their diversity to set you into turmoil, they can only disturb that which escapes, but never that which never escapes, which is firmly and constantly tranquil. If you think you need to eliminate the turmoil to seek tranquility, you will have to depend on a "ravine or swamp" as your hiding place, and depend on "blowing and spitting" to keep you wet. But there are none in the world who are not the Singularity—no self, no counterpart, no destruction, no completion. In all the sendings off and welcomings in, the destructions and completions, the turmoil is of itself in turmoil, and yet the tranquility is of itself tranquil. Even the greatest flood cannot wet the empty expanses of space, and a great fire cannot burn away the unified solidity of the Great Clump. Rising steep and solitary, it all forms a single vastness. When understanding reaches this point, it is like the moment when the sunlight first breaks through, the first moment of dawn, penetratingly and effortlessly reaching everywhere, a solitary light casting forth its radiance, forming a continuum of vast tranquility. Only the innate powers of a sage are able to fully take part in it.

6:39   WANG FUZHI: Since the Great Course is formless and cannot be seen, all that is learned, whether from bamboo and silk, bindings and manuscripts, ink and seals, recitations, direct hearing and seeing, or words and phrases, is just insubstantial echoes. What it all begins from is drift, murkiness, darkness, obscurity—one suspects something is there, but there never has been. The guesses and suspicions about beginnings and no beginnings were transmitted by means of these "transforming voices" [2:45]. Thus, these transforming sounds, though blowing forth like pipings from bamboo, never find that from which they sprout, and yet the Radiance of Drift and Doubt [2:29] has never ceased to be lodged in their self-transformations. So you may go ahead and lodge Genuine Knowledge in any symbolic language at all! It's just another case of reaching completion only through turmoil.

6:40   ZHU ZHENQING: Qin Shi's three cries [at Lao Dan's funeral at 3:8] were still a case of "letting the transformations frighten one." On the other hand, Yuan Rang's singing of the "Cat's Head Song" [at his mother's funeral; see *Record of Ritual*, "Tangong" 2] was ultimately a case of callousness. Now, where there is a morning there must be an evening—your clothes and hat and pendants and shoes suddenly lose hold of the body wearing them. This is the great vista of all motion and stillness. Where there is waking, there must be sleeping—father and son and elder and younger brother all go to dream their separate dreams of Heaven. This is the ultimate reach of converging and dispersing. Naturally content in happening to come into life, naturally following along in happening to pass out of life, for now you sing about it and for now you cry about it. Students must first understand what it means to sing with joy over death and mourn beyond measure over life before they can take part in the ultimate reach of the spirit, which can transform itself into both singing and mourning.

Lü Huiqing: Mice and insects are despised by humans, so humans hate the   6:41
idea that their vital energy and bodies will disperse to become the livers or arms of these creatures.

Lin Yunming: Mice have no livers. Insects have no arms.

Shi Deqing: The mouse liver is something extremely minute; the insect arm is something fragile and insubstantial.

Guo Xiang: In the Course of change and transformation there is nothing   6:42
that is not encountered sooner or later. Now you have encountered the state of having a human form. How could this be anyone's deliberate doing? Birth does not take place deliberately—the time just gives birth spontaneously to whatever is born. Is it not misguided then to labor yourself attempting to possess and control it?

Guo Xiang: Everyone knows that it is inauspicious for metal to be bound   6:43
exclusively to one particular shape. So once you realize you are no different from metal, the bond of the emotional dispositions can be untied. Once these are untied, there is nothing that is not all right.

Wang Fuzhi: These four took the great source, not their minds, as their   6:44
teacher. Every man has a mind, which makes him delight in life and abhor death. But it is not really life he delights in, it is *things*. The eye encounters them and colors take shape. The ear encounters them and sounds takes shape. The mind encounters them and attachments take shape, becoming tied up by things and not even wishing to disentangle itself from the dangling state it has put itself in. Tranquil Turmoil means that things bind themselves while I free myself, becoming a rooster, a crossbow pellet, a wheel, for all are everyday functions for me to lodge in, from which nothing ever escapes. Turmoil comes in from all directions, so all directions are tranquil. Hence the wandering can be unfettered and far-reaching, things and theories equalized, the world of men entered, emperors and kings handled—all Virtuosities fully intact within, with what is nourished unified within its master.[33] Being the generator and not what is generated, the destroyer and not what is destroyed, one fears no transformations—where then could one go that would not be acceptable?

---

[33]   A nod to the chapter titles of all the Inner Chapters.

6:45   GUO XIANG: For those who take heaven and earth as their bodies and vanish into each transformation, although the hand and foot have their different
duties and the five internal organs their varying offices, never taking part in one
anothers' tasks, nonetheless the hundred parts all harmonize into a unity. This
is being together in not being together. They have never deliberately done anything for the sake of one another, and yet both internally and externally they
accomplish what needs to be done. This is doing things for one another by not
doing things for one another. But if instead you labor your mind and your
willpower to help along your hands and feet, operating the thighs and elbows
to manage your five internal organs, then the more involved you become in
handling it all, the more troubled both the inner and outer parts will be. Thus,
a person who takes all the world as one body applies no love or deliberate activity to it.

6:46   GUO XIANG: He who knows the real point of ritual wanders outside the ordinary realm to handle what is within it, "holding to the mother to preserve the
sons" [*Daodejing* 52], matching up to the characteristic human inclinations
and proceeding directly forward on their basis. If instead you are constrained
by names and reputation, and pulled around by forms and regulations, filial
piety will not be based on sincerity and parental love will not be based on anything real. Then father and son, brother and brother, will only deceive one another about the real feelings in their breasts. How could that be the real point
of ritual?

6:47   GUO XIANG: Because he vanishes into each of them, there is no twoness between them [i.e., the energies of heaven and earth].

6:48   GUO XIANG: He tries to *distinguish between[34] life and death but is unable
to find anything to choose between them. They are like the coming of spring,
of autumn, of winter, of summer.

6:49   GUO XIANG: One who is always awake makes no resistance to wherever he
may go, so when others cry, he cries too. This is precisely how each thing takes
whatever suits it as "this" and "right."

6:50   GUO XIANG: I take each transformation, both life and death, as "me." Since
all are me, how can I ever be lost? Since I've never been lost, what worries can
I have? Because one makes no resistance, one cries when others cry. But because one has no worries, one cries without sorrow. There is nothing I fail to
take as me, so inner and outer are invisibly unified, past and present strung together on one thread, constantly renewed along with all transformations—so
how could anyone know where the "me" is once and for all?

---

[34] Alternate reading of the character rendered in the *Zhuangzi* translation here as
"simplify."

GUO XIANG: These three stories of death are all quite consistent with one 6:51 another. It's just that in each case a different kind of loss was being addressed, so in some cases they sang and in others they cried.

LÜ HUIQING: Knowing there have never yet begun to be any things, you no longer see any difference between inner and outer, life and death. Why must those who wander outside the lines necessarily delight in death to the point of singing at a corpse? Thus, in attending a funeral they may be like everyone else in crying, but they differ from others in that they are not encumbered by sorrow and grief. The story of Mengsun is used to show how those who have reached perfection do not separate themselves from agreement with the common world. Life is it, death is it, and crying is also it. *Even if you try to distinguish[35] them from others, it is impossible. The three friends, on the other hand, though not knowing how or why they were born or will die, took life as a loss and death as a return; this shows that they had not really achieved ignorance of how and why they were born and died. Delighting in return, sighing over being a human, they had not really achieved a state of *going after neither what went before nor what comes after. Mengsun, on the other hand, *really* didn't know how or why he was born or died, and so to him in life there was nothing to lose and in death nothing to return to. *Going after neither what went before nor what was to come, he had no reason to delight in death or sigh over life.

LI ZHI: Mengsun alone is awake, and this is why he cries when others cry. What does this mean? True sorrow is not sorrowful. True desolation is undesolated. True crying sheds no tears. True pleasure never laughs. True laughter makes no arrangements. *Discarding all secure arrangements and following along with the transformations of things,[36] you can enter into the clear oneness of Heaven. When you are dreaming you don't know it's a dream; so when you come to be awake, how could you know that it is wakefulness? This is why Mengsun is said to be the only one who is awake.

CHEN SHOUCHANG: When you come upon something that pleases you, the pleasure is there before you have time to smile. And when a smile does emerge on your face, the smile is there before you have time to put it in some kind of order. Pleasures and smiles emerge in the instant the situation occurs. The dreamer not reaching the realm of wakefulness is the same way.

GUO XIANG: He is new every day. 6:52

WANG FUZHI: This is the effect of forgetting life and death. What he calls "my teacher" is the Great Source in which the Heavenly and the Human, life

---

[35] See previous note.

[36] Li's creative reading of the line rendered in this *Zhuangzi* translation, "But when you rest securely. . . ."

and death are combined into one. That it doesn't take credit for the accomplishments of Humanity and Responsibility, that it is daily renewed and *determines the fate of the transformations of all things [5:4] is due only to the fact that it cannot be grabbed hold of as either life or death. Only when you wander together with it, and also forget it, can you accept all its exfoliations of Humanity and Responsibility, of right and wrong, without rejecting them, much less delighting in them!

6:53   GUO XIANG: The concept of "Humanity" is the trace left behind by an instance of unbiased love. The concept of "Responsibility" is the effect left behind by an instance of bringing something to completion. Love is not Humanity, but the trace of Humanity comes from love. Completing things is not Responsibility, but the effect of Responsibility emerges from the act of completing things. Maintaining Humanity and Responsibility is insufficient to bring about an understanding of real love and real benefit, which come from intentionlessness. Hence, they must be forgotten. But this is merely the forgetting of the traces and effects. It is not yet the wondrous comprehension into which one vanishes completely. So he has still come to penetrate them to the point of vanishing [into them].

6:54   GUO XIANG: Since no thing is not the same, he is never less than comfortable with any of them, so what could he prefer or dislike?

6:55   GUO XIANG: He who is the same as each transformation merely goes where each transformation goes. Hence, he is free of constancy.

RUAN YUSONG: "Same" is in terms of the synchronic. "Transforming" is in terms of the diachronic.

6:56   CHEN XIANGDAO: When the ocean is divided into all the rivers, we see the rivers and not the ocean. When the rivers combine into the ocean, we see the ocean and not the rivers. The Course is the ocean, and Humanity, Responsibility, Ritual, and Music are the rivers. When he forgot all of them, Yan Hui attained the Course. This was seeing the ocean and forgetting the rivers. But he had still not forgotten the Course itself until he reached the state where his body and understanding departed, forgetting both things and the mind, vanishingly free of all ties and fetters—in such a state, where could the Course finally reside? It is simply forgotten together with myself. This is why Yan Hui was indeed a worthy man.

LÜ HUIQING: It was "the same"—so he saw wherein all things are one. He had "no preferences"—so there was no end to his transformations. Becoming one with the *Great Openness by means of his nonconstancy—this means simply to be the same as every transformation.

6:57   WANG XUAN: When all your reasoning has been torn to bits, all that is left is this one reality, this one truth. When he says, "This must be what is called

Fate, eh?" it expresses his coming to the end of his rope and arriving at this word "Fate." When he asks, "Heaven? Man?" it is not just a way of expressing his depression; he is really seeking what has brought him to this condition of extremity and failing to find an answer. This rice bag of a foolish child has fallen apart completely; even the "deathless, deathless Dharma Body" is over-turned. But whether crying or singing, it is just a matter of entrusting oneself to whatever spontaneously obtains.

TAO WANGLING: When Mencius said [of Fate that it is] "what arrives although nothing makes it arrive," (*Mencius* 5A7) he said all there was to say about it. To find an ultimate foundation that gives what we get and takes away what we lose is not possible. Hence I ask: Is there really anything there to serve as the ultimate foundation, giving what we get and taking it away? For it is certainly not that Heaven controls our fate. When the realm of Principle[37] contrasted to human desires reaches an end, even the idea of "Principle" no longer applies. When the influence of acquired habit on the inborn nature comes to an end, even the inborn nature vanishes with it. Principle is itself the inborn nature; the inborn nature is itself Fate. All of them finally disappear into nothing together. When the three revert to a unity, a confused mass which is at all places at once, there is no longer any such thing as "Fate."

FANG YIZHI: Some say it would be better if this passage were omitted. I say: This is a man standing right at the mouth of the great furnace. When one comes to this point, one's true emotion comes forth inadvertently, and a completely unguarded cry of pain emerges. Would you say that "a white horse crying in pain under the glow of the clouds" is anything other than "the Great Source as Teacher"? If so, however much you spin your abstruse theories, you are still separated by an ever so thin layer from the real heaven and the real earth. You have then not yet perceived that in the Course there is only this one moon; there is no second moon.[38]

WANG FUZHI: When something cannot be avoided, we call it Fate. But there is no such entity as "fate." Having stumbled into having a human body, we are unable to determine the beginning of all that comes to provoke us into turmoil. Heaven and earth do not alter their minds because there are those in want or those who die. Hence, wealth and poverty have no foundation, life and death have no root, right and wrong have no standard, large and small have no limit. Joy and sorrow then have nowhere through which to enter. The ten thousand transformations are melded together, never really leaving their source.

LÜ HUIQING: The four questions [2:39] concern whether he knows what 7:1 all things are the same in affirming as right, whether he knows that he doesn't

---

37 "Principle" is *li* 理. See Glossary.

38 Borrowing the imagery of the Buddhist *Śūraṅgama Sūtra*.

know, whether all things are devoid of knowing, and whether knowing might not be nonknowing and vice versa. Wang Ni answer all four with "Don't know." For what all things are the same in affirming as right comes to rest in this not knowing. Wang Ni's "Don't know" was an embodiment of it through truly not knowing. "Youyu" — "joyful" — can also be read as meaning "Worry and Joy," while Mr. Tai means "Great Equanimity." The implication is that to possess the knowledge of the understanding consciousness with all its joys is no match for the Great Equanimity. The traces of Mr. Youyu's actions still affirmed the goodness of Humanity as a way to restrain others, so when others followed him, he could indeed win their hearts. But when you consider Humanity good and right, you cannot avoid regarding inhumanity as bad and wrong. Then *some are considered [truly] human and some are not, caging them in a chaos of conflicts. Mr. Tai slept without worry and woke without care, taking himself to be now a horse and now a cow, without disliking either. So his kind of understanding was reliable and without doubts, his Virtuosity genuine and unfeigned. Not knowing of any wrongness to inhumanity, what could ever compel him to negate and criticize other human beings?

LI ZHI: If you consider winning others over as right, you will have to consider those you do not win over as wrong. It is in this sense that Mr. Youyu could never get beyond criticizing others, considering them wrong.

WANG FUZHI: Seeing myself as myself and others as others, I see others as not me and myself as not others. I am right, the others are wrong, so I use my rightness to correct and govern the wrongness of the others, embracing Humanity and Responsibility to restrain the world. It is just this view that I am "not others, so others are in the wrong" that makes the borders that create the so-called Eight Virtues [2:33–34]. But if one stays away from the territories of these borders which establish self and other, right and wrong, the people will find their own contentment in being the people, the rulers in being rulers, peacefully awaking from their dreams so that all creatures may forget one another, just like the oxen and horses that do not mingle with human beings. Thus, his understanding was of the real substance of the feelings of all the people, and the Virtuosity that took shape from it was genuine. Wang Ni's four "nonknowings" were as follows: he knew no self, no others, no right, and no wrong. This and that were no longer coupled as opposites [2:17], so he vanished into the Great Source. This is how emperors and kings may enter the turmoil but remain ever tranquil, bringing tranquility to all the world.

7:2   GUO XIANG: If you entrust yourself to the rightness that is in all things, they complete themselves without requiring any labor from you. But if you try to control all the world with your one solitary body, nothing will be accomplished and you will be a failure at your task.

SHE DIQING: The nature of the people is like that of the birds and mice. If 7:3
a ruler tries deliberately to govern them, how could they fail to be alarmed?
How could they not wish to escape him?

GUO XIANG: To allow [creatures of] every nature to spontaneously grow into 7:4
being as they will is what it means to be unbiased. When your mind wants to
add something to them, this is selfish bias. Indulging your bias in the end never
produces the life of things, but following along with what is free of any bias
leaves all beings intact and complete.

LÜ HUIQING: The nameless man, like all who have embodied the Course,
had nothing he specially delighted in or was tired of. But this really means he
delights in and gets tired of things just like everyone else, for he delights in
chumming around as a human being with the Creator of things and in riding
off on a bird of unkempt air wisps when tired of it. Why? Because the survival
or perishing of such a person resides in his own hands, emerging and vanishing without trace. How could he bother himself over the handling of the world?

WANG FUZHI: Only one whose innate powers are intact but without taking
physical form [5:17], who does not delight in life or hate death [6:10], can nurture life, can nurture the people. He who thinks he can control life and death
pillages life. He who thinks he can control the people pillages the people.

GUO XIANG: Without a wise king, none in the world can find their sponta- 7:5
neous satisfaction, for it is actually the wise king who allows them to find it.
But he achieves this only through nondoing, by conversely going along with
the world. Since all in the world can thus go along with themselves, it seems
not to be the wise king's achievement.

GUO XIANG: This means that Liezi was not yet impregnated with the Course. 7:6

GUO XIANG: Not yet impregnated with the Course, he still had definite in- 7:7
tentions in his mind. Having definite intentions in mind and arrogant about
his one method, insisting the world believe in it, he could be caught hold of
to have his fortune read on his face.

SHI DEQING: Because he wanted to force people to believe in him, he arrogantly displayed his merits to them. Because he was unable to forget selfhood, and wanted others to know and appreciate him, people were able to get
hold of him and read his fortune on his face.

GUO XIANG: Like a sprouting, he neither moves nor straightens himself. 7:8
Blossomless like a dried-out tree, bodily energy stilled like wet ashes, this is how
the Consummate Person is when he is in the state of not responding to any
stimulus. The Consummate Person's activity is heaven, his stillness earth, his
motion the flow of water, his stopping the silence of the reservoir. But the silence of the reservoir and the flow of the water, the action of heaven and the

stillness of earth, all are one in being self-so, free of deliberate activity. Now Ji-xian sees him "sitting and forgetting" [6:54], dwelling there like a corpse, and says he's about to die; later, seeing the way his spirit moves into action and the Heavenly in him follows it, he says there is life in him yet. In truth he responded in each case without any deliberate intention, and the inherent principle in him spontaneously and obliviously matched the case, rising and falling with every change, making the world before him the only measure. Only in this way is one worthy to be a ruler of other beings, following smoothly along with every circumstance without anywhere being brought to an end. Thus he was beyond the fathoming of any fortune-teller. This is the main point of "Sovereign Responses for Ruling Powers."

LÜ HUIQING: The earth corresponds to the power of yin, which is by nature unmanifested. But by means of the patterns of the earth, it can be made known.

7:9   GUO XIANG: "Reservoir" here is simply a way of saying stillness and silence. Now, water is forever free of intentions, handing itself over to follow external things, so whether flowing or still, whether in the froth of the salamander's swirl or the splash of leaping dragons, it is always just like the reservoir, never losing its stillness and silence. When the Consummate Person puts it to use, he flows forth. When he lets go of it, he is still. Although the stillness and the action may be different, his unfathomable silence is one. So here three different states are mentioned to show that whatever ways the waves and currents may change, in whatever unruly alternations of order and disorder, one who dwells within the limits of each is forever undisturbed and satisfied, moored in his forgetting of all deliberate action.

LIN XIYI: In the *Liezi*, all nine names of the reservoir are listed. Hong Yechu thus said that the *Liezi* passage is superior to the *Zhuangzi*, but I'm afraid this is not quite right. If all nine names of the reservoir were listed without leaving any out, the prose would become humdrum. The marvel of Zhuangzi's style is that he can be exhaustive or nonexhaustive quite freely. Only those who are masters of literary art can grasp this.

SHI DEQING: The *whale in the depths of the ocean stands for perfect stillness, the initial state of meditative concentration. The clarity of the still water allows the images of all things to be reflected in it; this is Heaven's Soil, standing for meditative contemplation. Although the flowing water is in motion, the nature of the water remains transparent and clear. This is "the vast gushing surge in which no one thing wins out," standing for the nonduality of concentration and contemplation.

CHEN SHOUCHANG: The water of the salamander's froth is neither moving nor still, a symbol of the impulse that balances energies. The still water is a symbol of the impulse of the Virtuosity that blocks everything out. The moving water is a symbol of the impulse of all that flourishes. But although these three differ, they are one in being deep and unfathomable reservoirs.

LÜ HUIQING: In the patterns of the earth, yin wins out over yang. In the soil of Heaven, yang wins out over yin. But in the vast gushing surge, neither wins out over the other. And yet they are not unified either, which made him appear as an incoherent mess. Where neither wins out there is a certain evenness, however, so it is called the incipient impulse that balances all energies. The three reservoirs are an image for the mind's inherent goodness. Whether it is still, swirling, or flowing, it remains a reservoir. The vast gushing surge where nothing wins out is also like this[. . . .] Empty and serpentine in its twistings, admitting of no understanding of who or what—that is the state of no-mind and nondoing that constitutes his stillness. Endlessly collapsing and scattering, there is none to be known there as he who is scattering, and this constitutes his motion. Flowing away with every wave, there is none to be known there as he who is flowing. The shaman was searching for a fixed self somewhere in the midst of stillness and motion and found it nowhere. That is why he fled.

ZHU BOXIU: "The frothing of flowing water is the reservoir": this means a state where the upper part of the water is moving but in the bottommost depths it remains stored up in stillness, so the places of the swirling salamanders, of the still water, and of the top-flowing, bottom-still water are all to be called reservoirs[. . . .] "The reservoir of still water" is an image of "the incipient impulse of the Virtuosity that blocks everything out," "the patterns of the earth," in its complete motionlessness. "The reservoir of the salamander" is an image for "the incipient impulse of all that flourishes," "the soil of Heaven," in that although the water of the reservoir is unmoving, there is a salamander swirling around deep within it, meaning a slight activity within the stillness. "The reservoir of flowing water" is an image for "the incipient impulse that balances all energies," "the vast gushing surge in which no one thing wins out," in that the top half of the water is moving while the bottom half is still, stillness and motion thus finding their balance, which is used as an image for not yet emerging from the source: the Great Source and Teacher.

LI SHIBIAO: Zhuangzi puts this story in his discussion of "sovereign responses for ruling powers" because when rulers respond to the world they must be quiescent and unmoving, thus penetrating without obstruction whenever any stimulus is felt. It is all about retreating into the hiddenness. Hence both good and bad fortune equally present their difficulties, since in either case, once it starts to come forth from the source, all sorts of damage is incurred. If he labors himself for the sake of anything in the world, he will come to be knowable and divinable by others.

LI XIANGZHOU: Lin Xiyi says that when he reaches the stage of "balancing all energies" he stops at the half and half: it is half still and half moving. But I say that the "vast gushing surge in which no one thing wins out" is a state in which motion and stillness merge into each other—how can it be described as half and half?

FANG YIZHI: "The patterns of earth" and "the soil of Heaven" are a deliberately crisscrossed description [since we normally speak of "the patterns of Heaven" and "the soil of earth"], which brings us to the Great Mean that maintains the *harmony [i.e., the "vast gushing surge"] to transform them with its serpentine twistings. This is precisely what is meant by saying the Mean is not fixed in the middle, and balance does not cling to balance. Instead, it rides on the changes of each temporary situation.

7:11   WANG FUZHI: He begins with the patterns of the earth, his mind unmoved by all things. Suddenly the Heavenly Impulse emerges in the depths of his concealment, but he is in no hurry to show it. Then with an unwavering disposition he can place himself in the large and the small, the flowing and the still and the swirling, making no choice among them, thus bringing stability to all of them. This is what it means to join all the ten thousand transformations into one mind, knowing all and making use of all in the singularity of your nonknowing and uselessness [. . . .] When you are able to become the patterns of the earth, then the incipient impulse from the heels, the vast gushing surge where no one thing wins out, the wondrous function of the empty serpentine twistings, the source of all transformations—all of these will naturally appear of themselves. Hence, Liezi studied only the patterns of the earth and nothing more. Huzi needed no method besides the "wet ashes" to serve as the rooster by which to transform his hen's egg. The mass of chaotic confusion, the collapsing and scattering flowing away with every wave, the solitary form planted there in its place, all of these are the patterns of the earth. The essence of them all is simply the forgetting of life and death—which is why Jixian said he was "not a living being."

7:12   LIN XIYI: "Corpse presiding" means to be master. *"Not letting your reputation be your master" means the same thing as "doing good, but not to the point of bringing reputation" [3:3]. "Repository" means an accumulation. Earlier the text spoke of not planning affairs [6:6]: the meaning here is just that if one has no plans, what use is there for wisdom? If your mind is set on making plans, the plans accumulate there inside you. If there is occasion for a plan, then plan, but you should do so without applying any deliberate set intentions to it. Thus the text speaks of not being a repository of plans. Although things have to be done, do not take charge of getting them done. It is of this that the text says, "Not being the one in charge of what has to happen." Although man cannot live without some wisdom, he does not make wisdom his master, so he says, *"Not being mastered by your wisdom." For if the mind has any master at all, it becomes one-sided.

7:13   GUO XIANG: If you are not empty, you will be unable to follow along with all the varieties of full and substantial reality.

7:14   LÜ HUIQING: By "be empty," how could he mean that one should empty it? Rather, the mind is always empty from the start.

WANG FUZHI: This describes the real "chaos and confusion" [7:11]. Reputation, plans, things to be done, wisdom—these are all ways in which people think they can rule the world, but actually they bring only confusion. When we are emptied of these four, we are emptied of everything. Then although one may be a piping, one need not be tossed around by Heaven's blowing [Cf. 2:3–5].

WANG KAIYUN: When something is stored, there is gain. Where there is gain, there will certainly be loss and thus harm.

LIN XIYI: This passage just means that cleverness and sharp perception can encumber one. "Dropping away the limbs and torso, chasing off acuity" [6:54], one is then a Chaos, with everything mixed all together. This is originally a perfectly ordinary idea, but he lipsticks and powders it up with this tale of drilling holes, making it a marvelous work of prose. Swoosh, Oblivion, and Chaos are all metaphorical figures, not to be taken literally or analyzed rigidly; if you analyze them too rigidly, they become a dream described to an idiot. "Chaos" stands for the original vital force. All people have seven holes in their body, but when an infant is first born, although her eyes, ears, nose, and tongue are all there, she has no understanding; for her, Chaos is still intact. As soon as understanding sprouts, joy, anger, likes, and dislikes emerge: this is the drilling of the holes. When Mencius said, "The Great Man is he who does not lose the heart of an infant" [*Mencius* 4B12], he was speaking of the undrilled Chaos. Zhuangzi turns everything upside down, making it so strange and uncanny, but his prose is still quite marvelous. 7:15

LÜ HUIQING: The yang of the south is an image for manifest existence. The yin of the north is an image for unseen nonexistence. The center between them is neither existence nor nonexistence, which is why it can bring the two together. Although the manifest and the unseen may differ from Chaos, Chaos itself never considers them different from itself, never excludes them. This is why it is said to "attend to them quite well."

FANG YIZHI: Zhi Gong says, "Properly speaking, there should only be two; once you add a third, the whole thing is thrown out of whack. By whipping up a third one here, how many people Zhuangzi has drilled his holes through!" Zhuangzi cries out in response, "But it cannot be made clear without resorting to three! How could it be my drilling that made it so? It was already like this right from the beginning of the *Doctrine of the Mean!*" Zisi[39] says, "I didn't drill those holes! The whole *Book of Changes* was already that way!" Fuxi[40] says, "It wasn't me who drilled it thus! Everywhere between heaven and earth it has always been this way!"

---

[39] Grandson of Confucius, traditionally regarded as author of the *Doctrine of the Mean*.

[40] Legendary creator of the hexagrams of the *Book of Changes*.

SHI DEQING: This passage about Swoosh and Oblivion not only brings a fitting conclusion to the chapter on sovereign responses for ruling powers, but actually provides a general summary of the overall meaning of all seven Inner Chapters. They began with far-reaching unfettered wandering and finally resolved into the Great Source as Teacher, repeatedly speaking of how the petty understanding of the small consciousness harms the flow of life, how it tries to nourish life while forgetting the real host in which it flows, how it impairs the flow of life by favoring mere beings—all these obstructions to far-reaching and unfettered wandering are the fault of clever understanding and calculating skill. They are all holes drilled in Chaos, destroying him, so that the Heavenly genuineness is lost. In fact, from ancient times down to the present, in all times and places, from Yao and Shun on down, there is not one person who is not the driller of holes in Chaos, constantly destroying him.

GLOSSARY OF
ESSENTIAL TERMS

BIAN 辯. Debate, Distinguish, Demonstrate, "Back-and-Forth." The term literally means "debate" or "disputation," as engaged in by logicians of the day, including Huizi. It can mean "demonstration" in the sense of "demonstrating by means of debate which of two alternatives is correct." It is often used in the *Zhuangzi* as a cognate for the homonyms *bian* 辨 (meaning "to distinguish, to differentiate" and, by extension, to clarify by means of debate) and *bian* 變 (meaning "transformation"). Zhuangzi exploits this ambiguity, not least in the crucial line in Chapter 1, "riding atop the back-and-forth of the six atmospheric breaths" (1:8), where "back-and-forth" is meant to capture the sense of "debate" and "transformation," along with the implication of a differentiation between the contending positions.

CHANG 常. Constant, Sustainable. The more common translation as "constant," or even "eternal," can be misleading, for the term also means "common, everyday, ordinary" and at the same time has a distinctive value implication, that is, "normal." Bringing these senses together, it can be rendered as "sustainable" in the sense of what has the value of being capable of being maintained over a long period of time, without exhausting or destroying itself, particularly what can be maintained without special effort—hence a reliable and sustainable course of action. The term (or its cognate, in some versions, *heng* 恆) is central in the *Daodejing*, appearing in the first line of the standard current edition of the text, meaning, not "the Way that can be spoken is not the Eternal Way," but something more like, "guiding courses taken as explicit guides cease to provide sustainable guidance."

CHENG 成. Completion, Taking Shape, Accomplishment, Fullness, Maturity, Success, Formation, Fully-Formed, Perfection; opposed to *kui* 虧, lacking, waning (of the moon), incomplete, or to *hui* 毀, to destroy. Zhuangzi's argument in Chapter 2 plays heavily on the various implications of this term (see 2:21–22, 2:27, 2:35).

DAI 待. Depend On, Wait, Wait For, Attend To. The word means both diachronic "waiting for" and synchronic "dependence on," as well as "to attend to" someone, as one does to a guest. See 1:8, 2:44, 2:45, 2:48, 4:9, 6:5, 6:29, and 7:15. For Zhuangzi, the meaning of words "depends" on the perspective from which they are spoken (6:5). Right and wrong "depend" on the meaning

213

assigned to words, the primary designation of what is "this." The value of one's identity "depends" on the environments that affirm it. Liezi and Peng "depend on" the wind (cf. 1:8), just as Kun "depends on" the water. In all these cases, Zhuangzi regards dependence as an undesirable condition to be overcome. But the same word is used in the crucial line of Chapter 4: "The vital energy is an emptiness, a waiting for the presence of beings" (4:9). Freedom from dependence is attained not by withdrawal from interaction with things, but by emptying oneself of a fixed identity so that one can depend on—follow along with, "go by"—the intrinsic self-posited value of anything that comes along. See "Zhuangzi as Philosopher" at www.hackettpublishing.com/zhuangzisup for a fuller discussion of this point.

Dᴀᴏ 道. Course. Often translated as "Way," the term originally designated a program of emulation and study by means of which a particular set of skills could be cultivated (e.g., "the course of the sage kings," "the course of archery") or a process by which a particular type of valued result was produced ("the course of Heaven," which produces the seasons and thus the growth of all things). More concretely, it denotes a "road" or "path" and also means "to speak." In pre-Daoist thought it has a highly normative and ethical flavor: deliberate activity directed toward a goal that is seen and known in advance. Putting these implications together, it can be translated as "Guiding Discourse." Daoist use of the term, beginning with the *Daodejing*, ironically plays on this original meaning, reversing it to signify the nondeliberate and indiscernible process that is claimed to be the real source of value and being, on the model of the unhewn raw material from which a particular culturally valued object is carved. In the Inner Chapters it is used in both of these senses, along with a new sense distinctive to Zhuangzi: the process of producing not only valued things but also value perspectives and hence all the diverse values themselves. In the rest of the *Zhuangzi*, the earlier Daoist sense of the term is again prominent. See the Introduction and "Zhuangzi as Philosopher" at www.hackettpublishing.com/zhuangzisup for a fuller discussion.

Dᴇ 德. Virtuosity; usually translated as "Virtue." The original sense of the term is an efficacious power, "virtue" in the nonmoral sense ("by virtue of . . ." meaning "by the power of . . ."), which is closely linked with *dao*. If *dao* is a course of study, *de* is what is attained by successfully completing that course: the perfected skill thereby acquired. The term is thus often glossed with the homophone *de* 得, meaning "to attain" or "to succeed." Virtuosity is what one gets from a course. In the Daoist sense, it is the intrinsic powers constituting a thing's distinctive being, where a characteristic is regarded not as a property inhering in a substance but as a virtuosity, an effortless skill in a particular kind of efficacious nonaction. From an early period the term is also used to mean "moral charisma" or "noncoercive persuasiveness," and by extension leniency and kindness on the part of a ruler, as opposed to strict enforcement of penal law; here again this is looked at as a manifestation of the ruler's mastery and virtuosity in his practice of the "course" of true rulership.

Lɪ 理. Guideline, Coherence, Pattern, Perforations, the Way Things Fit Together, the Sense Made by Things, the How and Why of Things. "Principle" is
the most common translation of this term, but that word sometimes has misleading metaphysical connotations in English that are best avoided. In its earliest usages, the term was a verb meaning "to divide something up in a way that
made it valuable or useful," for example, carving a raw piece of jade into a ritual
pendant or dividing a field for agricultural purposes. By extension, it came to
mean the inherent lines or patterns in the raw material that might guide such
cutting most easily and effectively. The single occurrence of the term in the Inner Chapters (3:5, where it is translated "unwrought perforations") marks the first
appearance of the binome "Heavenly *li*" (*tianli*), which would later become a
central metaphysical category in Neo-Confucianism. But in Chapter 3, its meaning is more concretely related to the actual lines and patterns appearing in flesh,
guiding the knife to effectively and easily cut it. In later parts of the *Zhuangzi*,
the term becomes a more general philosophical term, referring to the discernible
guidelines in any object that allow one to take worthwhile action with respect to
it, or any guideline that can be discerned, such that acting in accordance with it
(or dividing along that particular line) will lead to a valued arrangement of things,
that is, to a "coherence." *Li* is a coherence in the sense of something valued,
something readable, or the lines according to which one may divide things up
so as to make them cohere into a desired whole. But like the term *dao*, it has a
strong normative sense, sometimes used "ironically" in Daoist works; a line or
continuity that guides action, that is, a guideline. As coherence, it is the sense
made by things, the how and why of them, the way they fit together, and a tracing of what patterns of action are workable with respect to this thing. It is translated differently according to the parallelism operative in each context.

Mɪɴɢ 命. Fate, Destiny. Literally, "a command," originally linked to Heaven
in the term *tianming* 天命 (Mandate of Heaven), which was used as a moral
justification for the Zhou overthrow of the Shang dynasty in the thirteenth century B.C.E. This term undergoes many of the same modifications that affect the
term "Heaven" in subsequent Chinese thought. In the Inner Chapters it is not
a preexisting plan inscribed in advance in some other, transcendental site, de-
termining what will happen, but rather the unknowability of the agent who
makes things happen. In the *Zhuangzi*, the term is sometimes explicitly disas-
sociated even from "Heaven" (6:57), underscoring the sense of "what happens
although I can find no one who makes it so," or more simply it is a synonym for
"the inevitable," that is, what no conscious purpose or activity, of any one particular agent, can change. That fate is not to be thought of as an agent that does
something or even accounts for anything is clear from Zhuang Zhou's contemporary Mencius, whose conception of Heaven retained a much more normative tinge than Zhuangzi's; Mencius states, "What arrives although nothing
brings it is Fate" (*Mencius* 5A7).

Qɪ 氣. Vital Energy, Atmospheric Conditions, Breath, Air, Life Force. A key
term in Chinese cosmology, sometimes speculatively traced to a root meaning

of the mist that forms into clouds, or even the steam rising from rice, in either case suggesting a vapor that takes various shapes and provides life (as rain or as food). It refers to air in general, but more specifically to the breath, and by extension the life force, the absence of which constitutes a living creature's death (referred to as "cutting off the *qi*"). Cosmologically, it comes to be regarded as the substance of which all things are composed, which is by nature biphasic, tending to expand into impalpable vapor and condense into palpable objects, spanning both the material and the spiritual; this is a meaning often encountered in the later parts of the *Zhuangzi*. It has no one fixed form and is composed of no fundamental building blocks such as atoms or particles; rather, it is constantly in a process of transformation. It also refers to weather conditions, and to the general "feeling" of a particular atmosphere either physically or stylistically. These implications are to be kept in mind in considering the various uses of wind imagery in Chapters 1 and 2. In Chapter 4 it is the "empty" condition, contrasted to the ear and the mind, with which one hears when practicing the "fasting of the mind" and which is "a waiting for the presence of beings" (4:9). Having no fixed form or identity of its own ("empty"), it is able to adapt itself to any and every condition.

REN YI 仁義. Humanity and Responsibility. The cardinal virtues of Confucianism, often translated as "Benevolence and Righteousness." *Ren* is originally the adjectival form of "human" (*ren* 人), initially used especially of the noble class as opposed to the common masses (referred to as *min* 民). Hence, the term means the demeanor of a true member of the nobility, someone who displays the character proper to a noble or, adjectivally, "noble." Confucius expands on this implication, using the term to mean something like "truly human" (note that David Hall and Roger Ames translate the term as "authoritatively human"), applicable to a virtuous member of any social class. The term comes to have the implication especially of kindness and humanitarian love. *Yi* can mean rightness, justice, or the doing of what one's particular role or rank requires. It is often glossed in early texts as "appropriate." The same word is also used to denote "meaning," as in the meaning of a word. Here it is translated as "Responsibility" to cover all these implications, with the full sense of "responding" in the forefront. The word basically means "responding appropriately," whether to one's position and role (duty), to the needs of the moment (appropriateness), or to the adjudication of alternatives (justice). The "meaning" of a word is also an instance of "doing what one should in response" to the word, the "appropriate response" to the use of that word. In some places here this word has also been translated as "justice" or "conscientiousness," according to the needs of the context.

SHENG 生. Becoming, Birth, Life, the Life in Us, the Life Process, the Process of Life, the Flow of Life. The term means both "birth, becoming, coming into existence," whether of a state or condition or of a living entity, and "life" in the sense of being alive. Hence, "life process" is sometimes used as a translation, sometimes "generation," "production," or the like. In the opening lines of Chapter 3 (3:2), in accordance with the "shoreline" and "current" imagery used, it is translated as "flow of life."

SHI/FEI 是非. Right/Wrong. Literally, "that's it/that's not it" (A. C. Graham), implying, "right/wrong." *Shi* by itself, or coupled with *bi* 彼 ("that, other"), can mean simply "this." The double meaning of "this" and "right" are key to Zhuangzi's argument in Chapter 2. For a full discussion, see "Zhuangzi as Philosopher" at www.hackettpublishing.com/zhuangzisup.

TIAN 天. Heaven, Heavenly, Skylike. Originally the name of the ancestral deity of the Zhou imperial house, whose moral "mandate" underwrote the Zhou overthrow of the Shang dynasty in the thirteenth century B.C.E. Like many ancient patriarchal deities, this collective ancestor was a sky god. With the rationalizing tendencies of the Spring and Autumn Period (770–475 B.C.E.), however, including the early Confucian movement, the naturalistic association with "sky" began to grow more pronounced as the anthropomorphic and morally retributive aspects of the term were dampened. In the *Analects*, Confucius sometimes uses the term with clear but possibly rhetorical anthropomorphic implications, but elsewhere in the same work he states that Heaven "does not speak [i.e., issues no explicit commands], and yet the four seasons proceed through it, the hundred creatures are born through it" (*Analects* 17.19). The naturalistic sense of Heaven as the plain process of the sky seems to be present in this pronouncement. Interpretive hedgings continued in the work of Zhuang Zhou's contemporary Mencius, representing what would later be deemed the mainstream Confucian tradition. Mencius sometimes reduced the meaning of Heaven explicitly to simply "what happens although nothing makes it happen" (*Mencius* 5A7). This is the sense of the term that emerges front and center in Zhuangzi's usage: the spontaneous and agentless creativity that brings forth all beings, whatever happens without a specific identifiable agent that makes it happen and without a preexisting purpose or will or observable method. This is "skylike" in the sense that the sky is conceived as the everpresent but unspecifiable open space that "rotates" tirelessly and spontaneously, bringing the changes of the seasons and the bounty of the earth forth without having to issue explicit orders, make or enforce "laws," or directly interfere: the sky makes the harvest without coming down and planning and planting; its action is effortless and purposeless. The Heavenly in all things is this "skylike" aspect of all things. The term "Nature" has been used by some early translators, but the implication of Nature as an ordered and knowable system, running according to something called "Natural Laws," which are rooted in the wisdom of a divine lawgiver, is profoundly alien to the Chinese conception of spontaneity, which excludes the notion of positive law as an externally constraining force. Since the term no longer refers to a particular agent, but a quality or aspect of purposeless and agentless creativity present in all existents, it is here often translated as "the Heavenly" rather than the substantive "Heaven."

YI MING 以明. Illumination (of the Obvious). Literally, "making use of light." The character *ming* is composed of a graph juxtaposing the sun and the moon; its most basic meaning is simply "light, brightness." It also means to make manifest, or to understand, or what *is* manifest, the obvious. The distinctive phrase *yiming* 以明 "using *ming*, because of *ming*," is repeated several times in Chapter 2 (2:15, 2:19, and 2:29) and is a crucial point of controversy for interpreters. *Ming* is contrasted to *zhi* 知 (see entry here) several times in the *Daodejing* (10 and 33; cf. also 16, 24, 27, 36, 47, 52, and 55, where the term denotes either a type of awareness with a positive connotation or manifestness per se), and there too *ming* is approved of by the Daoist while *zhi* is disparaged. In the *Daodejing*, it seems to refer to the type of awareness that does not cut names and identities entirely out of their unnamed contexts, thereby retaining a sense of their connection to the processes of the whole and their rootedness in the nameless. This is a type of nonknowing that is identified with the knowing of the sustainable (*chang*; see entry here). Zhuangzi does seem to inherit something of this contrast in his use of the term but gives it a twist more in keeping with his own way of thinking. Some take the term, as used at crucial junctures in Chapter 2 of this work, to indicate a higher, perhaps intuitive type of understanding, which transcends the relativism of perspectival rights and wrongs, a "Great Knowledge" somewhat similar to Buddhist enlightenment. But this seems to be inconsistent with Zhuangzi's relativist critiques, which must then be regarded as merely therapeutic and provisional. Understanding this term in its more basic sense of "obvious" resolves this tension. It then refers not to a deeper apprehension of the real, transcendental truth lying beneath the surface of appearances, but rather to attentiveness to the surface itself, the most obvious and undeniable feature of which is the disagreement between varying perspectives and their transformations. As such it is related to other distinctive and seemingly paradoxical phrases in Chapter 2, notably "the Shadowy Splendor" (2:37) and "the Radiance of Drift and Doubt" (2:29). Drift and Doubt are precisely what is obvious, and the radiance and illumination provided by this resolves the problems they seem to present, i.e., the uncertainty of multiperspectivism. This is still positively contrasted to ordinary *zhi* and does all the work attributed to *ming* in the earlier Daoist sense. (See "Zhuangzi as Philosopher" at www.hackettpublishing.com/zhuangzisup.)

YINSHI 因是.   Going by the Rightness of the Present "This." A special term of Zhuangzi's, repeated several times in Chapter 2 (2:16, 2:23, 2:24, and 2:33) but rarely anywhere else, it sums up his "Wild Card" way of handling the perspectival nature of value judgments (see "Zhuangzi as Philosopher" at www.hackettpublishing.com for a full account). *Yin* normally means simply "to follow" or "to go along with," but, as A. C. Graham has shown, it was also part of the technical vocabulary of the logicians of Zhuang Zhou's day, used to mean "to take as a criterion for a judgment, to go by." (See *Shi/fei*.)

ZHENG 正.   True, Right, Real, Correct, Straight, Aligned, Untilting. Normally translated simply as "true" or "correct," sometimes as "real" in the sense of "a true specimen of a given type," the term has special importance in Chapters 1 and 2 of the *Zhuangzi*, where it is sometimes the object of critique (2:39, 2:44), but sometimes used in a positive sense. In the latter case, given Zhuangzi's critique of normativity, the term is translated in accord with its more basic etymological meaning of "straight, aligned with." Hence, in the key line in Chapter 1, "to chariot upon what is true both to Heaven and to earth" (1:8; cf. also 1:4), the term is translated as "true," but this is to be understood in the sense of "aligned with" (as a rifleman's aim may be said to be "true"), rather than in the epistemological or moral sense.

Zʜɪ 知. The Understanding, Knowing Conscoiiusness, Conscious Knowing, the Understanding Consciousness, the Mind Bent on Knowledge, Consciousness, Intelligence, Intellect, Wisdom, Cleverness, Discernment, Knowledge, Know-how, Understanding, Comprehension. This is a crucial term in the *Zhuangzi*. The character can be pronounced in two ways, one being cognate with 智, usually translated as "wisdom." It denotes not a store of information but rather a *skill* in making "correct" distinctions concerning the character, behavior, and value of things encountered, and the successful know-how issuing from this recognition. Mencius, Zhuang Zhou's contemporary, defines it as the fullest development of the innate capacity to distinguish *shi* and *fei*, the key terms in the *Zhuangzi's* second chapter, meaning both the ability to approve and disapprove (and thereby to distinguish "right" from "wrong") and also the faculty of judgment that identifies what *is* or *is not* a certain thing or a member of a certain class. Sometimes Zhuangzi uses this positively charged term ironically, critiquing wisdom or "cleverness" in this sense.

In another pronounciation, the word means the faculty of cognition in general: what recognizes and understands on the basis of its knowledge, regards things as one way or another, and has opinions, views, and plans about things—the thinking mind. But the term also means *consciousness* in the sense of sentience or awareness as such. A few decades after Zhuang Zhou, the Confucian philosopher Xunzi will say, for example: "Fire and water have vital energy [*qi*] but not life; plants have life but no consciousness [*zhi*]; animals have consciousness but no sense of responsibility [*yi*]. Human beings have vital energy, life, consciousness, and also a sense of responsibility" (*Xunzi*, "Wangzhi"). The same word was used in this period in posing the question about whether the ghosts of the dead had consciousness or not. So the term should in all cases denote consciousness and its thinking, conceived as intrinsically a skill in making judgments and discerning objects by dividing down from a larger whole, and the capacity for successful action derived therefrom. The whole, undivided, would be impossible to discern; one could not be conscious of it. *Zhi* is the capacity to make "correct" divisions and select out particular parts from a larger whole. "The understanding" considered as a faculty of judgment, the capacity of the mind to identify and categorize things (somewhat in the sense of the German *Verstand*), is useful as a blanket translation for many of these senses. "Discernment," "wisdom," or "intelligence" is used as a translation when the sense of a skill in making correct distinctions is stressed. "Cleverness" is used when the sense of practical skill, or even cunning, is at the forefront. "Understanding," "conscious knowing," or simply "knowing" is used when the context implies a stress on the explicit holding of views about what is so and what is right. "The understanding consciousness" or simply "consciousness" is used when this process of knowing is viewed more substantively as the awareness that apprehends objects of experience about which judgments might be made.

About the Commentators

Cao Shoukun 曹受坤 (1879–1959). Late Qing dynasty and Republican period scholar and calligrapher, whose commentary on the *Zhuangzi* is often cited by Qian Mu.

Chen Jingyuan 陳景元 (also called Chen Bixu 陳碧虛; 1024–1094). Song dynasty Daoist priest, scholar, calligrapher, and music lover, appointed as a high-ranking secretary of Daoist affairs by Emperor Shenzong and held in high regard for his learning by Wang Anshi and other officials at the Song court, Chen was the author of commentaries on both the *Daodejing* and the *Zhuangzi*.

Chen Shouchang 陳壽昌 (also called Chen Songquan 陳崧佺, fl. late 19th century). Chen took the national exam and earned his *jinshi* degree in 1868, later becoming renowned as a calligrapher. His *Zhuangi zhengyi* was first published in 1887.

Chen Xiangdao 陳祥道 (mid-eleventh century). Song dynasty official and close associate of Wang Anshi, supporter of Wang's "New Studies," Chen authored a commentary to the *Analects* and also compiled a renowned and massive work on classical Confucian ritual.

Cheng Xuanying 成玄英 (fl. mid-seventh century). A Daoist priest of the early Tang dynasty, Cheng was the author of what became the official "subcommentary" (*shu*) to Guo Xiang's commentary, as well as commentaries on the *Daodejing*. Cheng employed Tiantai Buddhist ideas and the double negation method of the Chongxuan ("Redoubled Mystery") School of Daoism to develop and explain Guo's commentary, adding philological glosses and further points of his own.

Fang Yizhi 方以智 (1611–1671). Multifaceted genius of the late Ming—empirical scientist, phonologist, Confucian scholar from a distinguished family of the same, *Book of Changes* specialist, Buddhist monk in the Caodong (Sōtō) line of Chan (Zen), and author of the *Yaodi pao Zhuang* ("The Monk of Yaodi Roasts Zhuangzi"), one of the unsung masterpieces of Zhuangzi commentary. Fang was one of the first Chinese scholars to seriously engage Western scientific discoveries brought by Jesuit missionaries, accepting some of their findings in anatomy and astronomy, but remarking, "The Western Learning is skilled in measuring palpable objects [i.e., empirical studies], but clumsy in penetrating to the incipient impulses that make things so." He also made hands-on discoveries in the field of optics. In his early life, Fang produced classic works in the empirical sciences and phonology. His later philosophical writings combined Confucian, Buddhist, and Daoist elements into a creative and penetrating synthesis. Like many Ming loyalists, he became a Buddhist monk at the fall of the Ming, apparently to avoid trouble with the new Qing authorities. Unlike many such monks, Fang appears to have become enthusiastic and sincere about his Buddhist studies, and he remained a monk to the end of his life, which ended in apparent suicide while on the run under threat of arrest. His Zhuangzi commentary is a brilliant work, gathering comments from older commentaries and from his teachers and friends into a complex fugue of voices and adding his own sometimes critical, sometimes mocking, sometimes abstruse comments, in the style of Chan (Zen) Buddhist commentary, but with a strongly Confucian sensibility underlying it.

GUO SONGTAO 郭嵩燾 (1818–1891).   Qing dynasty diplomat and statesman, member of the Self-Strengthening movement in the 1860s, close associate of Zeng Guofan, whom he assisted in putting down the Taiping rebellion, Guo was also the first Qing minister to be stationed in a foreign country, serving as ambassador to England and France. His comments on the *Zhuangzi* are often quoted by his nephew Guo Qingfan, whose *Collected Commentaries to the Zhuangzi* remains one of the standard works in the field. Guo Songtao is also reported to be the first Chinese person ever to use a telephone.

GUO XIANG 郭象 (252–312).   Responsible for editing the original fifty-five chapter version of the *Zhuangzi* down to the current thirty-three chapter version, Guo Xiang is also the most influential of all its commentators, his work later being treated as the de facto "official" commentary when the text came to be recognized as canonical in imperial collections. His commentary is based closely on Xiang Xiu's lost work, to the point of raising suspicions of plagiarism. All later commentators may be assumed to have studied Guo's commentary closely. Guo's staunchly anti-metaphysical, anti-foundationalist, and antitheistic interpretation of Zhuangzi rejects any notion of the Course as creator or source of beings, and with it any ontological hierarchy between Heaven and Man or between the Course and things. Instead, he stresses the concept of spontaneity, or "self-so," (*ziran*,自然) reading Zhuangzi's Course as *literally* nonbeing, so that claims of the Course's creation of things are to be understood as meaning that nothing interferes with the self-so self-creation, and also intrinsic rightness, of each individual thing. "Self-so" is the antonym of deliberate activity and of the purposive knowledge that goes with it. All deliberate activity, in Guo's view, is based on the "traces" left by one particular self-so event on another, which come to inspire conscious esteem and emulation, thereby interfering with the self-so process that functions in the absence of cognitions, ideals, explicit values, and deliberate endeavors. Guo often interprets against the grain of the surface meaning of the *Zhuangzi* text, particularly when it is satirical or critical of Confucian sages or when it seems to advocate withdrawal from active involvement in the world of affairs. For Guo, the critiques in the text are merely of the sages' "traces," not of the sages themselves, who were themselves perfectly merged into their own self-so and thus perfectly right in all their deeds, but who thereby unfortunately, through no fault of their own, came to be valued and emulated by later people, thereby undermining and disturbing the self-so right-ness of these misguided admirers. Guo's expositions on the theme of the self-so, and his uncompromising relativism, remain unsurpassed among Zhuangzi's com-mentators.

Hu Yuanjun 胡遠濬 (1866–1931).   Eclectic scholar, painter, and poet of the late Qing and early Republican period, who advocated a syncretic approach com-bining Confucianism, Daoism, and Buddhism. His *Zhuangzi* commentary has a highly Buddhist flavor.

Jiang Yu 江遹 (ca. mid-eleventh century).   Song dynasty commentator on the classic Daoist text the *Liezi*, sometimes quoted by Jiao Hong.

Jiao Hong 焦宏 (1540–1620).   Jiao's *Zhuangzi yi* (Wings to the *Zhuangzi*) is a companion volume to his *Laozi yi* (Wings to the *Laozi* [*Daodejing*]). Both are ex-tremely valuable resources, compiling and preserving Jiao's own selections from dozens of no longer extant commentaries on these two Daoist classics, which are in many cases all we have left of the early commentaries. Jiao adds his own com-mentary as well, reflecting a learned and syncretic perspective on the text, com-bining Buddhist, Daoist, and Confucian ideas.

Li Shibiao 李士表 (d.u.).   Poet and author of the Southern Song dynasty, whose *Zhuang Lie shilun* (Ten essays on [passages in] the *Zhuangzi* and the *Liezi*) is collected in Jiao Hong's work.

Li Xiangzhou 李湘州 (also called Li Tengfang 李騰芳; 1573–1633). Prolific Ming scholar-official of Confucian orientation, whose commentary on the *Zhuangzi* is often quoted by Fang Yizhi.

Li Zhi 李贄 (also called Li Zhuowu 李卓吾; 1527–1602).   Ming philoso-pher, sometime semi-Buddhist monk, nonconformist and provocateur, self-proclaimed "heretic," often considered a far-left, fringe, or even post Confu-cian influenced by the more radical aspects of the Taizhou School of Wang Yang-ming studies. Li was an outspoken critic of orthodox Neo-Confucianism, particu-larly its villification of "private desires" as distinct from the Principle of Heaven. He was also an advocate of gender equality and an opponent of arranged marriage.

Lin Xiyi 林希逸 (1193–?).   A skilled painter, calligrapher, and poet, Lin's "oral commentary" on the *Zhuangzi* stresses literary and rhetorical features of the text, though sometimes with a relaxed attitude toward philological matters.

Lin Yunming 林雲銘 (also called Lin Xizhong 林西仲; 1628?–1697?). Qing dynasty poet, prose stylist, and literary critic, whose commentary on the *Zhuangzi* is especially sensitive to the literary and rhetorical aspects of the text.

Liu Chenweng 劉辰翁 (also called Liu Xuxi 劉須溪; 1232–1297). Late Song loyalist and patriot who became a recluse scholar and poet after the dynasty fell, often quoted by Jiao Hong and Fang Yizhi.

Liu Xianxin 劉咸炘(1896–1932).   A brilliant scholar of the early Republican period, Liu was chair of the Department of Philosophy at Sichuan University. Despite his early death he was an extremely prolific writer with almost unmatched knowledge of many fields in traditional Chinese culture.

Lü Huiqing 呂惠卿(also called Lu Jifu 呂吉甫 1032–1111).   A Confucian classicist, Lu was a high-ranking government official in the reigns of five Song dynasty emperors. As a close associate of the controversial Song reformer Wang Anshi, Lu was a staunch defender of Wang's "New Policies" and successfully defended them against the critiques of Wang's nemesis, the arch-conservative Sima Guang. In addition to a commentary to the *Zhuangzi*, Lu wrote exegeses of the *Daodejing*, the *Analects*, and the *Classic of Filial Piety*.

Lu Xixing 陸西星(also called Lu Changgeng 陸長庚 1520–1606).   Prolific author, theorist, novelist, and commentator, Lu was founder of the "Eastern School" of Daoist Inner Alchemy, known for its advocacy of sexual practices. His extensive *Zhuangzi Nanhuazhenjing fumo* (Ink aides to the *Zhuangzi*) utilizes many Buddhist and Daoist ideas to interpret the *Zhuangzi* with particular stress on its implications for spiritual cultivation.

Luo Miandao 羅勉道 (d.u.).   Ming dynasty scholar whose *Zhuangzi Nan-huazhenjing xunben* (Tracing back to the root of the *Zhuangzi*) focuses on close philological analysis of the text, attempting to steer clear of both empty praise of the literary wonder of the writing wherever it is hard to interpret and also of imposing anachronistic Buddhist and Confucian ideas onto it.

Ma Qichang 馬其昶 (1855–1930).   Late Qing dynasty and early Republican period scholar, historian, and literary figure, whose commentary offers extensive philological glosses of difficult passages in the *Zhuangzi*.

Qian Chengzhi 錢澄之 (1612–1692).   Ming loyalist who temporarily became a Buddhist monk and then a hermit scholar after the rise of the Qing, Qian was a poet and scholar who devoted himself to classical studies, with particular interest in the *Book of Songs*, the *Book of Changes*, the *Chuci*, and the *Zhuangzi*.

Qian Mu 錢穆(also called Qian Binsi 錢賓四 ; 1895–1990).   Great historian and Confucian thinker of the modern period, whose *Zhuangzi zuanjian* selectively compiles passages from many previous commentators and includes judicious glosses and comments of his own.

Qu Dajun 屈大均 (1630–1696).   Poet and scholar, Ming loyalist, and sometime Buddhist monk, Qu was one the "Three Great Masters of the Deep South [i.e., Guangdong]" in the late Ming and early Qing.

Ruan Yusong 阮毓崧(early twentieth century).   Active in the Yuan Shikai government, Ruan was a Buddhist scholar, a founding member of the Wuchang Buddhist Association, and a supporter of Taixu's interpretation of "Consciousness-Only" Buddhism.

SHI DAOSHENG 釋道盛 (also called Juelang Daosheng 覺浪道盛 1592–1659). Ming Buddhist monk in the Caodong (J: Sōtō) lineage of Chan (J: Zen) and Buddhist teacher of Fang Yizhi; his comments on Zhuangzi are often quoted by Fang.

SHI DEQING 釋德清 (also called Hanshan dashi 憨山大師; 1546–1623). One of the "Four Eminent Monks" of the Ming dynasty, Shi Deqing was a Buddhist monk renowned for his works on Chan (Zen), his spiritual autobiography, and his syncretic approach to Buddhism. More broadly, he viewed the three teachings (Buddhist, Daoism, and Confucianism) as forming a unity. His commentaries to both the Inner Chapters of the *Zhuangzi* and to the *Daodejing* are regarded by many as masterpieces, showing close attention both to the literary structure and to the religious and philosophical implications of the texts.

SIMA BIAO 司馬彪 (246?–306?). Late Han dynasty historian whose lost commentary on the *Zhuangzi*, one of the earliest on record, is preserved only through scattered quotations in other sources. Sima's interpretive glosses on obscure passages are particularly precious because of their early provenance.

SUN KUANG 孫礦 (also called Sun Yuefeng 孫月峰; 1543–1613). High-ranking official, literary critic, and prolific author of the Ming dynasty.

TAN YUANCHUN 譚元春 (1586–1637). Late Ming literary theorist, poet, and writer, Tan is a representative figure, along with Zhong Xing, of the Jingling School, named after the birthplace of Tan and Zhong, advocating individual expression and formal innovation rather than imitation of the ancients. His commentary on the *Zhuangzi* is often quoted by Fang Yizhi.

TAO WANGLING 陶望齡 (1562?–1609). Ming poet and scholar, and along with Yuan Hongdao a representative of the Gong'an (Koan; meaning "public case" in Chan [Zen] Buddhism) School of expressive innovation in poetry. Often quoted by Fang Yizhi.

WANG FUZHI 王夫之 (also called Wang Chuanshan 王船山 ; 1619–1692). One of the greatest philosophers of all Chinese history, Wang was a Ming loyalist who, after the advent of the Qing dynasty, became a scholar-recluse, devoting himself to his writings, which are voluminous and address an extraordinarily broad range of topics. Wang, who considered himself a Confucian, rejected the Cheng-Zhu Neo-Confucianism embedded in the official state ideology (and the civil service examinations) on philosophical grounds, as well as the doctrines of Wang Yangming and his followers, taking his cue instead from the *qi*-centered monism of the Northern Song Neo-Confucian Zhang Zai (1020–1077). Wang authored highly rigorous and insightful commentaries to the Confucian classics. He also wrote on history, literature, and, occasionally, Buddhist philosophy. Considered a rare traditional example of a true philosophical "materialist" after China's Marxist revolution of 1949 (he was a native of Hunan, Chairman Mao's home province), he was for many years one of the few classical philosophers whose works were in print in China (after being almost unknown prior to the twentieth century). His commentaries to the *Zhuangzi* are extremely innovative, original, and insightful, offering novel explanations and glosses of problematic passages, giving close attention to the structure of the text and the continuities to be found in apparently disparate passages, making keen judgments on the stratifications of the text as a whole, and developing his own philosophical interpretation that is nonetheless firmly rooted in the letter of the text. His distinctive *qi* monism, derived from Zhang Zai, is also much in evidence in his comments. The evocation of characteristic phrases and ideas from one part of the *Zhuangzi* text in his commentary to other passages helps illuminate the inner philosophical and literary coherence of the text in new ways. Many consider his *Zhuangzi jie* (and its companion volume, *Zhuangzi tong*) one of the true masterpieces of the Chinese commentarial tradition.

WANG KAIYUN 王闓運 (1833–1916).   Late Qing dynasty classicist scholar and philologist, author of many works on the ancient Confucian classics.

WANG PANG 王雱 (1044–1076).   Son of the controversial Song Confucian political reformer Wang Anshi, Wang Pang was well versed in both Daoist and Buddhist thought and wrote commentaries to both the *Daodejing* and the *Zhuangzi*.

WANG XIANQIAN 王先謙 (1842–1917).   Conservative classical scholar of the late Qing, opposed to radical reform movements of the day, Wang compiled and edited many selected commentary editions of classical texts. His edition of the *Zhuangzi* is still one of the most popular in general use.

WANG XUAN 王宣 (1565–1654).   Ming scholar and empirical scientist, early teacher of Fang Yizhi, often quoted in Fang's commentary under the name "Master of the Empty Boat" (Xudanzi 虛舟子).

XIANG XIU 向秀 (ca. 227–272).   One of the "Seven Sages of the Bamboo Grove," whose *Zhuangzi* commentary formed the basis of Guo Xiang's classic work, which was often seen as largely plagiarized from Xiang Xiu. Xiang's commentary is no longer extant but is often quoted in other sources.

YAN FU 嚴復 (1853–1921).   An enormously influential late imperial and early Republican period translator, scholar, and reformer, the first principal of what is now Beijing University, Yan introduced many Western disciplines, texts, and concepts into China through his translations, including Darwinian ideas (via T. H. Huxley) of "survival of the fittest" and "natural selection."

YANG SHEN 楊慎 (also called Yang Yongxiu 楊 用修; 1488–1559).   Prolific Ming scholar, poet, and classicist of broad interests and achievements.

YANG WENHUI 楊文會 (1837–1911).   Renowned Buddhist scholar of the late Qing dynasty, who traveled to Europe in 1878, bringing many technological inventions back to China, and collaborated on an English translation (from the Chinese) of the *Treatise on the Awakening of Faith in the Mahayana* attributed to Aśvaghosa. Upon returning to China, he obtained and republished over three hundred Chinese Buddhist Pure Land texts, preserved up to that time only in Japan.

In 1910 he became head of the Chinese Buddhist Association and had a strong influence on the revival of Buddhism at the hands of his students in the next generation.

Ye Bingjing 葉秉敬 (early seventeenth century).   Late Ming dynasty philologist, poet, and phonologist.

Yingningzi 攖寧子. Almost certainly not a real person. Dates as yet unknown.

Yuan Hongdao 袁宏道 (1568–1610).   Poet and author, representative figure of the Gong'an (Koan; meaning "public case" in Chan [Zen] Buddhism) School of expressive innovation in poetry, much influenced by Chan Buddhist thought and the iconoclastic post-Confucian Buddhist Li Zhi 李贄 , his *GuangZhuang* consists of seven short, highly literary, and quite unconventional essays on the seven Inner Chapters of the *Zhuangzi*.

Zhang Binglin 章炳麟 (also called Zhang Taiyan 章太炎 ; 1869–1936). Late Qing and early Republican philosopher and revolutionary, Zhang was a reform-minded Confucian scholar, strongly influenced by both Western philosophy and Yogācāra Buddhism. Zhang wrote a separate commentary on the second chapter of the *Zhuangzi*, offering a highly original and elaborate analysis of that chapter in terms of technical Yogācāra analysis of the mind into eight consciousnesses.

Zhao Yifu 趙以夫 (1189–1256).   Song poet and *Book of Changes* specialist.

Zhu Boxiu 褚伯秀 (late Southern Song dynasty, twelfth century?).   A Daoist priest renowned for his strict religious practice and eremitic lifestyle, Zhu wrote commentary that is believed to integrate and preserve the work of many earlier, no longer extant commentaries.

Zhu Xi 朱熹 (1130–1200).   Considered by some to be the greatest Confucian philosopher of all time, Zhu was responsible for the synthetic version of Neo-Confucianism that became the basis of the imperial civil service examinations for the last seven hundred years of Chinese imperial history, making his name all but synonymous with orthodoxy. He was in fact a brilliant thinker in his own right, and in spite of his official reservations about Daoist thought, had many important observations to make about the Daoist classics.

BIBLIOGRAPHY

Ames, Roger T., ed. *Wandering at Ease in the* Zhuangzi. Albany: State University of New York Press, 1998.

Cao Mufan 曹慕樊. *Zhuangzi xinyi* 莊子新義. Chongqing: Chongqing chubanshe, 2005.

Chen Guanxue 陳冠學. *Zhuangzi xinzhu* 莊子新注. Taipei: Dongda tushugongsi, 1989.

Chen Guying 陳鼓應. *Zhuangzi jinzhu jinyi* 莊子今註今譯, 2 vols. Taipei: Taiwan shangwu yinshuguan, 1989.

Chen Shaoming 陳少明. *Qiwulun jiqi yingxiang* 齊物論及其影響. Beijing: Peking University Press, 2004.

Chen Shouchang 陳壽昌. *Nanhua zhenjing zhengyi* 南華真經正義. Taipei: Xintiandi shuju, 1977.

Cook, Scott Bradley, ed. *Hiding the World in the World: Uneven Discourses on the Zhuangzi*. Albany: State University of New York Press, 2003.

Fan Gengyan 范耕研. *Zhuangzi guyi quangao* 莊子詁義全稿. Taipei: Wenshizhe chubanshe, 1998.

Fang Yizhi 方以智. *Yaodi pao Zhuang* 藥地炮莊. Collected in Yan Lingfeng, *Zhuangzi jicheng*.

Gao Jinsheng 高晉生. *Zhuangzi jinjian* 莊子今箋. Taipei: Guangwen shuju, 1977.

Graham, A. C., trans. *Chuang Tzu: The Inner Chapters*. Indianapolis: Hackett Publishing Company, 2001.

Guo Qingfan 郭慶藩. *Zhuangzi jishi* 莊子集釋. Taipei: Shijie shuju, 1982.

Hamill, Sam, and J. P. Seaton, trans. *The Essential Chuang Tzu*. Boston and London: Shambhala, 1999.

Hu Yuanjun 胡遠濬. *Zhuangzi quangu* 莊子詮詁. Anhui: Huangshan shushe, 1996.

Huang Jinhong 黃錦鋐. *Zhuangzi duben* 莊子讀本. Taipei: Sanmin shuju, 1986.

Jiao Hong 焦宏. *Zhuangzi yi* 莊子翼. Taipei: Guangwen shuju, 1979.

Kjellberg, Paul, and Philip J. Ivanhoe, eds. *Essays on Skepticism, Relativism, and Ethics in the* Zhuangzi. Albany: State University of New York Press, 1996.

Legge, James. *The Texts of Taoism: The Writings of Chuang Tzu*. Mineola, NY: Dover, 1962.

Li Zhi 李摯. *Zhuangzi jie* 莊子解. Collected in Yan Lingfeng, *Zhuangzi jicheng*.

Lin Shu 林紓. *Zhuangzi qianshuo* 莊子淺說. Taipei: Huazheng shuju, 1985.

Lin Xiyi 林希逸. *Zhuangzi Juanzhai Kouyi jiaozhu* 莊子鬳齊口義校注. Beijing: Zhonghua shuju, 1997.

Lin, Yutang, trans. and ed. *The Wisdom of Laotse*. New York: Modern Library, 1948.

Mair, Victor H., ed. *Experimental Essays on the* Chuang-tzu. Asian Studies at Hawaii, no. 29. Honolulu: University of Hawaii Press, 1983.

——, trans. *Wandering on the Way: Early Taoist Tales and Parables of Chuang Tzu*. New York: Bantam, 1994.

Moeller, Hans-Georg. *Daoism Explained: From the Dream of the Butterfly to the Fishnet Allegory*. Chicago: Open Court Press, 2004.

Palmer, Martin, with Elizabeth Breuilly, trans. *The Book of Chuang Tzu*. London: Arkana, Penguin Books, 1996.

Qian Jibo 錢基博. *Du Zhuangzi Tianxiapian shuji* 讀莊子天下篇疏記. Taipei: Shangwu yinshuguan, 2006.

Qian Mu 錢穆. *Zhuangzi zuanjian* 莊子纂箋. Taipei: Dongda tushugongsi, 1986.

Roth, Harold D. *A Companion to Angus C. Graham's* Chuang Tzu. Honolulu: University of Hawaii Press, 2003.

Ruan Yusong 阮毓崧. *Zhuangzi jizhu* 莊子集註. Taipei: Guangwen shuju, 1980.

Shi Deqing 釋德清 (Hanshan dashi 憨山大師). *Laozi Daodejing Hanshan zhu: Zhuangzi neipian Hanshan zhu* 老子道德經憨山註:莊子內篇憨山註. Taipei: Xinwenfeng chubangongsi, 1996.

Sima Biao 司馬彪. *Sima Biao Zhuangzi zhu* 司馬彪莊子注. Taipei: Xinwenfeng chubangongsi, 1987.

Tan Jiefu 譚戒甫. *Zhuangzi Tianxiapian jiaoshi* 莊子天下篇校釋. Taipei: Xinwenfeng, 1979.

Wang Fuzhi 王夫之. *Zhuangzi tong, Zhuangzi jie* 莊子通, 莊子解. Taipei: Liren shuju, 1984.

Wang Shumin 王叔岷. *Zhuangzi jiaoquan* 莊子校詮. Taipei: Zhongyang yanjiuyuan, 1986.

Wang Xianqian 王先謙, and Liuwu 弈劉武. *Zhuangzi jijie: Zhuangzi jijei neipian buzheng* 莊子集解:莊子集解內篇補正. Taipei: Hanjing wenhua shiye youxian gongsi, 2004.

Ware, James R., trans. *The Sayings of Chuang Chou*. New York: New American Library, 1963.

Watson, Burton, trans. *The Complete Works of Chuang Tzu*. New York: Columbia University Press, 1968.

Wu, Kuang-ming. *The Butterfly as Companion: Meditations on the First Three Chapters of the* Chuang Tzu. Albany: State University of New York Press, 1990.

———. *Chuang-tzu: World Philosopher at Play*. Studies in Religion/American Academy of Religion. New York: Crossroads Publishing, 1982.

Wu Yi 吳怡. *Zhuangzi neipian jieyi* 莊子內篇解義. Taipei: Sanmin shuju, 2004.

Xiao Tianshi 蕭天石, ed. *Daozang jinghua* 道藏精華, vol. 17. *Daozangben Nanhuajing: Zhuangzi baijia pingzhu* 道藏本南華經:莊子百家評註. Taipei: Ziyou chubanshe, 1993.

———, ed. *Daozang jinghua* 道藏精華, vol. 12, by Lu Xixing 陸西星. *Zhuangzi Nanhuazhenjing fumo* 莊子南華真經副墨, vols. 1 and 2. Taipei: Ziyou chubanshe, 1973.

Xie Xianghao 謝祥皓, and Li Sile 李思樂, eds. *Zhuangzi xuba lunping jiyao* 莊子序跋論評輯要. Wuhan: Hubei jiaoyu chubanshe, 2001.

Xuan Ying 宣穎. *Zhuangzi Nanhuajing jie* 莊子南華經解. Taipei: Guangwen shuju, 1978.

Yan Lingfeng 嚴靈峯, ed. *Wuqiubeizhai Zhuangzijicheng* 無求備齋莊子集成. 1st ser., 30 vols. Taipei: Yiwen yinshuguan, 1972. 2d ser., 42 vols. Taipei: Yiwen yinshuguan, 1974.

Zhang Songhui 張松輝. *Zhuangzi yiyi kaobian* 莊子疑義考辨. Beijing: Zhonghua shuju, 2007.

Zhang Taiyan 章太炎. *Qiwulunshi dingben* 齊物論訂本. Taipei: Guangwen shuju, 1970.

Zhou Jinran 周金然, Yuan Hongdao 袁宏道, et al. *Nanhuajingzhuanshi wai erzhong* 南華經傳釋外二種. Taipei: Xinwenfeng chubangongsi, 1987.

INDEX

233